The Builders of Camphill

The Builders of Camphill

Lives and Destinies of the Founders

Edited by Friedwart Bock

Floris Books

First published in 2004 by Floris Books
© 2004 Friedwart Bock
Reprinted with corrections 2005

British Library CIP Data available

ISBN 0-86315-442-5

Produced by Polskabooks in Poland

Contents

The publishers would like to thank the many people who kindly supplied photographs for use in this book. Particular thanks go to Agathe Dawson and to Karin Gretton for many of the photographs in 'The Youth Group in Vienna' and 'Thomas Weihs' chapters respectively.

Preface

The pioneering work of the Camphill Community over sixty years in caring for both children and adults with special needs has been one of the major initiatives that has changed the way society approaches such individuals. It is therefore timely that this book should appear describing the pioneers and founders of the movement who had such social insight and concern ahead of their time. This arose from their relation to the work of Rudolf Steiner and the Anthroposophical Movement that he founded, giving them insight into the soul and spiritual background of individuals with special needs. The indications from spiritual science for effective methods of care was developed over the years and put into effective practise, bringing meaning and social integration to the lives of many that might otherwise have remained as 'problems.'

Rudolf Steiner described how those taking up spiritual science, and the path of initiation that may accompany that, eventually face a threshold where everything they have felt to be most essential in outer life is stripped away — either physically or in their inner attitude to it — so that they face a kind of personal abyss. This can lead to the birth in them of something higher which comes to be experienced as truer to their own essential being than all they had previously regarded as their self. The founders of the Camphill Movement went through this experience outwardly and physically in a very real sense, fleeing Vienna in 1938 in the face of the advance of Hitler (for most were Jewish). All personal possessions and the very environment that had given meaning and security to their lives was abruptly lost, to be exchanged for life in Scotland, and later on internment of the men when war broke out. This was indeed an outwardly experienced initiation of a kind, which so many others suffered in many other ways in that war. But they came to Scotland with a purpose which they accomplished beyond what might have been expected. This is characteristic of approaching the threshold of inner existence: there must be an inner strength of purpose, and above all love for humanity, if the higher self is to be found in place of what has been lost.

For them to enter Britain initially it was necessary to obtain entry visas, and Cecil Harwood — Chair at that time of the Anthroposophical Society in Great Britain — was instrumental in so doing, for he knew the Home Secretary. He once said that it was really he who started Camphill! The relations between the Anthroposophical Society and the movement were not always harmonious, so it is important to know of this action by its Chair. In the 1970s strenuous efforts were made on both sides to heal a gap that had grown up between the movements, and several courageous deeds made that possible, for example by Thomas Weihs, so that since then we have enjoyed a fruitful harmony of spiritual striving.

All pioneers have to make hard decisions if the enterprise is to continue, and in Camphill one of these decisions concerned money. I was told by Anke Weihs that one day Karl König told them there was no money to pay them wages. They continued to work without, and from this external necessity grew a resolve to continue to live in community that way — not by necessity — but as an ideal which has lived to this day. Thus may outer hindrances and conditions be spiritualized by free deeds. Rudolf Steiner expressed an ethic for community life as 'The healthy social life is found when in the mirror of each human soul the whole community finds its reflection, and when in the community the virtue of each is living.' This has lived at the centre of Camphill life, and their relation to money is seen as one expression of it, although of course such an archetype can find expression in diverse ways in different situations. The point is that when an idea becomes an ideal which is practised faithfully great strength ensues, and that has surely been witnessed throughout the history of the Camphill Movement. The biographies in this book not only shed light on the origins of the movement and what kind of people founded it, but also on how individual the ways of realizing a common ideal may be.

Nick Thomas
General Secretary of the
Anthroposophical Society in Great Britain

Introduction

All understanding begins with admiration.
We cannot make our own what we do not understand.

Goethe

Those who have died live on as their contributions continue to inspire future generations. This book is concerned with a group of people who built a modern Christian community. Their primary task was to work with people with special needs, and for this they are best known.

Humankind walks a lonely road, and new communities are able to face the challenges of isolation only through striving and working together.

When Karl König's biography was completed in 1992, its author Hans Müller-Wiedemann expressed two wishes. Firstly, the biography should be translated into English and it should become available to readers in the West. This was achieved in 1996. Secondly, a book should be compiled that would describe the lives and contributions of the group of younger people around Karl König. Hans used the image of the sun in the centre and the planets that circle around it. He offered to help with the book but he died before the project could be realized. Thus the book has become our legacy.

We found it right to include a chapter on Karl König in this volume as he was the central person in this process of community building. We thank Christof Andreas Lindenberg for letting us use *Karl König — A Portrait* which he wrote for the fiftieth birthday of Camphill.

The small editorial group (Marianne Sander, Cherry How and myself) had the task of finding authors who would write the individual chapters and guiding the project. The search was long but rewarding. Those who have contributed have our warm thanks. None is a professional writer and for each of them it was a deed of friendship to write their chapter. The authors have also drawn on the contributions of others who had known the founders and the stories told are coloured by their experiences. The chapters vary in length and style, but this is not a sign of rank or importance.

Special thanks go to Sally St Clair and Christine Polyblank for reading and assisting with editing the manuscripts.

The reader will discover a many-faceted picture of a modern community that began with this group fleeing from Austria shortly before the outbreak of the Second World War, and eventually making their way to Scotland. In *Fragments of Camphill* Anke has described what now lay before them:

The labour of hard, practical work,
The labour of learning to live together,
The labour of getting to know Anthroposophy.

The seed of these labours has borne fruit across the world.

With gratitude and appreciation for those portrayed in this volume.

Friedwart Bock

The Youth Group in Vienna

John Baum

The biographies in this book belong together. The Youth Group that went on to found Camphill met in Vienna over the course of a little more than a year, as the storm clouds of the Second World War were gathering. This chapter describes the coming together of the group, as well as following those who stayed a shorter time in Camphill, or who found their own separate path in life.

Karl König has described the atmosphere of that Vienna into which the founders of Camphill were born, starting some years earlier with the arrival of the eighteen year old Rudolf Steiner to study at the Technical High School:

After having completed the first moon-node of his earthly life the young Rudolf Steiner came to Vienna for the first time, as a young student. It was the year 1879, at the beginning of the Age of Michael, almost exactly to the week ... This Vienna was beginning to take on the traits of a metropolis ... and becoming the centre of a mighty empire, of the Austro-Hungarian monarchy. It was a town in which an extraordinary life took place, a town in which numerous very important people gathered. A town which got its inner character from such circles as the one which formed at No. 5 Colloredogasse where Eugenie delle Grazie lived ... If one sees this in connection with all that the Vienna of that time represented, something appears of a renewed life which can be experienced as a reborn Athens of the fifth and fourth centuries BC ...

... It is very interesting if one begins to divine that not only human beings reincarnate, but also that beings of towns reappear, and that they reappear together with essential people who lived within them ... Now we should try to experience how the young student Rudolf Steiner entered into the world of Vienna, came into the circle of Eugenie delle Grazie, but also into the circles of the University and of the Technical High School and was surrounded by something which had been Athens two millennia before ...

... Every thirty to forty years the 'image of reincarnation' of a town changes. It changed for Vienna already at the beginning of the

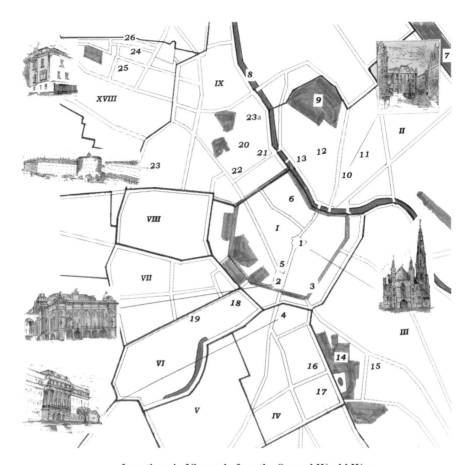

Locations in Vienna before the Second World War

Greater Vienna is divided into 23 districts or Bezirke. Districts I to IX comprise the centre

I Inner Town
1 St Stephen's Cathedral   **2** Opera   **3** Ring Road
4 Technical High School (Rudolf Steiner)
5 Maysedergasse 5 (Anke Weihs (née Nederhoed
1937–38)   **6** Gonzagagasse 5 (Lisl Schauder (née
Schwalb)

II Leopoldstadt 7 Danube   **8** Danube Canal
9 Augarten   **10** Glockengasse 1 (Karl König/
König's Shoeshop   **11** Rotensterngasse 4 (Karl
König 1902–10), Rotensterngasse 22 (Trude
Amann, née Blau)   **12** Malzgasse 2/2 (Barbara
Lipsker (née Sali Gerstler)   **13** Untere
Augartenstrasse 1A/5 (Hans Schauder)

III Landstrasse 14 Belvedere garden/Botanical
gardens   **15** Gerlgasse 10 (Thomas Weihs)

IV Weiden 16 Theresianumgasse 3 (Peter and
Alix Roth)   **17** Karolinengasse 7 (Marie Korach,
née Blitz)

V Margareten

VI Mariahilfer 18 Mariahilferstrasse 3 (Carlo
Pietzner 1915–26)   **19** Mariahilferstrasse 49 (The
Christian Community

VII Neubau   **VIII Josefstadt**

IX Alsergrund 20 Berggasse 19 (Sigmund
Freud)   **21** Hahngasse 3/3 (Alex Baum)   **22**
Wasa grammar school, Wasagasse 10 **23** General
Infirmary **23a** Realschule, Glasergasse 25 (Karl
König, Alex Baum)

XVIII Währing 24 Colloredogasse 5 (Eugenie
delle Grazie/Rudolf Steiner) **25** Anastasius
Grüngasse 49 (Karl König and his family, April
1936–May 1938) (Here the Youth Group held all
their meetings) **26** Hasenauerstrasse 21 (Karl
König and family, May –August 1938)

Map: Fred Halder

eighteen-nineties. Then Vienna became something entirely different. When one walked, for instance, at the beginning of the century through the General Infirmary, then one could immediately and directly experience that this is a place which carries in itself again what once, a century before Christ, had been the region of the temple of Jerusalem. Vienna carried in itself a Jerusalem-like destiny at the turn of the century. Therefore it was also filled with so much old Jewish Destiny ...[1]

Karl König

Karl König grew up in Vienna's 2nd District, Leopoldstadt, the Jewish district. The Danube Canal separates the 2nd District from the centre of town. Hans Schauder, who grew up in the same district, has described in his biography how he had the feeling of living on an island. Inwardly, König left the 'Jewish island' of Vienna when he found Christianity. His mother, Bertha König, described in her autobiography how she and his father found a large picture of the Christ hanging in his cupboard. Outwardly, Karl König left the 'Jewish island' after a quarrel with his teacher at the Realschule (secondary school), following which he said to his mother: 'I won't go to my school any more. I have quarrelled with my teacher and I want to go to the school in

Taborstrasse, one of the main streets of Leopoldstadt. Where the road forks the Glockengasse goes off to the right. Karl König's parents had a shoeshop in Glockengasse 1, at the right rear of the building. Photo: P. Ledermann, 1908

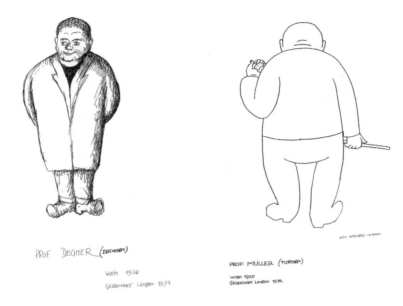

PROF DEGNER (ZEICHNEN)

WIEN 1920
GEZEICHNET LONDON 1974

PROF. MÜLLER (TURNEN)

WIEN 1920
GEZEICHNET LONDON 1974.

Prof. Degner (Art) Prof. Müller (Gymnastics). Two of the special group of
teachers at the Glasergasse Realschule. Vienna 1920.
Drawings by Eric Walters-Kohn

the 9th District.' His mother went to speak to the headmaster of the school
and he agreed to meet the young Karl. The headmaster looked him up and
down, and he was allowed to change schools.

In 1920, when König was eighteen, he took the Matura, the school-
leaving examination, and passed with distinction. He studied Latin for a
year (which was neccessary, because he had gone to the Realschule, not
the Gymnasium, or grammar school) before studying medicine and qual-
ifying as a doctor in 1927.

The 'Old' Youth Group

Hans Schauder lived in the 2nd District, right beside the Augarten Bridge,
which connects it with the 1st and 9th Districts. When he was ten years
old he was walking, with his mother, past the Wasa Gymnasium which
was near the Realschule in the 9th District, but a little nearer the inner city.
He should have gone to the Leopold Gymnasium, which lay in the Jewish
district, and was attended mainly by Jewish students and which Sigmund
Freud had also attended. Walking past the Wasa Gymnasium he experienced what he has described as a moment when destiny intervenes. He
saw a distant cousin leaving the school and immediately said to his
mother: 'I want to go there.' His mother took the ten-year-old Hans to see

Wasa Gymnasium. (From the booklet given out when the Wasa Gymnasium was 50 years old in 1931). Drawing by Franz Heidrich

the headmaster of the Leopold Gymnasium, but nothing would make him change his mind.

At the Wasa Gymnasium Hans Schauder became friends with Rudi Lissau, Bronja Hüttner and Edi Weissberg, who were all in the same class. This friendship endured for life.

Bronja was one of the star students in Greek and Latin in the class. Rudi's father and uncle were among the eight people who, early in the twentieth century, founded the Theosophical Society in Vienna, in order that a platform could be provided for Rudolf Steiner's activity in Austria. Rudi as a child, had sat on Steiner's lap, and as a boy had been presented to Steiner. He had received membership of the Anthroposophical Society as a gift from his mother for his eighteenth birthday. Even before he was eighteen he had tried to persuade the other pupils to read Steiner, as Hans has recorded in his biography. In the last years of his life, looking back, Hans described Rudi:

Rudi Lissau was a leader intellectually, because of his connection to Anthroposophy, but also purely in a physical sense. He arranged walking tours and then led them. He walked up to the Zugspitze, and usually one only got there by the funicular railway.[2]

In 1920 Alex Baum had begun attending the same Realschule in the Glasergasse that Karl König had just left, a short walk from Hahngasse where he lived. He remained at the school until 1924, when at fourteen, he

A group on a walking tour arranged by Rudi Lissau in May 1930. Front from left: Alex Baum, Fritz Kalmar, Hans Schauder. Standing from left: Knut Grab, Erich Huppert, Ilse Lederer, Karl Frucht, Marianne Hochdorf, Edi Weissberg, Bronja Hüttner, Rudi Lissau

Alex Baum and Hans Schauder in Ischl in July 1929. Alex was 18 and Hans 17 when the picture was taken

*At a young socialist camp for city children ca. 1930-31: Sali (second from left,
standing), Lisl (right standing), Trude (right, behind)*

started work in a factory. By early 1929 Alex had become part of the group
which had formed at the Wasa Gymnasium. In July of that year Hans
Schauder was convalescing in the mountains at Ischl. One Sunday Alex
visited Hans there and a street photographer took a series of pictures.

As an old man, Hans, while describing Alex, began to sing a popular
song from the Vienna of the 1920s, adding: 'Edi Weissberg would have
sung like that. Also others in the group, but no one ever heard Alex Baum
sing like that.'

Sali Gerstler (later Barbara Lipsker) met Lisl Schwalb at a camp for
socialist middle school pupils. Trude Blau (later Amann) also met Lisl and
Sali at the socialist camp, around 1930–31. Both Sali and Trude lived in
Leopoldstadt; Trude in the same street in which Karl König was born and
adjacent to the street where the Königs had their shoeshop and where Karl
König grew up, Sali a few streets away.

Hans Schauder has described in his book *Conversations on
Counselling* how he heard, from Bronja, about his future wife, Lisl
Schwalb. He remembered standing at a certain place and hearing bells
ringing, and having the feeling that this was the girl he had been waiting
for:

On a Sunday outing in May 1931: from left: Robert Schwalb (Lisl's brother), Hans Schauder, Rudi Lissau, Sali Gerstler (Barbara Lipsker), Alex Baum, Hanna Förster, Hanna Lissau

All I can say for myself is that when I started to know Lisl I had one of the three big dreams of my life, in which I dreamed that I had waited five hundred and forty years to come to earth in order to meet her and to be there when she was here — and we were born and grew up within a mile of each other, across the little Danube canal.[3]

Lisl lived in the 1st District, not far from the Augarten Bridge, which Hans had to cross to visit her. Of Lisl's special contribution to the group, Hans recalled:

Lisl was a culturally gifted, knowledgeable person in a non-intellectual way. She brought her interests, nature and culture, into my life, and into the group in a naive, loving way. She showed me the world. Lisl was deeply concerned with culture, in a natural way, and transferred this to the other members of the group.

That I met Lisl at the end of my school time is the most important occurrence in my life. We read much poetry, especially Rilke. The interest in culture, music, art and nature came from Lisl, and I shared it.

In the summer of 1930 the four who formed the nucleus of the Youth Group took the school-leaving examination, the Matura, at the Wasa Gymnasium. Hans Schauder met Hanna Förster on the first day entering the Medical Faculty of Vienna University. Rudi Lissau explains how they met:

There were two schools with different heads and the students had to choose. One was under Prof. Tandler, a famous teacher and politician. Socialist students usually chose him. Then each student was allotted a desk which could be locked so that he could keep his belongings there.

As it happened — or, as karma directed, Hans Schauder's place was next to Hanna Förster's. They became friends and Hanna heard of an alternative form of medicine. Soon she joined Dr Wantschura's group of students of medicine. Every week when she came home from the meeting her sister Hedda was waiting in bed to hear her account of how the proceedings had gone. It was not long before she too became a member of the group and finally Hedda Förster became my wife.

Hans has described Hugo Frischauer as drifting into the group:

He was the joker of the group. Every group has its clown. He had a tremendous sense of humour, always telling jokes, and everyone would burst out laughing.

He drifted through life. He met anthroposophy, but his relationship to it was light-hearted, playful. He enjoyed it, he believed in it. He enjoyed life in his own way.

Hans could not remember Willi Amann as really part of the group in Vienna. Willi, who at that time was studying law in Vienna, was the son of Dr Amann, the translator of Thomas Mann's work into French. Trude's sister Lizzi was going to spend a weekend together with Willi's brother Ernst. Willi was going with them and when they came to collect Trude's sister, Willi persuaded the young Trude to come. They became friends. In 1936 Willi helped Trude on her way to Arlesheim by hitchhiking with her to Switzerland.

In his biography Hans wrote this about the Youth Group:

At school, I generally met with my fellow Jewish pupils in a group of friends. Many of us young Viennese Jews then became followers of Rudolf Steiner's anthroposophy, but not all of us of course. Edi Weissberg, for example, later became an important and famous representative of Jungian psychology after his exile to America. We met every Sunday to go walking in the Vienna Woods. Later, when we were already students, we sometimes encountered Nazis, who early on felt confident out here in the open, during such walks. Occasionally they shouted 'Jewish pigs' and spat at us.

We met again in the evening after such walks. These evening meetings were great cultural events. On one occasion I recited a whole drama from beginning to end and my friends listened with rapt attention for the whole of the three acts ... We also read poetry of course. We made music, played the piano. I was still able to sing at that time and performed Schubert. These regular meetings in Vienna, where Nazism was already beginning to make its pernicious influence felt, were like an oasis for us into which we withdrew regularly every Sunday. First there was always the walk in the Vienna Woods followed by the cultural programme in the evening.

Surprisingly, we never thought or talked about our Jewish origins at these meetings. Not even when we felt under pressure from the Nazis. I believe that we were all especially receptive towards

Rudolf Frieling and his wife
Margarethe in Vienna in 1930

intellectual and artistic influences, and that may have been connected
in some way with our Jewish origins; but all of us considered that we
had severed those connections. Our assimilation, our blossoming in
the spirit and culture of Vienna — for that was the way that we were
assimilated — made us particularly receptive with regard to music
and literature.[4]

Hanna Lissau can be seen sitting on the far right of the photograph
(page 18), on the periphery of the group, just as she was in life. She chose
a destiny quite unlike the others, as described by her brother Rudi. Hanna
Lissau was born in 1914 and did not like the Jewish element in Vienna.
Instead of studying, Hanna wanted to work with the Christian
Community priest, Hilmar von Hinüber, among unemployed people in
the Ruhr district in Germany. But she was prevented from doing this
when the Nazis came to power in Germany. She went instead to
Arlesheim and worked for years at the Sonnenhof Curative home.
Following the Annexation of Austria, Rudi decided he must leave the
country as soon as he could. At the time, he was working in a school for
blind children. The headmaster begged Rudi to take his eighteen-year-old
son with him. They travelled to Arlesheim and then to Paris. Rudi had to
wait in Paris for a permit to enter Britain. The headmaster's son stayed
on longer than he had intended before travelling to Israel. Hanna got to
know him and they fell in love. He was proud of his Jewish faith, and for
her this was a revelation. Later, Hanna worked with Madame Vachadze,
a curative teacher, in a home in the French countryside. After the occupation of France the local police warned her that they would have to
come in a few days' time and arrest her. But they revealed to her at the

same time how she could escape across the Pyrenees. Hanna said to the others working in the home: 'I have never liked Jews, but I will stand by them now.' When the police came, she was prepared. Hanna was taken to Drancy, a collecting camp near Paris, and from there to Auschwitz on September 9, 1942. She died there on October 14, 1942. Hanna, who had chosen to stand by the Jewish people in their hour of need, died in the place that epitomized the Jewish fate in the Second World War. Madame Vachadze later wrote that she had dreamt that Hanna sat at the head of a table, passing round bread and saying, 'Now I know that I am a Christian.'

In 1927 the Christian Community in Vienna was founded with Dr Rudolf Frieling (1901–1986) as one of the first priests. He had a powerful impact on the lives of many people. Hans Schauder describes his meeting with Rudolf Frieling in his biography:

The personality of this man represented a major experience for Lisl and myself in our youth. Of all the people I have met he is probably the person most worthy of veneration. From that moment on I started to read the Bible properly. When for the first time I entered the room in which the Act of Consecration of Man was celebrated at the Christian Community in Vienna, I had a very intense feeling of finally having reached home after long wanderings. I took part in the Act of Consecration of Man celebrated by Frieling. That was a truly sacred celebration. My religious feelings thus were awakened relatively late. Before that I was at a loss and not particularly interested. We were sent to the Temple when I was at school but that was such a monotonous experience for me, that I resolved never to go back again. (Incidentally, Lisl, quite independently of me, had had the same experience of monotony.) I never felt the need to keep to the religion of Moses.[5]

By 1936 the group had been together for a good seven years. Most were born well before the First World War and could remember the Austro-Hungarian Empire. Trude Blau was some years younger than the others, having been born in 1915. She joined the group at fifteen and by the time she was twenty-one, in 1936, she had already made her way to the Sonnenhof to become a curative teacher.

Trude Blau's experience in this special Youth Group, which met when they were all teenagers is revealing. Hans Schauder invited her to a Shakespeare performance, then to the opera, and finally to the Christian Community where, while listening to Frieling's address on the Christ, she felt her Jewishness fall away. Later on, he invited her to a talk by a curative teacher, and from that moment she knew that that was to be her task in life. Through their Sunday outings and cultural evenings they became Viennese. Through their interest in anthroposophy and Christianity they

Karl König in Vienna 1936

found their own path in life, quite distinct from the heritage into which
they were born.

When Karl König met them he saw them as a group that had been
together many years, so he called them the 'old' Youth Group, in contrast
to the group that was by then forming around him.

Rudi Lissau recalled an experience from that time:

*So far we had not thought much about the future. Hedda was keen to
be an actress, while I lived and worked in an institute for blind children.
Meanwhile the threat to Austria's independence grew.*

*One evening we had been together and were walking home together,
she to her mother's flat, I to the Institute for the Blind. She began to cry
and told me of her worries for the future: 'Hitler will invade, there will
be war and we want to be happy.' I argued that the European countries
would never permit this, but Hedda's fears could not be assuaged. Finally
I said, 'If you stop crying, I promise you I shall go abroad on the day
Hitler comes.' She stopped crying and we became the first members of
the group to imagine a life outside Austria. But where could we go? She
thought of a South Sea island, I would not leave Europe. She had been an
au pair in England, I had relations there and so we began to improve our
English.*

The Youth Group around Karl König

Karl König had to leave Germany in 1936. For seven years Pilgramshain had been the home of the König family. In the short time between his graduation in 1927 and settling in Pilgramshain, König worked at Ita Wegman's Clinical Therapeutic Institute in Arlesheim, near Dornach in Switzerland. It was there that he met his future wife.

In Vienna, Karl König met Rudi Lissau and told him that he would like to start a Youth Group. Would Rudi come and bring his friends? König later wrote:

Every Saturday evening twenty to thirty young people came together. It had started with a small nucleus of about eight to ten students I had already known before I returned to Vienna. While I was in Pilgramshain, I had visited my home-town once or twice a year to see my parents and to meet old friends. During these visits, I had become acquainted with this small group which was studying Anthroposophy and whose members asked me to help them in their attempts to understand Rudolf Steiner's work. They were a closely-knit little community and deeply connected to one another. A rather melancholic mood prevailed among them but they were earnestly striving young people.

To this nucleus, others soon attached themselves and a few months after I had arrived in Vienna, another deeply connected group of young men and women appeared on the scene. They were just the opposite of the original band. They lived in style, enjoyed life and had a good amount of savoir vivre. Two of them, Peter Roth and Thomas Weihs, were in their last year of medical studies and others were around them. Carlo Pietzner was a graduate of the Arts School, Alix Roth was working as a photographer, another as a musician and a few more related to them. With this group, a fresh new wind blew through the 'old' Youth Group and our evenings extended far into the night. We studied and read together, discussed the problems of the day, cultural and artistic as well as scientific. I was very grateful to destiny for entrusting these outstanding representatives of the younger generation to my care and guidance.[6]

Rudi Lissau has recorded that this was a tense time in the Anthroposophical Society, which had split into different factions after Rudolf Steiner's death in 1925. Meanwhile, he was glad of the opportunity to work with Karl König, whom he described as an extraordinary figure. On meeting him, the eye was drawn from his huge head, with its mane of beautiful hair, to his very slight frame, and finally to his feet, which were crippled. Whenever he spoke he said something fascinating and new.

Members of the 'old' Youth Group had started to meet with Karl König, and this created an opportunity for others to join. The newcomers, born in 1914–16, were younger, in their early twenties. They came from families that had lived longer and were more established in Vienna. This is apparent in the locality in which they lived. They did not come from Leopoldstadt, the Jewish district in the north-east of Vienna, or from Alsergrund, in the north, where many assimilated Jews lived. South-east of the centre of Vienna is a beautiful park called the Belvedere, to the west of which, in Wieden, the 5th District of Vienna, Peter Roth and his sister Alix lived. Marie Blitz (later Korach) lived close by, and was a childhood playmate of Peter and Alix. Thomas Weihs lived to the east of the park, on a road leading directly to it, in the 3rd District of Vienna, Gerlgasse. Carlo Pietzner was born nearby, in a house on the Mariahilfer Strasse. Carlo was friends with Peter Roth in their youth and spent holidays at the country estate of the Roth family. Carlo even met Thomas Weihs briefly whilst at school. Thomas, Peter, Alix and Marie, although all of Jewish descent, were recorded as being members of the Protestant church, a further sign of their families' assimilation into Viennese society.

Stella-Maria Hellström, who grew up in Vienna, tells how the two closely-knit groups came together. Her stepfather, Marius Widakowich, who in 1936 was working as a self employed engineer, has described his role:

When I was trying to get orders, I met an ELIN co-worker called Schwarzmann. He was interested in me, as I had my own inventions, which he asked me to help develop. Ernst Weihs, Thomas's brother, worked as an engineer under Schwarzmann. People in the Anthroposophical Society told my parents about Karl König who had just recently come back to Vienna. I was friendly with Ernst and soon took him to a lecture, which took place in Karl König's house. Afterwards Ernst said that his brother, Thomas, who studied medicine, might be interested in the lectures.

When the König family moved back to Vienna in May 1936 they settled in a villa in the 18th District, near Alsergrund. As a child, Stella-Maria Hellström was a patient of Karl König and also a playmate of his children. She writes:

Karl König's family came to Vienna from Germany after Hitler's activity had begun there. They moved into a wonderful villa which was not so far from our house. Their house had central heating! All the rooms were warm — what a dream! My second father soon came there on evenings when Karl König held courses for students and other interested people. It was my second father who told Thomas Weihs's brother, Ernst Weihs about them. Thomas knew Peter Roth. My new father met in the group each week, without knowing that he had led two people to Karl König, who later would be founders of Camphill.

I was soon allowed to experience Karl König as a doctor. In the warm, beautifully ordered waiting room, was a large aquarium with many different fishes. I felt that these quiet, peacefully swimming fish gave the waiting room the right atmosphere for waiting. Karl König lifted me in a fatherly fashion onto his knee and laid his enormous cold ear onto my chest ... I can feel it still today. Soon I was allowed also to go up the beautiful winding wooden stairs to where the family had their private rooms. For me it was a great source of wonder to climb up there because Karl König's wife was the most beautiful woman I had seen in my short life. A real queen, tall, slim and with black hair that shone. When I first saw her, the sight took my breath away and I was filled with awe. The oldest daughter, Renate, was just a little younger than I was and soon I was invited as playmate to the Königs. I was always very proud and happy when I could visit, could never see enough of the 'queen' and enjoyed the warm, special atmosphere. Another important person contributed to this atmosphere, a small, delicate woman called Sali Gerstler. She helped in the house and especially with the children, perhaps also assisted Karl König in his surgery. She was modest, quiet, with warmth and a strong, loving radiance and much humour. She gave the feeling of absolute safety.

After a conversation with Peter Roth, Andrew Hoy described the Youth Group:

A group of young people and medical students began to meet with Dr König regularly and some of them joined the Youth Group. Among them were Peter, Thomas, Alix, Carlo, Alex Baum, Sali Gerstler (Lipsker) who looked after the König children, and Trude Blau (Amann) who was soon to leave to study at the Sonnenhof. Anke was a patient of Dr König but did not belong to the Youth Group ... Mrs König, who was to play such a vital role in the development of Camphill, did not participate in the group ...

In the period leading to the takeover of Austria by the German army — the Anschluss or 'unification' — there was a considerable division within Austrian society as well as in Germany as a result of Hitler's determination to seek the total extermination of the Jewish society which tended towards intellectualism while the trend of these countries was nationalistic. The universities emphasized this general ferment. The work with Dr König created a true island of peace within this ocean of upheaval. Each week Dr König gave a lecture on animals in the Town Hall of Vienna. These lectures were well attended, 100–150 people from Dr König's patients, the doctor's groups and the youth groups and anyone interested. Dr König gave the Youth Group the task of connecting themselves to a number of young artists and intellectuals who had died around the time of the First World War. These young

*people had possessed exceptional abilities and Dr König felt they were
the true bearers of the light age. Members of the Youth Group gave
presentations about this earlier group. They included the painters Franz
Marc and Ernst Macke; Hellingrath, who edited a book of Hölderlin's
poems; Otto Braun, a youth of eighteen years who wrote poems and
fragments which were published after the war and brought him
considerable renown; and Ernst Trakl, an Austrian poet who died in
1914 but not as a result of the war. Dr König also encouraged the Youth
Group to relate to the group of Romantics at the time of Goethe.*[7]

Barbara Lipsker confirmed that all the Youth Group meetings were
held in Anastasius Grüngasse 49 in the 18th District of Vienna. Karl König
was well aware that Rudolf Steiner, after coming to Vienna to study in
1879, frequently visited the parallel street to Anastasius Grüngasse,
Colloredogasse, where in No. 5 the poet Marie Eugenie delle Grazie lived.
Rudolf Steiner had written:

*In the home of Marie Eugenie delle Grazie I passed some of the
happy hours of my life. On Saturdays she always received visitors. Those
who came were persons of divers spiritual tendencies. The poet formed
the centre of the group. She read aloud from her poetical works; she
spoke in the spirit of her world view in most positive language. The light
of these ideas she cast upon human life. It was by no means the light of
the sun. Always, in truth, only the sombre light of the moon ...*[8]

Remembering the Youth Group's meetings in 1936–38, Barbara
Lipsker wrote:

*Every week one of us brought a leading thought, verse, a sentence from
the Bible, a poem, a significant thought from a book. With this content we
would live then throughout the next week. The verses of the Calender of the
Soul began to sound: Man–World, Ego–Cosmos, divining a reality, which
was to be grasped anew. Christmas 1936 drew near. Trude and Hanna
(Lissau) were already in Arlesheim to learn about curative education.*[9]

Karl König recorded what the group meant for him:

*We began to like each other and to meet as often as our work would
permit. During the year 1937, this Youth Group became a source of
great satisfaction to me. I was able to mould a younger generation and
lead them step by step to an understanding of the spiritual realities of
the world.*

*In the course of this year it became evident that we ought not only to
study together but that we should in time do some common work. We
expressed it, in that we said: We do not want to read Anthroposophy; we
want to live it. We decided to aim at starting a home for handicapped
children.*[10]

Hans Schauder, looking back near the end of his life, described the
development of the group:

*The core of the first group went to the Wasa Gymnasium, a poor
secondary school. The only good thing was that some great personalities
had attended the school, such as Stefan Zweig. Here was the first karmic
meeting: a group was at school together. The school group developed
into König's Youth Group. Out of this developed the founder group of
Camphill. König had the ability to integrate people.*

*The group was an archetype. I use my imagination, I may be right, I
may be wrong. I have the feeling that the majority had a connection to
König in a previous life. When König came to Vienna from Pilgramshain
in Silesia the group formed itself — a karmic group, connected to each
other.[11]*

The Annexation of Austria

The Austrian chancellor Kurt von Schuschnigg's efforts to prevent
German absorption of Austria were successful until he lost the support of
Mussolini in 1937. In February 1938 Hitler forced him to take the
Austrian Nazi leader into his cabinet. The government ordered a referen-
dum (which was cancelled soon after), to be held on Sunday, March 13, to
decide Austria's future. But much was to happen before that. The writer
Carl Zuckmayer (1896–1977) wrote:

*In the night leading up to March 11, 1938 a very fierce south wind
blew up, an arid Föhn storm, as if it was coming from the desert. It blew
across a cloudless sky, it blew the whole of the next day. The wind swept
countless election handbills through the streets like so many dead leaves.
Paper in bundles, crumpled paper, smooth or in shreds — paper was
drifting everywhere. It dropped like dirty snow from the lorries, which
carried groups of workers from Wiener Neustadt through the city in
order to demonstrate against Hitler and the government by way of
invisible speech choirs.*

*It had become public knowledge that the socialist workforce was
prepared to vote for Schuschnigg and for Austria although they had not
forgotten the bloody February of 1934.[12]*

As the sun went down on Friday, March 11, Chancellor von Schuschnigg spoke on the radio and announced that he had resigned:

*The German government today handed to President Miklas an
ultimatum with a time limit attached, ordering him to nominate as
Chancellor a person to be designated by the German government and to
appoint members of a cabinet on the orders of the German government;
otherwise German troops would invade Austria. I declare before the
world that the reports issued about Austria concerning disorders created
by the workers and the shedding of streams of blood, and the allegation*

*that the situation has got out of control of the government were lies from
A to Z. President Miklas asks me to tell the people of Austria that we
have yielded to force ...*[13]

While he was speaking two of his own guards stood at his side, bearing the swastika. When the microphone was switched off they arrested
him.

In his biography Hans Schauder tells of the atmosphere in Vienna that
Friday evening as they were on their way to the Youth Group meeting:

*Lisl and I went there by tram and had no idea how fateful that
evening would be for us. When we got on the tram, we felt immediately
an immensely oppressive and spectral atmosphere. Something quite
different, which had never been there before, spread through this
Viennese tram. It was full and there were no seats left so we were the
only people standing. Everyone stared silently at us. No one said a word.
And then we saw that all of them without exception had pinned on a
swastika. Some had very small ones acquired from somewhere at the last
minute but most had large ones.*[14]

When the Youth Group met for the last time on that Friday evening,
March 11, 1938, the annexation of Austria had begun. By candlelight,
behind closed curtains, the group met. Karl König later noted:

*On the evening of the occupation when the Austrian government had
to resign and the new Nazi leaders assumed power, our Youth Group
assembled. We read a lecture of Rudolf Steiner's together. It was one in
which he speaks very powerfully of Michael the Archangel.*[15]

The meeting that evening was long. The plan to leave Austria, and to
meet in another country and to work together, was decided. This had
already been discussed in January and February of that year. They went
out into the night full of an inner resolve, not yet knowing where they
would meet. Hans Schauder continues:

*The meeting at Dr König's ended very late. Lisl and I no longer dared
to take the tram home so we walked back through the nocturnal city; she
as my protector. It was a terrible walk. Both of us were now completely
alone with our fear. I still remember our awful loneliness on that Vienna
night in the empty streets.*[16]

Carl Zuckmayer wrote of that evening:

*That evening all hell broke loose. The nether world had opened its
gates releasing its lowest, most revolting and most filthy spirits. The
city became transformed into a nightmarish painting by Hieronymus
Bosch. Lemurs and semi-demons seemed to have crawled out of dirty
eggs and from swampy holes in the ground. Incessant yelling and
hideous hysteric screams issuing from the throats of men and women
filled the air. This screeching continued day and night. All human
beings became faceless and resembled distorted grimaces: some full of*

fear, others full of lies and again others full of wild triumphant hatred.
In the course of my life I had seen plenty of human dismay and panic.
During the First World War I had experienced a dozen battles,
incessant bombing, death by poison gas and combat assaults. I had
witnessed the unrest of the time immediately following the war — the
crushing of uprisings, street battles and battles in halls. During the
Hitler riot in 1923 in Munich I was among the people in the streets. I
lived through the first period of Nazi rule in Berlin. None of those can
be compared with these days in Vienna.[17]

After the Annexation of Austria

The first to leave Vienna after the German Army marched in on Friday, March 11, 1938 was Rudi Lissau. Shortly after the Annexation he travelled via Switzerland and France to England, where he later married Hedda Förster. Rudi joined Wynstones School during the War and was an upper school teacher at Wynstones for decades. Many of the first generation of children born in Camphill went to Wynstones and had Rudi as their teacher. In Vienna Rudi had made it clear that his work did not lie with handicapped children. Rudi worked unstintingly for anthroposophy, celebrating in June 2003, both his ninety-second birthday and seventy-four years as a member of the Anthroposophical Society. Rudi has described himself as Camphill's 'first friend.' His wife, Hedda, died in 2002 and Rudi on January 30, 2004, two-thirds of a century after the Youth Group formed in Vienna. Rudi was central in the very first beginnings of the Youth Group and the last to die.

Bronja Hüttner left Austria in October 1938 and lived for many years in Britain before returning to Austria. She was very active in the Waldorf Kindergarten movement from its pioneer days, and became well known as one of its representatives. She will be long remembered for her extraordinary ability to create beautiful little dolls out of wool. She died in a Village Community in Austria in 2000.

Edi Weissberg, who qualified as a doctor in 1936, worked in 1937 as Karl König's assistant. He fled to America in August 1938, where he became well known as Edward Whitmont. From 1940 he studied homeopathy; and his increasing interest in analytical psychology led first to a correspondence, and then to a meeting with Carl G. Jung. He trained in Jungian therapy and eventually became an eminent Jungian analyst, critical of anthroposophy. Edward Whitmont wrote several books, including *The Symbolic Quest: Basic Concepts of Analytical Psychology* and *Return of the Goddess*. He died in 1998.

Hanna Förster, who was born Protestant with no Jewish connections, qualified as a doctor. The Nazis were keen to make use of every doctor so she was sent as far away from Vienna as she could be, namely to Bremerhaven in the northern tip of Germany. There, she was given the task of running a hospital. She did this throughout the War and, during this time, made contact with other anthroposophists in the area. When the War was over she decided to remain in Bremerhaven having by then made a number of friends, also interested in anthroposophy, who remained close to her throughout her life. She ran her own anthroposophical medical practice in Bremerhaven for over fifty years and was active in the local anthroposophical group in all its different activities. She never married. She turned ninety in November 2001. Hanna died in 2003.

Hugo Frischauer followed the group, leaving Vienna in March 1939 and was present when Kirkton House was officially opened on Whit Sunday, May 28, 1939. Hugo was interned in Canada together with Alex and Willi. On his return from internment he did not go to work in Camphill. He sang in the chorus of an opera company, and later became a teacher of English as a foreign language. Hugo Frischauer died in the 1990s.

Willi Amann escaped to Britain and lived in Kirkton House before he was interned in Canada. On his release he married Trude in June 1941, the first marriage in Camphill. Hans Schauder described his long-time friend:

Willi was the gentlest person I have known. He would never say an unpleasant word about anyone. Owing to his gentle and submissive nature he was not so appreciated as he should have been. Dr König did not know what to do with him. Eventually he became a gardener.

Hans Schauder escaped to Switzerland via Italy. Once in Basle he prepared for his final examinations in medicine. Meanwhile, Lisl found shelter in Williamston, the manor house near Kirkton House, leaving Vienna for Insch, near Aberdeen, in Scotland in September 1938. Rudi Lissau tells how she, and the others, came to Scotland:

The move to Scotland came about through the member of the group who all her life felt little real relation to Rudolf Steiner's work: Lisl Schwalb, who was to marry Hans Schauder. She had for a short time worked at the Clinic at Arlesheim, and while there was asked by an elderly couple to help improve their knowledge of German. They were called Haughton and were landowners in Aberdeenshire. He was an Englishman, a natural gentleman, who loved his garden which during the summer was open to visitors. Gardening was one of two activities which filled him with joy, painting was the other. His wife was a Scotswoman, very proud of her Celtic origin. She was known to have some trace of clairvoyance. She was strong-willed and temperamental.

She presided over the house, that almost constantly had visitors, friends of the family who would stay for weeks, sometimes months.

Lisl Schwalb wrote to the Haughtons and asked for a job at their house. She got the job and arrived at their house in Aberdeenshire.

On the eve of Michaelmas, September 28, 1938, just days after Lisl had arrived in Williamston, Karl König wrote to the young people from Paris:

I have been in Paris for exactly one week. During this week it has come about that to begin with our work shall start in France. When I crossed the French border eight days ago, I felt received by the French landscape as never before. The width and breadths of the pastures, the beauty of the hills, the trees, the sky with its clouds above — these were a first welcome ...

This is a strange country. I believe that it will have great significance in the next decades, because all signs point to it being the space where the spiritual rebirth of Middle Europe will take place. Much is to be found here of holiness and of healing. The ancient stream of the wisdom of Mary continues to live here and the grace that emanates from it is noticeable everywhere. The true stream of the Mother is at home here. But this Motherhood is sorrowful, like Herzeleide after Parsival has ridden away from her. He has forsaken the mother and seeks the way to the Holy Grail. It is also the image of the Pieta *which constantly rises upwards in the soul when one seeks 'La France.'*

I believe that you should take into your hearts this image of the mother who weeps for her son, this will help us further. It may be that we are permitted to go there in order to comfort this sorrowing mother.

Please start learning French industriously. Please read as far as it is possible for you, the story of Parsival, particularly the version by Wolfram von Eschenbach ...[18]

However, this move to France was not to be. Rudi continues: 'Soon Lisl told the Haughtons that there was a whole lot of friends who wanted to settle in Britain, intent to start curative work.'

The same good ideas often come to different people at the same time. The political climate in France soon made any chance of work there impossible. Karl König travelled to Switzerland, still wondering where the unknown place of work would be:

One day in October, when I was staying at the Clinic in Arlesheim as a guest of Dr Wegman, she said to me: 'Why do you not try Scotland? I have a friend near Aberdeen who may be willing to help you to start work there and to build up a new future." I looked at her with great doubts and asked her if she knew how difficult it was to obtain an entry-permit for Britain. She dismissed these thoughts and said something to the effect that if there is a will, the way ought to be found.

To my great astonishment two days later, I received a letter from the British Consulate in Berne saying that I and my family had been granted permission to enter the country and to settle down there permanently.

I soon received my permit, discussed my immediate plans with Dr Wegman who furnished me with a letter of introduction to her friends ... I arrived in London on December 8, 1938 ...

To this very day I do not know for certain who it was who made the application to the British Home Office on my behalf. I had hardly ever contemplated settling down in Britain. My eyes were turned towards France or Switzerland ...

A few days after my arrival in Britain, I travelled to Scotland and via Aberdeen reached the country estate of Williamston near Insch. Mr and Mrs Haughton, Dr Wegman's friends, received us (I had travelled with Mr Roth, the father of Peter and Alix Roth) with very great kindness. They had already accepted one of the members of our Youth Group as a permanent guest ... They also showed me a house, an empty old manse, quite near to their own house which they proposed to acquire for us and to adapt so that we could start with our work as soon as possible.[19]

Rudi takes up the tale:

The Haughtons were willing to help. Twenty minutes walk from their house there was a manse, which was empty, (Manse is the name for the house of the local Church of Scotland minister). This manse became the first home of the members of the Vienna group in exile. Lisl Schwalb stayed with the Haughtons.

Meanwhile a few people of local standing in the town of Aberdeen had heard of the group, felt sympathy for these refugees and their social intentions and provided help and advice. When war broke out all 'enemy aliens' were registered and graded. With the standing of the Haughtons and the Aberdeen solicitor the members of the group were allowed to continue as before.

Anke Weihs — then Ann Roth, had come to Britain with Peter the summer before. She describes the beginnings at Kirkton House:

On March 30, 1939 — the fourteenth anniversary of Rudolf Steiner's death. Mrs König, Alix Roth and I moved into Kirkton House. When, almost strangers to one another, we stood in the chilly little candle-lit entrance hall that evening to speak a prayer together, past and future seemed poised on a knife's edge; our single lives, embedded as they had been in a seemingly secure European context, had come to an end. Our lives as participants in an as yet unborn spiritual adventure had taken their first infinitesimal but irrevocable steps into a more than uncertain future ...

Dr König and Peter Roth joined us a day or two later and we were now five. At the end of our first week at Kirkton House, there was an eclipse of the sun ... The four König children came up from Williamston where they had been staying and a few weeks later, Marie Blitz joined us. The house was full of life and our daily existence together began ...

On May 10, just about six weeks after we moved into Kirkton House, our first handicapped child arrived and with him, our chosen vocation advanced to meet us ...

May 28 was Whit Sunday, one hundred and eleven years and two days after Casper Hauser's sudden appearance in the streets of Nurnberg. Six children and fifteen adults gathered in Kirkton House for its dedication to the task of curative education.[20]

Those who took part in the consecration of Kirkton House signed their names afterwards: Mr and Mrs Haughton, Mr and Mrs Roth (Alix and Peter's parents), Margarete Blum (Peter and Alix's Hungarian grandmother), Kalmia Bittleston, who had been nursing at the Clinic in Arlesheim, Hugo Frischauer, Elisabeth Schwalb (later Schauder), Peter Roth, Ann Roth (later Anke Weihs), Alix Roth, Marie Blitz, Tilla König, Karl König and one whose signature is difficult to decipher. Six children were also present: Clara Renate König, Bernward Christof König, Andreas Daniel König, Anna Veronika König, Peter Bergel and Rudi Samoje. Karl König addressed the small group who were present:

It is significant that we are here in Scotland where the mighty Hibernian mysteries were at work which, although springing from pagan sources, absorbed Christianity and helped to christianize Britain.

Rudolf Steiner spoke of two streams of Christianity: a blood stream coming from the east and beginning with the disciples, which spread westwards over Europe as the Grail stream of Christ. The second stream coming from Ireland, Scotland and Cornwall, spreading down over the continent to unite with the other stream in Middle Europe ...

We should not feel that we are bearers of a mission but should rather try to bring about a meeting of the British Spirit with the Spirit of Middle Europe. A uniting of what within the German language is dreamt and thought, with what the British person is able to put into deed.

We should promise ourselves not to try and create a Middle European island in this place. Rather, to try as best we can, to act for the good of this land, this country ...[21]

In 1940, Lisl Schwalb travelled from Scotland, across France, to collect

Hans. She found she was crossing a country on the verge of collapse. On the journey back from Switzerland to Scotland, Hans and Lisl stopped in London and were married by Alfred Heidenreich in the Christian Community. Meeting them in Scotland, Karl König expressed his disappointment that they had not married in Kirkton House and made it a community event. Hans and Lisl went to live not in Kirkton House, but nearby in Williamston, perhaps an indication of what was to come. Rudi and Hedda also spent a short time in Williamston.

Rudi continues:

Half a year later France had fallen, and the speed of the collapse made the authorities take another look at the refugees.

Most male members of the Group were confined in a hotel at Douglas on the Isle of Man, with the exception of myself, who was taken to a different camp, also on the Isle of Man. There I formed new connections, which at the end of the War brought me back to Vienna.

Hedda and I did not join the work of Camphill, but our personal relations to the members of the Group continued for the rest of our lives.

The married men, Karl König, Thomas, Hans, Peter and Rudi were interned on the Isle of Man. The unmarried men, Alex, Willi, Hugo and Carlo were interned in Canada. Carlo had never come to Kirkton House and before internment had lived in the Lake District. He was interned longer than the others, because he was not Jewish. Carlo arrived at Camphill October 18, 1941.

Hans Schauder, while interned on the Isle of Man with the other married men, wrote and performed a musical sketch. It was not difficult to guess who was being made fun of. Hans was very apprehensive as to how Karl König would react, but apparently when he saw it, König roared with laughter and asked him to perform it again. Some months before he died in 2001 Hans asked that a copy of his musical sketch should be given to the Karl König Library in Camphill, Scotland.

The stories of the other members of the Youth Group who founded Camphill are told in separate chapters.

Camphill

It was the women who first actually moved into Camphill House. The connection with the Haughtons came to an end. Barbara, who had spent the Kirkton House time working for a family in England, soon joined the other women; 'Frau Doctor,' as Tilla König was called, Anke, then known as Ann or Ännchen, Alix, Trude, Lisl and Marie.

When Hans Schauder was released from internment he joined Lisl in Camphill. In the autumn of 1940, he wrote a poem for Karl König's birthday. It is entitled 'Herbstzeit' — 'Autumn' and is a witness to the enthusiasm that fired the founders. Here is the last verse:

Herbstzeit

Mögen Geistesflammen
unsere Seelen
eng zusammen
schmieden.
Leuchten soll das Wahre
als das Brot
auf dem Altare
den wir in Gemeinschaft bauen.
Jugend-feuerkräfte soll sein
in dem Kelch
der starke WEIN
den ER uns zu Kämpfen wählt.
Schwertes Engel
Michael.

Autumn

May spirit flames
weld
closely together
our souls.
The truth shall shine out
as the bread
on the altar
which we build in community.
Youth's fiery powers shall be
the strong wine
in the chalice
which He will choose for our battle.
Angel of the Sword —
Michael.[22]

Chailean 'Anne' Weihs, born in July 1940, daughter of Thomas and his first wife Henny, was the first child to be born after the move to Camphill, whilst the men were interned. In February 1942 Lisl and Hans's twins, Agathe and Bridget, were born. In June 1943 their third daughter, Ethne was born.

Trude and Willi Amann married in June 1941. The next weddings in Camphill were of Barbara and Bernhard Lipsker in December 1942, and of Thesi and Alex Baum in February 1943.

After the christening of Agathe and Bridget Schauder, in Camphill, 1942.
Hans and Lisl hold their daughters

After the christening.
Barbara Lipsker holding
her goddaughter Agathe.
Alfred Heidenneich, the
priest of the Christian
Community looks on

Some leave Camphill

Hans and Lisl became undecided about staying in Camphill. Hans spoke to Karl König who then offered him responsibility for the medical work, but there were basic disagreements between them. In a conversation in 1994 with Nora and Friedwart Bock, and Deborah and Tom Ravetz, Hans, after recalling that Karl König did not want him to leave, described the exchange of words that followed:

Karl König said: 'Don't you think that I understand things much better than you, that I can judge them much better?' I said: 'Yes, very much so. But I have to make my own mistakes, otherwise I will not learn anything.'

A compromise was sought. Hans and Lisl Schauder, with Willi Amann, Mary Dinnie, Aletta Adler, Freda Walker and Hanne Moody, together with a group of children, moved to a large, rented house, known as Auchindoir Lodge, in a very beautiful part of Aberdeenshire, near Rhynie. When the lease ran out the group working there did not wish to reintegrate with the others in Camphill, and so they began to search for another estate. South of Edinburgh, Garvald House, a sixty-acre estate with three cottages, a lodge and a walled garden was found. In September 1944 the work at Garvald began.

After Willi's marriage to Trude had broken up, he moved to Garvald with the Schauders, and a new life began for him, here described by Hans:

Willi married again, a beautiful girl, Renate, who came to Garvald with a child, whose father had been a soldier who died in the landing in Brittany. They teamed up, both a bit lost.

Garvald became Willi Amann's life. When he retired in 1982 he kept in close touch. In the last conversation he had with Hans, shortly before his death in 1999, they talked about their departure from Camphill. Well over fifty years after they left Camphill, the parting of the group was still painful to talk about. Renate had died several years earlier.

Hans and Lisl Schauder continued their work at Garvald for some years, before moving to Edinburgh where Hans developed his work as a counsellor. His gift for quiet listening has helped many people. In remarkable discussions with the Catholic University Priest, Marcus Lefébure, which are recorded in *Conversations on Counselling*, Hans elucidated his ideas on counselling.

Near the end of her life, Anke Weihs visited Hans, and they looked back at the events of forty years before when Hans and Lisl had left Camphill, and a warm reconciliation was possible. Hans had followed the development of Camphill with great interest for well over half a century and continued to feel very much part of it. He died in July 2001, nearly ninety years old. His last years had been lived alone after Lisl died in 1993.

Anke

Anke was not part of the Youth Group in Vienna. She was a patient of Dr König's. She met Alix in the photo studio where Alix worked. Peter's first sight of Anke left a lasting impression. His sister, Alix, years later told Claudia Pietzner what had happened:

Peter saw Anke's picture on a front cover of some magazine, grabbed the magazine, ran to the photo studio, threw the magazine on the table and said to me: 'I have to meet this woman!'

As with many stories, in the retelling they begin to live a life of their own. Rudi tells a different version:

Alix worked in the photography studio of Carlo's father, Atelier Pietzner-Fayer. One day, her brother Peter said, 'I will take you out tonight. I will call at 6 o'clock at the Studio.'

When he came Alix still had some work to do and gave him some pictures to look at. When she came back, Peter had the pictures in front of him: 'That is a fantastic woman; can you introduce her to me?'

'Yes! But you won't have a chance — she's a dancer!'

Anke became friends with Peter and then Thomas, and had met Carlo at an artist's party. Yet Anke was never invited to join the Youth Group.

A play for Michaelmas, written by Karl König, was first performed in Camphill in 1942. Looking back at the Youth Group in Vienna it is revealing to see the first cast of the play:

The Guardian — Karl König
The Mother — Tilla König
The Prince — Carlo
The Knight — Thomas
The Man — Peter
The Virgin — Anke
The People — The others

In the play the Virgin is hidden until near the end. When she does appear, she says the words: 'I have been waiting ...' Anke had not taken part in the Youth Group, yet was central from the beginning of Camphill. Perhaps she had indeed been waiting for her role.

Karl König

(September 25, 1902 – March 27, 1966)

Christof-Andreas Lindenberg

During the period of twenty-seven years from 1939 to 1966, the life of Karl König and the unfolding and growth of Camphill is so interlinked as to be one story. To tell this part of König's biography is to relate the birth of a worldwide movement of homes, schools and villages on four continents; the manifestation of an impulse. The fact that König was solely responsible for the development of Camphill is balanced by the fact at the very core of the impulse; the community idea. Thus the story of the founding group of young people, most of whom had been part of a study group of friends around the Königs in Vienna from 1936 to 1938, is an integral part. Interrupted in their studies by the annexation of Austria to Nazi Germany, many of the group gathered again with the Königs just before the Second World War in a small manse in the north-east of Scotland, to work together for an ideal. Then are the stories of those who joined the founder group after the War, and of the many who came thereafter to take part in the growth of Camphill as their own unfolding destiny. Community building is the inherent force in a growth process involving many, not only one man. However, this introduction offers a picture of one man's unique contribution to Camphill and its taking root in twenty-two countries. It is true to say that the continuing development of some one hundred Camphill Centres is due to all those, handicapped or not, who form the living communities in each place, while Karl König is rightly referred to as the Founder of the Camphill Movement.

He was small of stature, but great in bearing. How was the controversial figure of Karl König experienced? Many instances come to mind, for instance, the lectures. The Camphill Hall is filled to the last seat. Dr König steps forward, a folder held tightly under his left arm, then walks with his customary deliberation to the table. There follows a brief rearrangement of his space: the glass of water, the flower vase, sometimes the position of the whole table is slightly altered, no matter how carefully some old hands

Karl König as a child with
parents and neighbours.
Vienna, 1906

have prepared everything. Having arranged his books, he clasps his hands behind his back, straightens himself up as if in a moment of decision, fastens his gaze on a point in the distance above the audience and begins, often in a kind of questioning tone, perhaps: 'Dear Friends, I have the impression that it would be necessary for us to turn to the coming Easter Festival ...' He immediately takes the listeners right into the pursuit of a quest connected with the seasonal festival ahead. König was deeply conscious of the signs of the times. In lectures we often had the impression that he seemed to read them from a place behind us and, as his gaze indicated, a little above our heads. In beginning his talks in this way, Dr König freed us from our more narrow concerns and we found ourselves living in the present moment with the spirit of the occasion.

He shunned figures of speech or intellectual excursions. He was very direct. Often quoting Steiner verbatim, he linked these passages with the situation we found ourselves in at the time. König's impulse showed the immediate relevance of Steiner's words to the moment. He demanded our alertness at such moments. His eyes could send out a choleric message to the person interrupting him by a cough or nodding off to sleep. Once more attentive, we would follow the images König painted before us, forming bridges to his thoughts. For example, he once described the seasons of the year in their outgoing movement from winter to summer, adding the image of the arterial blood stream going from the heart to the outer capillaries. Likewise he compared the descending, centring half of the year towards Christmas to the venous blood returning to the heart. Progressing

Karl König (second row, far right) as a medical student in 1925

further he spoke of the possible threshold experiences when going from one half of the year to the other, then which kinds of mental illness pictures may arise: the schizoid tendency in entering the ascending half of the year, the manic-depressive tendency crossing into the time from the height of summer to midwinter. Such complementary images often helped us to grasp his thoughts in greater depth.

He was also most adept at acting the animals he described, so that we had the impression he became the sparrow or the squirrel he was talking about. A zoologist at heart, he deemed it a privilege when the opportunity came to turn to the animal world. He delighted his listeners. Whether in a light or grave mood, most of his talks were addressed to our potential to become more awake and useful in our anthroposophical striving. His public talks never failed to inspire a moral enthusiasm, often changing people's lives there and then.

When I think of the writer Karl König, the concentration visible in his posture, the deliberate way he held his large fountain pen, how both his arms were bending in action filled with utmost intensity, I know that I witnessed a man of will. Through writing he was in touch with the whole world; he prepared the founding of centres, he startled the experts with his medical papers, he comforted parents and taught out of his self-acquired anthroposophy. A close friend of his told me König's secret of getting so many helpers: 'He always answered their letter of inquiry quickly.' Indeed, a look at his desk showed that he always seemed to be up to date. To anyone visiting him this was a marvel. To some of us who knew the number of letters and papers he dealt with daily, it was beyond comprehension that he accomplished the work in the time available.

As early as 1942, when the first Down's syndrome children came to Camphill, he researched this condition with profound interest. He loved these children and he inquired into the riddle they posed. Seventeen years later he was able to write and publish *Der Mongolismus,* a first clinical study to appear in German. Like other pioneers in curative education before him, the enigmas he encountered stirred the physician and human-itarian in him to put questions and investigate possibilities of help and healing.

He regularly wrote, with new insights, about the spastic child, the thalidomide child, the contact-disturbed conditions he met in the thou-sands of children that came to him. Apart from his peripatetic consulta-tions he treated many children in the community setting of Camphill schools. He would hold conferences with resident or visiting physicians and work with those who looked after the children. Then he wrote down the appropriate treatment and educational methods for each child. He brought about many opportunities in which to share his ever present spirit of inquiry. This corresponds to an unwritten law in community liv-ing: one's own question gains by the same measure by which it is seen to be living in others. I believe that König wrote all his books out of such recognition; thus his books are not his creations alone. This is not only so for the study in child psychology, published as *Brothers and Sisters,* in which almost every co-worker helped him by supplying the data, but also for *The Human Soul,* and for perhaps his most outstanding book, *The First Three Years of the Child.* His insights were 'ploughed under,' as it were, in seminars, and worked through in a supplementary way tak-ing into account the experiences of others, thus ever linking his creative thoughts with life experience.

For some years I was with Dr König on the editorial board of *The Cresset,* a quarterly journal of the Camphill Movement. There I wit-nessed his will in action. For issue after issue he wrote the leading arti-cle and showed concern to the last dot with the contributions of other writers. While always welcoming initiative, his expectations were high and his scrutiny could be severe. In those days I also experienced his choleric side: Dr König could give an almighty row!

Karl König documented his wide interests in hundreds of articles that ranged from his erstwhile professional interest, embryology, to history, or human biography and, as expressed in his very last essay, zoology. Some

Karl König with Albrecht Strohschein and Walter Johannes Stein (centre)
at Pilgramshain, 1932

things were written by the medical doctor, others by the pedagogue, or
the researching natural scientist. He wrote petitions for the social standing of the handicapped person. Other writings were prompted by his
ever-growing concern for the suffering of humanity and the needs of the
earth. Any attack on the dignity and integrity of man called him to speak
and write. He often wrote a long lecture, complete with quotations. When
having to give the same talk in another town in a slightly different context, he would write it out again, tirelessly. Here was a man who always
managed to link his active thinking with the will to write. This had far-
reaching consequences.

In contrast to all that stands the artist-writer. In more quiet moments, or
when he was ill, Karl König created poems or lyrical stories. Friends put
together a volume of these for his sixtieth birthday. Among his best contributions are the festival plays which, even now, bring about a community-
forming moment in the season of the year they are highlighting in village or
school. König wrote the plays with a particular cast in mind, but they remain
relevant for subsequent generations. Some of these plays are more like pag-
eants, involving the whole community, the most famous being the midsummer St John's play. Gradually the players form into the Bell of Mankind,
singing, swinging and intertwining, and ending in a circle of oneness. No
words can express the experience of an unfolding community in these celebrations, as spoken word, movement and song come together harmoniously.

Karl König with his
daughter Veronika in 1938

In September 1952, on his fiftieth birthday in Camphill House, Karl König agreed to play a piano duet with Susi Lissau, a rare pleasure for us. Then he told us that, as far as he was concerned, he never aged. As a child and throughout adolescence he always felt himself to be the same unchangeable self. While he assumed this to be generally valid, we realized that it was perhaps more true for him than for others. A photograph from 1927 shows the young man of twenty-five with an expression of someone in his late forties; deep wrinkles and a moustache complete the impression. Already as a child he had a wise, knowing look in his eye.

Karli, as his mother called him, was born on Thursday September 25, 1902, to parents who owned a shoe shop in Vienna. 1902 was the year in which the Swedish educationalist Ellen Key proclaimed the Century of the Child. Though well loved and cared for, he did not have an easy childhood. Being an only child, born with slightly crippled feet and over-awake in his senses and soul, he looked into the world with precocious wisdom. There was something special about him. When the two-year-old curly blond-haired child sat in his push-chair outside the shoe shop, a psychology professor, strolling by, was so impressed that he went into the shop to inquire to whom this child belonged. He told the proud mother: 'He will be a very famous man in later life. In my whole career of studying heads I have never come across so special a form as this child's head.'

The growing child did not mix much with other children, but helped his parents in the shoe shop. Once he said, 'My school years were not altogether smooth-running.' The parents witnessed with concern his all too early independence. They found a picture of Christ in his cupboard when

The König family and others at Kirkton House 1940.
Back: Unknown, Anke and Peter Roth, Tilla and Karl König.
Front: Marie Blitz, Peter Bergel, Andreas, Veronika and Christof König.

he was eleven years old. Although he underwent the customary Jewish bar mitzvah at the age of thirteen, he had already begun to find his own way to the Christian religion.

His social awareness at the beginning of the First World War made him a young St Martin, sharing his cloak with the beggars he saw all around him. He refused to eat his mother's home-baking when he thought others were starving. He spoke up when he witnessed cruelty to animals and sometimes got into trouble with the police for doing so. König described himself as self-willed. Then, there were the increasing migraine attacks. As he grew up, his mother noted: 'There was such sadness in him, as if he had to carry the whole pain of the world alone.'

His eyes saw, and his ears listened to the problems of his time, long before he was a grown man and could really do something about it.

Towards the end of his school time Karli was deeply immersed in reading Haeckel, Freud, Buddha and Lao-tze, Dumas and Balzac, and especially the New Testament, seeking his way. His library grew when, after a quiet and successful matriculation, the eighteen-year-old youth studied all necessary basics for natural scientific research, with as he expressed it, 'a primeval force' that took hold of him. He was then in his pre-medical year. When he discovered Goethe's scientific writings he compared his enlightenment with what he had earlier experienced when discovering The New Testament.

Karl König with Trude Amann, Alix Roth and Thomas Weihs, 1958

In 1921 he heard the name of Rudolf Steiner. He found a group of students and doctors who discussed Steiner's lectures related to a study of man. Then came the important discovery on reading Rudolf Steiner's *Philosophy of Spiritual Activity.*

'Here,' he said, 'is all I myself have noted down on nature's creative force and on human thinking.'

It was an overwhelming experience. He wanted to meet Rudolf Steiner. Sadly, he was unable to go to Steiner's East-West Congress in Vienna in June 1922, and thus missed the only opportunity he might have had for such a meeting.

While still a medical student he became a teacher and research worker. For three years he was engaged at the Embryological Institute of Vienna. There the twenty-three-year-old student published his first research papers. When König graduated from medical school in 1927, Alfred Fischel, the Dean of the University, wished to employ him as an assistant at the Embryological Institute, as long as he would keep anthroposophy to himself. This condition decided Dr König to decline the offer. He had become a member of the Anthroposophical Society and would follow a different calling. In the summer of 1927 Dr König gave his first lecture in

Portrait of Karl König by
Trude Fleischmann

a sick children's hospital. His name rapidly became known, and, indeed, the call did come.

Dr Ita Wegman, then leader of the medical section of the School of Spiritual Science in Dornach, Switzerland, came to Vienna on a brief visit during which, she met Dr König. She straightaway invited him to work at her Clinical Therapeutic Institute in Arlesheim, near Dornach. He accepted at once.

In the weeks that followed, destiny played a significant hand. On entering the clinic he met his future wife, Tilla Maasberg, a nurse, who had arrived from Silesia that same November day.

On the first Advent Sunday, he witnessed the Advent Garden where he saw very handicapped children walking with lighted candles in a spiral-shaped garden of moss. What moved him on seeing this celebration is best described by himself, foretelling his life's work: 'In this hour I made the decision to dedicate my life to the care and education of these children. It was a promise I made to myself: to build a hill upon which a big candle was to burn so that many infirm and handicapped children would be able to find their way to this beacon of hope, and to light their own candles, so that each single flame would be able to radiate and shine forth.' In the clinic he was able to deepen the anthroposophical approach to medicine. This was reflected in a series of articles on embryology, the foremost subject on his mind at the time. König the writer emerged.

A little over four weeks after the Advent Garden experience in the Sonnenhof he was encouraged by Dr Wegman to hold his first lecture in

*At the site of Camphill Hall
in April 1961 with some
members of the Movement
Council*

the makeshift lecture hall of the Goetheanum, Dornach, during the Christmas Conference. The title was 'World Evolution as reflected in Embryological Stages of Development.' This saw his role as lecturer begin. A lecture tour to Breslau, in consequence of the Dornach lecture, was to lead him to the place of his future work. For seven years Karl and Tilla König would put their efforts into the newly founded curative home, Pilgramshain, in Silesia, working with handicapped children. Destiny had spoken; a life of dedication to the child in need of special care and to the integration of the handicapped person was born out of these portentous weeks in Switzerland.

Dorothea von Jeetze, having lived until 1993 in Camphill Village Copake in America, was our living link to those days. She told how Dr König, on his tour, visited the small children's home run by the Maasberg sisters. On Ascension Day in mid-May, he was asked to take up work there, but he could not imagine practising in so small a place. That very day, Joachim and Dorothea von Jeetze came to offer their nearby mansion house and park at Pilgramshain for the Maasbergs' work in curative edu-

All the co-workers and children in Pilgrimshain, c. 1930.
Karl König standing fifth from the left, back row.

cation. Now König felt doubly attracted. He was already feeling drawn to Miss Tilla Maasberg and to her Moravian-Bohemian Brethren background, but here, too, was the offer of a castle and grounds. Great moments call for quick decisions: the curative home at Pilgramshain was started that August, and in September Dr König joined the venture. He married Tilla the following year. As well as being the physician for the home, he built up a medical practice in the area which, in the next seven years, was to draw some 40,000 patients. The requests for lecturing increased.

Little is written about the years in Pilgramshain, but what becomes clear is that Dr König gathered more essential experiences and material for a medical approach to mental retardation, as well as organizational insight in residential care. Still to come was community living, both from a social and a spiritual standpoint. Dr König was thirty-three when, under political pressure, he decided to leave Germany for Austria. The arrival in his home town promised a new beginning. However, things turned out very differently.

The two years in Vienna became a period of inner and outer preparation. What formed as the main element for the future around the busy physician was a group of young people, most of whom were to become lifelong friends and co-founders. The Jewish background of many of them meant that they soon felt the mounting pressure from Nazi Germany.

However, the fire of the forge of their hearts was kindled by Dr König's weekly talks, and their discussions. Thus the smithy of the future was active from without and within. On the day of Austria's annexation to Germany they were ready to disperse, bound by their inner commitment. The date was March 11, 1938, a kind of eleventh hour for the whole of Europe. The future depends as much on silent deeds silently recognized as it does on strategies and actions. A little band of people left home and country to kindle a community fire which continues to burn in many countries, in many hearts.

Dr König could be a difficult person to approach. Yet every time, on entering his room, one was at once reassured by his welcome. He seemed to know one, and in the brief time allotted, usually half an hour, unspoken doubts were dispelled and superficial analyses of a situation corrected. Meeting him, one felt warmer. This must have been the experience of the many thousands of people who sought his counsel, whether in a personal meeting or by writing to him; the meeting of warmth through being recognized. We often witnessed it when he spoke to children; a bridge of warmth was created in that moment.

Dr König always had a lot of things on his mind. In the course of a day he would meet very many destiny stories, some disturbing matters, would be faced with a variety of difficult situations, while having to plan lectures, courses, journeys and confirm the work and direction in the new places. However, in a private meeting an individual was always met with his undivided attention and love. The accompanying challenge to do better was not the main thing which was taken away, but rather the thought that one had untapped resources for doing infinitely better; an enthusiasm and confidence engendered by the increased flowing warmth. A phenomenon of the Camphill Movement is the uninterrupted growth in the number of people coming to join the work. Dr König had the rare gift of knowing almost all the many co-workers by name. He knew the people who supported the work, the parents, and the very many special children and villagers; in their turn they all felt known by this man of the heart. His unbounded human interest penetrated the whole movement. And he always included those who had died.

Near the end of his life, Karl König wrote:

Only the help from man to man — the encounter of Ego with Ego — the becoming aware of the other man's individuality without enquiring into his creed, world conception or political affiliations, but simply the meeting, eye to eye, of two persons creates that curative education which counters, in a healing way, the threat to our innermost humanity. This, however, can only be effective if with it a fundamental recognition is taken into consideration, a recognition which has to come out of the heart.

*Karl König in
America 1962*

It is difficult to imagine the change from Vienna city life to that in a
remote granite manse in the north-east of Scotland; out in the windblown
countryside, without amenities or electric light. From March 30, 1939, the
growing group of Austrian refugees learnt, day by day, to handle broom
and hoe and create a home for twelve children in need of special care.
Thirteen months later, the men in the group were interned as enemy aliens.
During their six-month absence, the women brought about the birth of
Camphill. On June 1, 1940, the move into Camphill House and estate near
Aberdeen took place. The way that led from the humblest of beginnings
to that spiritually determined beginning is what makes that day a true
birthday, and justifies using the name Camphill to cover the whole world-
wide movement.

When he was applying for planning permission, Karl König wrote
down as the purpose of the intended work: medical, curative-education
and agricultural pursuits. That gave freedom for future development. Long

before the Camphill Villages came into being, Dr König, Thomas Weihs and others had deepened their knowledge of biodynamic agriculture. König arranged medical conferences for doctors, nurses and therapists, and, with the many helping physicians, laid a foundation for the gradual development of the science of curative education. This is taught in the International Camphill Seminar held in many countries.

Dr König became ill in 1955. Recovering, he entered the most intense period of involvement in the expanding Camphill Movement. During his last eleven years he was able to help in the threefold ordering of life within the centres, as well as establishing villages and schools in Germany, the United States, Switzerland, Ireland, Holland and Scandinavia. His heart was worldwide, but his focus and will were directed to the immediate surroundings. A fine example of his greatness was his ability to delegate and foster responsibility for the impulse and all realms of work. He gave up his chairmanship of the Camphill Movement, acting as *primus inter pares*. From the beginning, the Camphill work was built, formed and carried by many people. At the end of his life the king in him had fully united with the shepherd. In 1965 he said again that the handicapped children and adults are our true teachers, and that he too was learning daily from the life together with them.

I have tried to sketch the man of imaginative thought, the man of determined will, and the man of great heart to paint a portrait of a unique brother for those in need. Only by surveying the whole development and present position of the Camphill Movement can Karl König's contribution be rightly estimated. However, it stands out clearly that one man in particular was able to bring down the right thoughts and perform the necessary deeds at the right moment. Thus Karl König, in the years from 1939 until his death on March 27, 1966, was the ongoing founder of the worldwide Camphill Movement.

Tilla König

(March 9, 1902 – September 17, 1983)

Margarete von Freeden

Tilla König's life spanned a large part of the last century with its two great wars. She was born in Silesia, in Central Europe, and died in the most southern part of Africa, a remarkable Michaelic signature.

Matilda Maasberg was born into a Bohemian-Moravian family, the fourth child of seven. This middle child was different, her complexion was darker, her eyes were large and melancholic and she was extremely shy and sensitive. Her father used to line up the family and then point to Tilla, as she was called, and say 'This child we found under the hedge — she is not really ours!' This was said in jest but for a time she believed it. The family came from Silesia, a beautiful fertile land with great farms and estates, rolling hills and forests. It bordered on Poland and Czechoslovakia and became Polish after the Second World War. This land had become home for the Moravians who had been banned from many other parts of Europe. Tilla was born in Gnadenfrei, a typical Moravian settlement, with its large whitewashed church, the houses of the Brothers and those of the Sisters, the large cemetery at the edge of the village with its wrought iron gate and its inscription, within the centre the Lamb holding the Cross. The graves were simple, no ornaments, just plain flat gravestones between rows of lime trees. Often these graveyards of the Moravian Brothers were set on a hill from which one had a wonderful view of the sunrise and sunset. On Easter morning the brass band would be there to welcome the rising sun, a symbol of the Resurrection of Christ.

The childhood years of Tilla were joyful and protected. Her father ran a large factory that wove materials for curtains, bed linen, towels and tablecloths. Her mother was young and devoted her time to the children. They would go off at weekends with a pony-trap to a holiday house in the nearby hills known as the 'Waldhaus.' She and her younger brother Heiner were the best of friends — there was only one year between them, and there was a deep bond of destiny that united them. He too was a very melancholic child who later, in his early twenties took his own life.

The co-workers at the Waldhaus prior to the move to Pilgramshain.
Standing: Albrecht Strohschein, Maria Maasberg, Hermann Kirchner.
Sitting: Sister Annegret, H. Weiss, Mrs Strohschein, Tilla Maasberg 1928

After the end of her schooling, Tilla was meant to go to a sort of finishing school, where girls learnt all about running a household. She was
desperately unhappy and broke off her training to come home. Instead she
went to Berlin to train as a children's nurse. This became her vocation in
life. She learnt a great deal in the children's hospital and got on well with
the professors. Her special love was the work with the premature. After
her training she was called home to help her second sister Lene who had
married young and had had two children and then twins. She was not coping because of TB that she had contracted. After that the call came from
her oldest sister Maria, who had trained as a social worker, to help her start
a Children's Home in their holiday house, the Waldhaus. Both Tilla and
her sister Maria had met the Christian Community in Breslau and had
become members. They were also beginning to become interested in
anthroposophy. In November 1927 Tilla went to Arlesheim to take part in
a course for Curative Teachers run by Dr Ita Wegman. She arrived in
Arlesheim on the same day as Dr König arrived from Vienna and was put
up in the same guesthouse. Thus destiny led them together.

Both Tilla and Dr König took part in the same courses in eurythmy, lyre,
painting and many other subjects. To Tilla, Dr König seemed a lot older
than she was and it was only later that an intimate friendship grew up
between them. In the spring of 1928 Dr König visited the Curative Home
in the Waldhaus that was being run by Maria and Tilla together with

Tilla with Renate 1931   *Tilla with Andreas and Veronika, Vienna 1937*

Albrecht Strohschein who had taken part in the original Curative Course with Rudolf Steiner himself. During this visit Dr König met Gnadenfrei, the Moravian Church, the Maasberg family and Tilla's second eldest sister Lene who was dying of TB. This was a fated visit. The serenely beautiful and cultured land of Silesia made a deep impression on Dr König. The heart-religion of the Moravian Church awakened in him a deep Christianity that he had been looking for since his early childhood. It was through meeting Tilla and her home background that his heart gained a new dimension — in her presence he felt his heart melt and widen. During this eventful visit, the von Jeetzes (big landowners in Silesia), came to offer their great home — known as Pilgramshain, with its hundred rooms! — to the seedling work that had started in the Waldhaus. This offer enabled the work to grow. It also expanded the deep bond that had begun to weave between Tilla and 'Markus' (that was the name she liked to call him). It led to their joining in the new pioneering work of Pilgramshain, which began in September of that same year.

In May 1929, Tilla and Markus were married and lived in a small house together with the Strohschein family, close to the mansion where they worked. Dr König was a man with a mission and he warned Tilla that it would not be easy to be married to him. But her love for him was steadfast throughout the ups and downs that this union held in store for them. Even during their short honeymoon in Vienna he would go off to his old university and study, while she wandered around in the strange and unfamiliar streets of Vienna. Tilla's shyness would get the better of her at times and when there were too many visitors, she would run away into the fields and woods and Markus would have to go after her, find her and bring her home.

For seven years Tilla and Karl König lived and worked in

*The Kirkton
House group.*

*Standing:
Willi, Peter,
Anke, Thomas,
Alex, Tilla*

*Sitting: Trude,
Marie, Alix*

Pilgramshain. König was often away on lecture tours, or seeing to his enormous practice that had grown up during this time. Their first three children were born during these years. Tilla was a very good, devoted mother and kept the home going while König branched out further and further with his ideas and ideals.

In 1936 the family had to leave Pilgramshain due to political pressure. They moved to Vienna as poor as church mice. Work had to start all over again. König's renown for being a good doctor spread quickly and his practice grew. The family had to move into a bigger house and Dr König needed an assistant. These were busy and turbulent years with much work and insecurity. Tilla built up the home, providing the ethos for all the work, for the study groups, and for the constant flow of people that came seeking help. On March 14, 1937, Veronika was born — their fourth child, a blond curly-headed girl who was loved by everyone.

But life became very stressful due to the political situation and in 1938 when Hitler came to Austria Dr König had to flee and leave a mother with four young children behind. And it was only at the beginning of 1939 that Tilla could again make a home for her family, following the invitation of Mr and Mrs Haughton, friends of Ita Wegman's, who had made an old manse available for the König family and the founder members of Camphill, and even, in May 1939, the first child in need of special care.

Tilla belonged to the group of brave women who had decided to move to Camphill without their men, who had been interned on Whit Sunday 1940. Tilla had the ability to create order, peace and culture wherever she

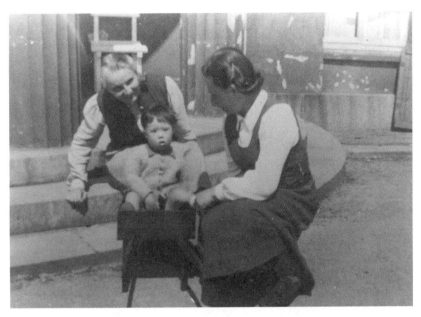

Tilla at Heathcot with Alix Roth and a pupil

Tilla at opening of Camphill Hall, September 1962

went. This and her warm humour made a wonderful basis for the coming work.

Anke Weihs relates an incident from the very early days in Camphill:

The furniture stood in the entrance hall of Camphill House like an accumulation of druidical monoliths. So Alix and I, inspired by Tilla, began to shift it, not without long strategic arguments as to which end first. One evening at 11.30, we moved an enormous and solid cupboard down the long drive to the Lodge on a wheelbarrow. It was one of those long light Scottish summer nights. Imbued with some kind of superhuman strength that was not our own, we had shifted furniture all day. Finally, we reached the Lodge and unloaded the cupboard. Down the drive came Mrs König to inspect our labours, saying she was too tired to walk up the drive again. So we put her into the wheelbarrow and wheeled her home, stopping every few yards, bent double and helpless with laughter ...[1]

In 1948–49 the first larger influx of young co-workers arrived mainly from Germany where the currency reform had made it possible to leave the country. It was the generation that had grown up in the war. Order, peace and culture were sorely missing, but the constant effort of community building, not just in theory but the daily handling of one's moods and emotions, the daily rubbing along together, the faith that had to be practised between people, the awareness for the needs of the other person, all this had to be learned.

With her sense of order and her devotion to the smallest thing, the detail, Tilla stood like a pillar of strength. She became the 'Mother' to all the young mothers, showing them how to care for their children.

In 1950 a new dimension was added to the spreading work of Camphill when Dr König was asked to start a hostel for St Christopher's in Wraxall, near Bristol, and Tilla offered to pioneer this work. This venture did not last long — Tilla was called to Thornbury Park to start a place for very young and frail children with cerebral palsy. Gisela Schlegel talks of this time: 'I was one of the lucky ones to go with Tilla König to build up a house community around the children with cerebral palsy who were so very much in need of care.'

The idea was to combine it with the long-planned nurses training, but this was not yet to be.

Meanwhile Tilla watched the co-worker children grow into a lovely but unruly bunch of children who did not know of order, peace or culture.

Christof, her eldest son, remembers from this time:

Mother had the idea to start a hostel for all the Camphill co-worker children, and this came next in The Grange at Newnham-on-Severn in Gloucestershire.

I was in Sweden at the time, and she wrote to ask me if I would want to help her with this. I decided I would, and came back. She was concerned that these children would have a proper home life, and go each day to Wynstones School on the train and bus. The children loved the Grange and Mother put her all into making their life full in all respects. I have no doubt that Mother brought more into Camphill than she is credited with. I have no doubt that the idea to start Camphill with disabled children came from her initial work with her sister in the family holiday house, The Waldhaus in Silesia which father visited before the move was made to Pilgramshain. The element of the Brudergemeinde also came from Mother and her family into the weaving of the fabric of Camphill which started to happen from that time onwards in thoughts and ideas. So Mother made a huge contribution to all that has to do with the care of the handicapped child, the aspect of devotion and of prayer, the aspect of order and beauty, the aspect of devotion to small detail. With Mother this became a real art form, which could stand on equal terms with writing, painting, sculpture and all the other arts. She was a homebuilder and a homemaker, and this too led to significant contributions to community building. Mother, as far as I can remember, was not ambitious, and was happy to be in the background, and because of all this her role was not always apparent in the building up of the Camphill Community.

Because of Father's other preoccupations, she played the main part in my upbringing. She was our educator as well as our Mother. Cleanliness, order and beauty were all around. We had many tasks to perform, in the house as well as outside. We cleaned our shoes, helped with washing up and cleaning, made our beds, helped to rake leaves, helped with preparing vegetables; we had to have put all our belongings neatly away before going to bed and being settled. Settling was a very special time for us, with a prayer for each of us written by Father, and one for the whole family, and songs. But before this could happen, everything had to be put away; we had to make friends if we had quarrelled so that we could be settled in harmony, and be prepared for the night and sleep.

We had to play our part in the house community we lived in, and did not feel separate from it. We were fully part and parcel of the whole extended family, and made to play our part as everyone else. All this was a wonderful gift for our life, and I know that none of us ever regretted having been brought up in Camphill.

After the Grange Tilla spent some time in Delrow in its early period when it was still finding its direction. This was not a happy time for her. But then Tourmaline in Botton Village, Yorkshire, was built for her in 1964. There she found a new home. She no longer had to pioneer but could unfold and live and share the many ideals that she carried in her heart. From there she undertook her journeys to her children, till finally she decided to spend her last years with them in South Africa.

Tilla with Kate Roth.
Around 1963

Tilla had not lost her sense of fun. Her son-in-law Julian Sleigh remembers a typical story from the final years in South Africa. He describes how it was always a bit of a palaver to get Tilla to the Hall for community events and celebrations. One had to get the car out, help Tilla into the car, drive the (short) distance, help Tilla out of the car and into the Hall, park the car, and so on. One day a play was to be performed in the Hall and Julian was responsible for getting everything set up and ready. He didn't really want to rush back at the last minute to bring Tilla in the car. Remembering the story of the move to Camphill when Anke and Alix, amid much hilarity, brought a very tired Tilla back from the Lodge to Camphill House, Julian quipped to his daughter Veronica, 'I'll be busy in the Hall; why don't you bring Grandmother over in the wheelbarrow.' He didn't give it another thought until, as people were beginning to arrive, he caught sight of Tilla and greeted her. 'I feel a bit wobbly,' she told him. 'The ride in the wheelbarrow was rather unsteady. Is there some place to sit down?' Although quite frail, she was a good sport.

Renate writes:

In March 1966 Markus died of a heart attack. They had not lived together since she had moved south to Wraxall in 1950. Their lives and tasks had spread out and widened — but they remained faithful to each other. Markus would visit regularly; he would phone her every few days and there was a steady correspondence between them. In 1965 during my stay in Botton with our first three children — while Julian was training for the priesthood — I had my first conversation with my father about this fact that they could not live together. He was very open and told me that her melancholy temperament pulled him down and he could only manage a few days at a time. It would have the effect of laming him in his spiritual endeavours. Tilla bore this as her cross; she was strong enough to carry it alone and she always kept faith. Never ever did I hear an unkind word spoken to or about Markus. She was also deeply connected to Peter Roth who was like her Father Confessor, or a younger brother to her; and to Thomas Weihs who recognized her courageous pioneering strength, underlying the nurturing mother role she had taken on in this lifetime. On the day of Thomas's death, June 19, 1983, Tilla fell and broke the neck of her femur. She never really recovered from this, became confused, and died three months later on September 17, 1983. She, Tilla, had been born in March and died in September. Markus was born in September and died in March. Thus their destinies intertwine and form a whole.

Barbara Lipsker

(August 8, 1912 – May 25, 2002)

Cherry How

Looking back over the course of her life, Barbara once said that she owed her destiny to her handicapped brother and her damaged knee.

The family lived in the Jewish Quarter of Vienna, Leopoldstadt, between rivers. They were exceedingly poor and hungry, and yet her tales from her childhood are filled with fun, laughter, singing and street games with hordes of other children. Barbara, then known as Sali, could run very fast, but one day aged five or six she fell and hurt her knee. This blow developed into TB of the knee joint and from then on her memories were filled with pain and sleeplessness. 'No more freedom to run and jump.' [1]

For many years after that she was in pain and could hardly walk. She had to endure a lot of treatment; once, for six months, being in plaster to the waist. She was sent on holidays arranged for poor children to have the experience of sun and sea, and to spas for iodine therapy. Although she came from a Jewish family, it was assumed she was Catholic because she had fair hair and blue eyes, and so she was taken to Mass. She loved the whole experience; the candles, the kneeling, and making the sign of the cross were possibly her first introduction to Christianity. But this stopped when her mother came to visit.

Later, at about the age of nine, Barbara was sent to Italy with other sick children and was there for four months. She later recalls:

A young social worker looked after us. On her bedside table lay a small black book, red where the pages met. I could not withstand the temptation to look into it. It was a New Testament. How could I know the meaning of it? But I can never forget it. I still see the many little paragraphs which I certainly could not read, but I was sure that they held something holy.

Barbara was born in the summer of 1912 into a Hasidic Jewish family in a little town in Poland called Brzozow. She was the sixth of eight children. When the First World War broke out, the family fled to Vienna, the centre of the Austro-Hungarian Empire, to escape the advancing Russians

Barbara (front left) at Rimini, July 1929

and their pogroms. She wore all her clothes at once, and could hardly move for the bulk of them.

In the house in Vienna there lived about twenty refugee families, all blessed with many children. We played any free moment, we did not need any toy — the world was full of magic and wonder in spite or perhaps because of all poverty. The courtyard — grey, grey asphalt and grey stone walls all around, was a fairyland to me.

It was empty apart from a plain wooden contraption on which the housewives hung their carpets to beat the dust out of them (There were no hoovers yet). That wooden contraption had a magic power: it was a castle, it was a ship, it was a house, a mountain, a forest and we children were the princes, the knights, Red Indians or robbers; everything was alive with splendour, with colour, with beauty and delight.

Then, one morning, I went down as usual, waiting for my sisters and friends to go with them into our fairyland. They came, we began to play — and nothing happened! The wooden contraption remained the wooden contraption, the walls remained grey stone walls, the ground under our feet was hard and grey — the world was grey, without light, no splendour, no magic. The innocence of my childhood came to an abrupt end. I must have been around ten years of age.

Barbara found the travel and hospital treatments a welcome change from her home life, and in consequence the estrangement from the devout

On an outing with some of the 'old' Youth Group in 1932.
From left: Edi Weissberg, unknown, Robert Schwalb, Barbara.

Judaism of her family increased. Her father was a strict Hassidic Jew and observed all the correct Jewish practices. Amongst his peers he was a well-respected scholar. For a while he had been a flour merchant, and later he had a shop selling kosher meat, where Barbara's brother also worked. But for a lot of the time there was no obvious source of income and the family, with eight children, existed in two rooms. Beds were erected every night and space was short. Her mother was a simple and innocent woman devoted to her family, yet unable to create order or culture in the home. Later, Barbara's older sisters were able to some extent to organize the family, managing to ensure that Barbara received appropriate medical treatment.

Her father, although deeply religious, was tyrannical. It was impossible to disobey him, so the family pretended to follow his way, while in their hearts rejecting his strict Judaism. She said of this period:

My life was a lie. It is probably from this time that I developed something of an inferiority complex on the one hand, on the other hand a covering up of my real being, a difficulty just simply to be.

As a child, because of her knee, Barbara literally could not get away from her father's oppressively fundamentalist practices. She longed for peace, order and harmony. She and her sisters were intelligent and questioning, hungry for culture, and sensing there was something more to life. How could she free herself?

I sometimes wonder which angel took me. Meanwhile I grew inwardly

*Barbara's brother
Moritz Gerstler with
Hans Schauder in
1934*

more and more a stranger *in my family, longing for friendship, for
someone with whom I could truly share, in whom I could confide. The
bond of love between sisters and brothers was a natural, a strong one
but did not reach into the dim longing of my young soul.*

However, because of her lameness she was often away from home, and
this enabled her to experience different ways of life. On one of her trips to
Italy Barbara met Lisl Schwalb. They shared a room and became close
friends, and their friendship continued back in Vienna. Lisl's home
became Barbara's second home, she slept and ate there and came to appreciate Lisl's simple, warm, intelligent parents.

From her early years Barbara had longed for the experience of community life. It was the time of the Zionist movement and groups of young
people were emigrating to Palestine:

*... putting all their enthusiasm, all their youthful conviction into making
the desert earth, converting it into fruitful ground through the work of their
hands. Communities of young people were doing this! I listened
fascinatedly, being much too young to join the heated discussions. In my
young and longing soul an image began to form: human beings, living
and working together for a great ideal, in peace and love, not minding any
hardship. Yes, this I would do when I was grown-up: I would learn to
become a gardener and then join such a Community!*

This search for a deeper kind of friendship is characteristic of Barbara's
life: she always wanted to have a more profound relationship with people.
She made up for her missed schooling by reading everything she could
find, and in her imagination new worlds opened up.

Barbara while working for the König family in Vienna in 1937

Barbara's younger brother Moritz was a handicapped child in need of special care. Because the family was poor, and because at that time there was little provision for such children, he was cared for at home.

But something else happened which was to become the slowly rising star on the path of my earthly destiny. Somebody who knew of our sorrow about Moritz gave us an address of 'some people' who did some special things with handicapped children. It turned out to be the Viennese centre of the Anthroposophical Society, where a lady doctor, Maria Glas, and her husband Norbert, and also a certain Dr König were active. Moritz was introduced and consequently received treatment in curative eurythmy. It was 1928, 1 was fifteen years old. Pilgramshain, where Dr König was to be medical officer began its work and Moritz became one of its first pupils. I did not meet Dr König at that time but the little bit I heard about Pilgramshain resounded in the very depth of my soul, calling forth a dim longing as if for a lost paradise.

Following a visit to Pilgramshain my mother told me of the impressions she received there and once again I experienced something like a great wondering: is it possible that such a life does exist

Passport photo from 1938

*somewhere on earth and who are the chosen people who are permitted
to take part in it? — From that date I made every effort to take on all the
correspondence with Pilgramshain if it was only for the sake of contact
with this place.*

While Karl König was in Pilgramshain, he would go to Vienna to visit
his parents, and this was how Barbara met him.

*In utter shyness, full of awe, this first impression of Dr König entered
my soul. Who was he? I cannot remember the exact circumstances
surrounding this meeting — but I know that this short young man who
appeared so wise and serious made a deep impression on me. He
awakened ideals and longings in my heart and mind which I was as yet
unable to grasp.*

Later, as the Nazis became more powerful in Germany, Moritz had to
return home and Barbara took on the care of her brother. The difficulty of
this situation led her to a crisis of health and strength through which her
friends supported her. Eventually, the family reluctantly decided to place
Moritz in an institution. He died there of TB in 1937, thereby escaping the
horrors of Nazism.

*I never forget how he looked at me when I visited him a few days
before his death. It was a sad, knowing, promising look: He, and my ill
knee guided my destiny through childhood and youth.*

Moritz was important in the line of destiny that linked Karl König and

*Barbara with
daughter Agnes,
Murtle 1944*

curative education, and Barbara and her circle of young friends. This now included Lisl, and Lisl's future husband Hans Schauder. Out of this circle came the First Youth Group.

After she finished school Barbara took a commercial college course and began work in an office. However, she really wanted to work with children, and so in her free time she went into the park, where children gathered around her for ring and ball games.

The stress of caring for Moritz had led to a deterioration in the condition of Barbara's knee, and through the help of friends she was treated in a sanatorium in the Tirol run by doctors Norbert and Maria Glas. It was Advent 1933 and she was twenty-one years old. This was an important time for Barbara. She met people interested in Rudolf Steiner and received anthroposophical treatment. She celebrated Christmas for the first time and gloried in the beauty of nature she found in the mountains.

Barbara had the growing conviction that she wanted to work in curative education. She wanted to go to Holland to work in the Zonnehuis but when she was refused a work permit she was shattered. 'What was I to do? I *had to* get away!'

Barbara spent time visiting her sister in France, and on her return to Vienna she studied to qualify as an English language teacher. But she still longed to work with young children, and finally won a place on a Kindergarten training course, by gaining a special exemption from the gymnastic examination.

'My becoming a Christian more or less happened naturally,' she said once. Despite still living at home, she was longing for a different life without knowing how really to achieve it. Her friendships in the Youth Group were her lifeline:

In the evenings when we were returning late on our way home we were a noisy company full of abandon, or we observed the starry sky learning to orient ourselves among the constellations. Every Thursday night many of us gathered in the rooms used by the Christian Community for the wonderful evening sermons by Rudolf Frieling, Rudolf Köhler and, a little later, of Josef Kral. These men were the priests in Vienna at that time.

New worlds opened up for us. Sometimes I would tell my friends of Dr König and of my brother whom I loved so much. Three of the friends were studying medicine and as a result of their growing interest in Anthroposophy two of them took part in a conference for medical students in Arlesheim. It was there that they got to know Dr König. The ring began to form.

At first, they met for long conversations in cafes with Karl König. They began to turn to him for advice. Meanwhile, he gave lectures in the city.

For us he was the person who made one feel known and appreciated ...

We asked Dr König to meet our whole group and it was from that time onwards that we had meetings together whenever he came to Vienna. Very frequently he gave lectures in Anthroposophical circles or also public lectures and we would meet afterwards in one of the Viennese coffee houses, sitting together for hour after hour to discuss world perception, political questions or very personal questions together. There was one man who could listen! He never smiled at our questions which may not have been all that world-shaking, but he entered into them and taught us to distinguish the essential from the inessential. The horizon of our consciousness became ever wider and richer; in the personal conversations the first glimpses of the light of self-knowledge began to show. We could also turn to him as a doctor and receive help. It seemed that our lives gained a new dimension, a new meaning.

We endeavoured to recognize the signs of our time and its demands upon us. To experience the leading time spirit, to call upon our will to become awake. Every week one of us brought a leading thought, a verse, a sentence from the Bible, a poem, a significant thought from a book. With this content we would live then throughout the next week. The verses of the Calendar of the Soul began to sound. Man — World, Ego — Cosmos, divining a reality which was to be grasped anew.

Because he was Jewish, Dr König could not continue working in Germany, and so his family moved back to Vienna. He asked Barbara to help his wife look after their children. At last, in May 1936, Barbara could rent a small room and move away from home. Soon she was asked to move into the Königs' house as a permanent helper.

There Barbara found the peace, beauty, order and culture she had longed for. Tilla König later said that she had never had such an orderly helper, and this impulse to create order remained with Barbara for the rest of her life.

I was now able to get to know Dr König more closely in a quite different situation. The house, 49 Anastasius Grün Street, was bright and friendly. It was furnished simply but tastefully and artistically. The financial resources were rather limited to begin with. Dr König insisted nevertheless to pay my monthly salary even though I refused it adamantly.

The children lived in a very large nursery with a big sunny terrace. A corner of that room was now my room. A bed, a table and chair, a bookshelf, cupboards on the landing. When the children were asleep, I could enjoy my corner in peace, the peaceful breathing of the children adding an atmosphere of homeliness and 'belonging.' Otherwise the days were fully lived in the house community. The number of patients increased daily, Dr König was incredibly busy. That determined and influenced the rhythm and atmosphere of the house greatly. After breakfast, when Dr König had his quiet half hour I had to keep the children absolutely still, which was not an easy thing with the lively, temperamental children. What was this half hour, what was Dr König doing and why had it to be such a holy time? Very gradually new concepts, new experiences began to widen my consciousness.

The way Mrs König ran her household, her harmonious, even movements, how she dealt with her children, approached her husband, cared for meals, the beauty and order of the house — always with the attitude of devotion in the actual doing. What a lot I had to learn! And I absorbed it eagerly, full of wonder! These were new worlds! I loved the children and thought I could never again love children so dearly.

When I look back now I realize that my move to the König family marked a new road, or rather the road leading to Camphill. All my searching, my longing for culture, for beauty, for order, for friendship — although already met in various ways before, was now gathered up here like in a haven from where streams of new life were flowing out.

This new road inevitably led Barbara away from her parents. They could never quite believe in her conversion to Christianity. Once, they visited Dr König in an effort to reconcile their daughter to the family, but although she did continue to see them, the separation was irrevocable. Later, they fled east together with their youngest son and all three were lost in the Holocaust. They were not the only members of Barbara's family to undergo such great suffering during this terrible time.

To the end of Barbara's life it was a source of sorrow to her that she had not considered or helped her parents enough.

What have I done to my parents? It weighs heavily on my conscience, what could I have done? Have I tried?

The pain I inflicted on them is a guilt I have to carry, which I hope and pray will be redeemed one day.

But Barbara had found a new 'home' and a new 'family' in the circle of friends who regularly met in the Königs' house.

It was where, somewhere, my life started.

Also the circle of young friends found now something like an earthly home: we became a real youth group. One evening every week, I believe it was Friday, we met at the Königs' house to work, study together, have inspiring conversations and learned, learned about the world, about ourselves. Dr König was just ten years older than myself — he was thirty-four at that time! One could have the impression that he had actually never been young in the ordinary concept of 'young' but that he was born into this world wrapped in wisdom, the stars of his earthly task around him, increasing in strength and in clarity.

The weekly meetings became essential in their lives. 'One was sustained by them.' Meanwhile, the idea was gradually coming about of doing something meaningful together. On the fateful evening of March 11, 1938 Barbara was in the Königs' house. Outside, the crowd shouting 'Heil Hitler' could be heard. The voices resounded with fanaticism and Barbara remembered thinking to herself: 'If I were young and not Jewish I might also have followed the crowd.' She sensed there was something very powerful at work. Everyone was fully aware of what had been happening in Germany. Barbara always left the house carrying The Calendar of the Soul by Rudolf Steiner and The New Testament in case she was arrested.

These last months in Vienna were a very dark time. Persecution of the Jews started from the moment Hitler marched into Vienna. Our little shop, the source of our daily bread, was attacked and closed down. Already you saw old men down on their knees scrubbing the stones. Rows and rows of young and older men — people you knew — were marched off — where to? You heard screaming and weeping — loud shouting of Heil Hitler! *There was a knock at the door — a group of men outside when I opened. 'Is there any man in your flat?!' 'No' I answered completely calm and cool. They looked at me suspiciously, I made a gesture like inviting them in — they went. Aba, my brother stood hiding behind the bathroom door. All male beings from the twenty-three flats of our house were walked off.*

My parents were not up to date with tax paying. One day a few men appeared and took everything that could be moved away with them: furniture, books, clothes, lamps, linen etc. I stood and watched them, angry and speechless. Finally I said: 'Do you know what you are doing, are you considering what consequences such deeds will have for you?'

They smiled contemptuously, uneasily and carried on, leaving us an old table, a few old chairs and our beds. They did not take me along. Were we protected? How could we escape into safety?

We met almost every day. Dr König drew the outlines of the work our group was going to take on. The East was barred for us, we might go to an island: Cyprus perhaps? We would have to take European heritage, culture with us, work on the land, share our lives with handicapped children. We would do all the work ourselves, receive no pay; farmer, teacher, priest, doctor, all would carry the community; our way of life would be simple in Christian brotherhood. We warmed to the idea enthusiastically, connected by an inner will that need not be spoken. Finally a request for entrance as a group was sent to Ireland, which was turned down. But there was no time to be lost, we had to leave Austria individually as soon as possible, especially the men.

Barbara received a work permit as a 'Nurse Maid' which enabled her to leave Austria in December 1938 for Britain. But 'when I sat in the train and we crossed the German border into Belgium I cried bitterly ...' Arriving in London on December 30, she was reunited with the Königs and Peter Roth. From there she journeyed to Oldham, to the Wrigley family, and later worked with the family of Adam and Gisela Bittleston. Visiting her friends in Kirkton House she found herself impatient to join them. Finally, on December 30, 1940 Barbara arrived in Camphill, 'my ultimate home!' She was one of the last of the group to find her way there, and said of this time 'It was not always easy because something had already formed itself without me, I had to find my place.'

She later saw this as a signature in her life, that she was someone who 'nearly' or 'just' made it, or even 'just missed' it.

Once she dreamt that she was walking over a narrow bridge across a chasm. On the other side stood the Friend of God, a spiritual teacher from the end of the fourteenth century to whom she felt a strong affinity. There was a handrail to help her, but the last part had fallen away and in her dream she only just managed to get across and reach safety.

This element of uncertainty is reflected in her birthday and in her name. Her exact birth date is not known, although it was always celebrated on August 8, and her given name turned out not to be her 'real' name. Frau Sabine, an elderly woman and close friend of the König family, became a mother figure for Barbara in Vienna. 'It was she who knew that my real name was not Sali but Barbara Sybille.' This name means 'the wise or prophetic stranger.' Certainly, Barbara was not at home in her birth family; she always felt she was searching for something else and was a stranger in her surroundings.

One friend, sitting by Barbara at the end, as she lay in Glencraig Chapel, felt that he was looking at *l'inconnue,* the archetypal woman who

Barbara with Karl König after the christening of her daughter Agnes

goes through history but is never really known. She had also sometimes asked herself, 'Who am I really?'

The sixty-two years following her arrival in Camphill would be a quest to discover this. When describing this time she wrote:

I stand before the house and have the intense experience of 'knowing' the place, of having come home. I walk behind the house, look down to the River Dee, look across to the gentle hills on the other side and the feeling of knowing the place intensifies.

Barbara embraced her new life, cooking and doing housework and caring for children, as she had done in Vienna. She was one of the few among the pioneers of Camphill who had had experience of working with children and it was her natural gift to relate to them. Community life was ordered: hard work, study, festivals, Services, the building of friendships.

Everything we did was important, special, nearly sacred and had to be done at its best. If it was not so we either confronted each other or were in a most definite way put straight by Herr or Frau Doktor. The sense of calling increased, community consciousness spirit began to work more strongly.

When Heathcot was established in 1942, Barbara was asked to move there, away from Camphill. It was a difficult wrench, but she found it a happy time. She shared her room with six children, some of whom were very frail: 'It was a holy task!'

*Barbara with
Marianne Gorge at
Mourne Grange in
1982*

*At the same time a clear little light, a steady inner flame had begun to
burn, caused by the first beginnings of an inner path under the loving
guidance of Dr König and by the growing enthusiasm and willingness to
sacrifice one's self-will to the spirit will.*

At the end of 1942 Barbara married Bernhard Lipsker, a Jewish refugee
from Berlin, a clever man who at the time was working in the garden.
'Bernhard had a vast universal knowledge, but his outlook into life was
burdened — it challenged me to convince him of goodness and hope.' But
only eight months later, riding a bicycle with no brakes, Bernhard was run
over by a car and seriously injured. He lay deeply unconscious. Barbara
was expecting her first child, and 'a time of deep trial followed' which
influenced the rest of her life. Bernhard eventually recovered but always
needed support.

In spring 1944, Barbara took on a new challenge when she and
Bernhard, together with a group of co-workers and nine children, were
the first people to move to Murtle House. It was the beginning of a new
venture, and it was very much thanks to Barbara's dedication, vision, perseverance and experience that it could develop in spite of very difficult
circumstances. But it was demanding work for Barbara, with an invalid
husband, a small baby and another child expected. She asked Dr König if
she could be relieved of her responsibilities, and eventually the family
went to live alone in Heathcot Garden Cottage.

This move brought about a rift with Dr König that lasted for several years and caused her great heartache. But despite her dedication to him and to the Community, Barbara had the courage to do what she knew was needed. This small woman was not afraid to stand up to a man when necessary. Further moves followed: back to Murtle, and again, back to Heathcot.

Looking back, what Barbara managed to achieve was extraordinary. She was certainly overworked. She was matron of large houses of up to sixty people, she was mother to her own children and, in addition to all this, took other children into the family. She gave herself fully to other people, especially the young co-workers around her.

Barbara and Bernard's second daughter, Elizabeth, was born in 1946, and a third daughter, Veronika, in 1948. Barbara and Bernhard are remembered by their children as wonderful parents who created a strong family life with love and stability, not an easy task amidst the demands of the growing community. Bernhard died suddenly in 1979.

As early as 1936 the first Youth Group had performed the Oberufer Christmas plays together and this tradition continued in Scotland. From the beginning, Barbara always played the part of Mary, and it came to seem as though that role belonged to her. She embodied the modesty, purity and innocence of Mary with what can only be described as a lack of worldliness. These qualities were to remain with her throughout her life. But she was also very down to earth and had the complementary qualities of motherly warmth and security, which acted as vessels for something higher to be born on earth. She later wrote about that experience: 'The holiness of being Mary accompanies me through the whole year.'

These qualities made Barbara a capable, loving mother to her own and many other children. This motherliness streamed out into whichever community Barbara lived. She strove to uphold the value of making a real home whenever the possibility of institutionalism threatened.

Whilst fully valuing the leading male spirits of Camphill, Barbara always paid tribute to the women. It was they, after all, who had taken the courageous step to move to Camphill estate in June 1940. Tilla König, a role model for the young Barbara, was strongly influential in the style of childcare, home and culture that developed in Camphill. There were other women, several without children of their own, who followed this example and also brought in different feminine attributes: perceptiveness, faithfulness, protection, morality.

As early as January 1939 the young Alix Roth wrote to Barbara, not yet in Camphill:

We women have an important and great task. We cannot be protective enough, warm and tender just when the world becomes ever heavier, harder and more dismal. In this world in which the men find it hard to work, to the end that sometimes they will almost lose heart. Much will

*Barbara with her
husband Bernhard at
Thornbury*

*depend on us in Scotland — apart from the work — to create the right
atmosphere.*

'To create the right atmosphere' was another task that Barbara consci-
entiously strove to undertake.

*Barbara eventually had a well-earned sabbatical. She took her family
to Botton Village for a year, just when it was starting. She did the
laundry for the Community on an old fashioned copper boiler, and
always said it was the best time in her life.*

*Though she loved Botton and village life, the children tugged at her
heartstrings. So she left the Village and working with adults, and took
her family to Thornbury. Now her greatest challenge came. She was
principal, administrator and leader of the school, which did not sit well
with her inner discipline of service.*

*Then Dr König sent her to Glencraig, in Ireland. Here she could
practise Community building in a way that suited her. Together with*

*Hans Heinrich Engel, she could bring to life an inner attitude of service
for the good that pervaded the whole Community. First as a children's
housemother, then as a housemother in the village, then for a short time
as a workmaster, she carried out her conviction that the human being,
with all his faculties and failings, is the highest spiritual achievement on
earth, and as such, must be challenged, revered and honoured no matter
who that human being is nor how expressed.*[2]

Her unassuming manner belied the considerable worldly and esoteric
tasks that Barbara fulfilled. She carried them out scrupulously. Although
she was not a naturally gifted speaker, her contributions on special occasions or festival days were plain-spoken affirmations of Community values and the work involved in striving towards them, which inspired and
recalled the listener to the fundamentals.

Entrusted in the early days by Dr König to take on one of the important
tasks in the developing Community, she accompanied that Community
with awareness throughout those sixty-two years. She felt an immense
responsibility to what Karl König had initiated, and upheld the work from
its beginning, to the end of the twentieth century and the end of her life,
as she felt he had wished. Barbara's contribution was formally recognized
when, in 1984 she received an M.B.E.

Yet she did not hold on to the past, she accepted that the forms and
expression of Camphill would change. 'Camphill as we know it will die,
but it must die victorious.' She would say: 'We must sacrifice ourselves
before we are sacrificed,' using the example of the Green Snake in
Goethe's Fairy Tale who dies so that something greater can develop.

Barbara felt a particular affinity to and responsibility for the anthroposophical, spiritual and religious life, and she committed herself to several
tasks of anthroposophical service. She was fully involved in Councils, and
management issues, although often what she contributed was the morality
around which issues could be resolved, rather than brilliant strategies.

Karl König himself characterized Barbara: 'The voice of conscience
who decisively helped us forward in times of need.'[3]

Barbara was able to do this equally both in the esoteric and the exoteric
field. Her allegiance was well balanced between the 'other' world and this
one. The realm beyond the threshold was a complete reality for her, but at
the same time she was devoted to this earth. She delighted in the beauty
of nature, and children were always her special joy and concern. She took
responsibility for the struggle and pain of life down to the smallest detail.
Nothing was too insignificant for her. Although she found administration
an onerous task, it fell to her to carry many of the burdens of running
Glencraig after Hans Heinrich Engel's death in a tragic accident in 1973,
until in time others joined the community and could take on administration duties.

It is an interesting motif of her destiny that Barbara, the archetypal mother, found herself on several occasions having to assume a role traditionally occupied by a man. For virtually all of her married life it was Barbara who had to be the organizer, decision-maker and stable element of her family because of her husband's accident, from which he never fully recovered. Then later in Glencraig it was Barbara, meant to be a support and complement to the gifted young doctor and superintendent Hans Heinrich Engel, who had to assume a leading role. After his death she found a way, with others, to meet the supreme challenge this brought to Glencraig and to encourage and empower much younger people to grow into responsibilities which they found themselves facing. For the next thirty years she watched over generations of young co-workers who, with her support found in themselves unknown resources with which to fulfil their own destinies as well as to serve the community.

'Going to talk to Barbara' was an intrinsic and indispensable part of community life. Many have described how they were met with a warm and personal interest. Barbara never failed to get to the heart of a problem, even if the person concerned didn't know what it was! Her penetrating gaze and questions meant it was at least possible to see a way forward, if not an immediate solution. An individual was not dressed down, but pulled up, up to the higher self, the realization of which suddenly felt possible because Barbara had seen it. What was heard was not necessarily what was wanted, but was always what was needed. At the end there would be the admonition: Be well. One was not 'let off' but was left free, invested with significance and empowered. One could go on!

What Barbara had to say could be accepted because of her example. She had high expectations of herself and of others. She had learned how to make her own will subservient to the outer demand, her own wishes to what was needed and right, and she managed to do it with joy and enthusiasm. In this way individual and community destinies became woven together in a way which many experienced as a fulfilment of the ideal of the Camphill Community: free, yet in service, so that the greater good for individual and community was realized. In the last phase of her life she had to learn how to adjust to the failure of others to live up to her high expectations. Things Barbara took for granted were not done or valued. 'It's a matter of course,' she would say, but it was not so for everybody. Eventually, she learned how to free herself of the burden of expectation while retaining her love and interest. This process was made easier by her declining powers: sight, hearing, movement, smell, taste all diminished. She suffered from this, but it was necessary in order to let go, as she drew ever nearer to the world beyond the senses.

The order with which Barbara lived her life also characterized her last months on earth. Although she had for years been asking plaintively 'Why must I live so long?' the beginning of the end came quickly and she, while welcoming it, was somewhat taken aback by this reality. Failing health, the discovery of a serious condition, a few weeks in hospital: but then, back home with enough time for family and friends to visit and make their farewells, and last precious weeks spent with her three beloved daughters and their families. With deep gratitude she insisted on thanking everyone who came to give their thanks to her. Then, Barbara herself, in full consciousness, asked for the last anointing, which took place on Whit Sunday 2002. Exactly one week later she took her last breath with peace and dignity: 'The door is open.'

It was Saturday, May 25, the birthday of Count Zinzendorf, one of the personalities Karl König called 'stars' of the Camphill Movement. It was Zinzendorf whom Karl König experienced in the night of August 29, 1940 instructing him to establish a meal on earth, which later came to be the Bible Evening, so that human beings might learn how to become 'true men.' Throughout her life Barbara observed the Saturday with a Bible Evening in some form, even on holiday.

May 25 was also the death day of Alix Roth, Barbara's friend from Vienna. They had been the last of the group to leave Austria at the end of 1938. They had attended the Act of Consecration of Man together at Michaelmas that year.

The twenty-sixth of May is celebrated as the day on which Kaspar Hauser appeared in Nuremberg in 1828. This foundling youth *(c.* 1812–33) touched those who met him by his exceptional human qualities. As Camphill developed he became the symbol of the redemption of damaged bodies, souls and destinies, and their contribution to society and world history. The Bible Evening and Kaspar Hauser were among the Camphill impulses most precious to Barbara.

Karl König often told Barbara that she belonged to *'den Stillen im Lande,'* those quiet humble people who serve humanity. In one sense this was the character and mission of Camphill itself. However it would be wrong to fail to see the greatness in this. Barbara herself exemplified what a mighty force this stream can be. Humble, modest, simple, but also someone devoted to the being of Michael in the aspect of earnest judge, seeker for truth and the one who prepares the way for the Christ.

Thus, with complete appropriateness, Barbara departed at Whitsuntide: the Festival of Community, of the Holy Spirit, of the fulfilment of the Christian year. How often did she say: 'You know, the flames were perceived on the heads of *the others'* or, 'Pay attention to the Spirit wind, it will lead us'?

In Barbara one could experience the light of wisdom and truth, a warmth of interest in everyone and everything, and the fire of an individual will to bring the spirit to earth.

Barbara in 1998

For Barbara, Karl König was the most significant person in her life: friend, mentor, example, inspiration, admonisher; they had a strong personal relationship.

He recognized every small, honest effort, every tiny progress in one's development and was in a nearly knightly way always at one's side, obviously full of joy. But he could also be pained and dark, when one failed out of negligence and laziness. He was a constant mirror, but also the Community as such took on this function of a mirror ever more.

Dr König was always there when my soul faltered. I often came to visit him, having to walk up the steep stairway towards his room. He would stand at the top, stretch out his arms, helping me up the last steps. Then we would sit in his room, chat a little and discuss earnest issues of destiny, of Community concerns. I treasured these hours of growing friendship, spiritual uplift and guidance.

He could be harsh, once saying at a time of her perceived weakness, 'Why are you so faithless?' Then, Barbara felt ashamed and searched her innermost soul. But at the harrowing time of Bernhard's accident he was a support.

For me personally an unforgettable time full of anxiety, facing up to destiny, being carried and supported by unbelievable love! Especially Dr König is next to one, practically day and night.

At the end of her life Barbara characterized Karl König as a 'caller,' someone challenging other human beings, as John the Baptist did when he cried out, 'Change your ways! Make His path straight!'

Dr König again and again made us aware of the fact that we were preparers and that each person who wanted to follow that way should offer something of himself.

In this way, personal self-transformation came about in Karl König himself as much as in everyone else.

The early longing for friendship which was first met by Barbara's school friend, Hertha West, and Lisl Schwalb, then by the members of the two Youth Groups, grew into a powerful force for the rest of her life. Thomas, Peter, Anke, Trude and all the others were lifelong companions and confidants. In the 1980s Barbara enjoyed holidays with Thomas, Anke, Peter and Kate. She remained close to the adult König children, particularly Renate and Christof. She travelled to Edinburgh to meet Hans and Lisl Schauder after many years of estrangement since their departure from Camphill, and there was a degree of reconciliation.

All these years I was sustained, helped, carried by faithful friends. How did I deserve it? [During] My whole life friendship was holy to me, mutual understanding, soul-communication without words, to be in one accord with another soul — I received so much! Did I also give it?

To that, her friends would resoundingly answer, Yes!

Early photographs of Barbara show an open-faced young woman with a high, broad, clear brow framed by fine, light hair. To the very end of her life she retained her soft, smooth complexion, with hardly a line, never looking her age. She was always immaculately dressed. She preferred simple dresses and blouses, together with one favourite piece of jewellery. Everything was spotless and tasteful, giving an impression of modesty and timelessness. Her expression was warm and sympathetic, but what one remembered was her gaze, mild, yet earnest, direct and uncompromising.

Small in stature, yet somehow immensely impressive, Barbara walked with a limp because of her damaged and stiffened knee. She was unable to kneel down, and she sometimes asked herself what deeper significance this had. Outer activities in life which are restricted or have to be sacrificed often bring inner deepening through the self-denial and suffering they necessitate. In an inward way Barbara refined the qualities of devotion, humility and reverence into powerful instruments of service. All this was balanced by a striking uprightness and a dignity that radiated from her person.

Barbara has described how at times in her early life she managed to overcome her physical limitations; for instance, once, when in charge of a handicapped boy, she had to quickly learn to climb fences or risk losing him completely. And her early efforts to achieve her goals despite her physical disability, such as gaining exemption from gym, and then later convincing an eminent surgeon to operate on her knee without payment, surely strengthened the forces of will which accompanied her all her life.

In her funeral dress of cream raw silk she looked like a priestess of some Greek mystery, immensely old and wise, yet also fresh, unlined and youthful: Iphigenia reborn on Tauris. In Greek mythology the maiden Iphigenia sacrifices herself so that the Greek ships could sail to Troy. But the goddess Artemis rescues her to serve as a priestess on the island of Tauris. This story was an inspiring image for Camphill in the early days, and one Barbara often spoke about as an example of freely serving the needs of the time. Her illness meant that in the last two months of life the yellow of jaundice tinted her body and complexion. One friend saw this as a manifestation of the inner substance of Barbara's life. Her long years of self-discipline and dedication, all undertaken in complete freedom for the sake of anthroposophy and Camphill, had transformed all resistance into light and love. And so her soul shone out radiantly, the ordinary substance of a life transmuted alchemically into gold, into a transparency and grace that pointed to the future.

The first to meet Karl König, one of the last to leave Austria, the last to arrive in Camphill, among the last to leave the earth: this is Barbara, truly the first and the last.

'I was graced to be guided: I was allowed to find it.'

Barbara said that she felt she had received a great deal of grace in her life but that she had had to ask herself: did I make enough of it? She herself felt that she had never fulfilled her promise and that in some way Dr König was disappointed in her. She often asked herself: Was it a failure of will? My pride and intellect?

Barbara always loved Rudolf Steiner's *Calendar of the Soul* and felt very challenged by the verse belonging to the week of her birth. Early on, Karl König gave her two books on the occasion of her birthday and wrote her birthday verse in one of them which she felt expressed her life's challenge: how to be worthy of the gifts and blessings that she was privileged to have.

Barbara was very clear about the goals and impulses the first group in Camphill set themselves. First, to serve the earth through the hallowing of everyday life, the devotion to ordinary things. Next, to uphold the best in each other through faithfulness to the higher being. Lastly, to take up the challenge of self development, of change and transformation in oneself. Throughout her long life Barbara practised these with dedication and strength of will. They did indeed 'found and form her soul, a garment worthy of the spirit' and they became enshrined in a community of mutual commitment devoted to the good on earth.

Gradually the inmost task of the Community: service for the coming about of the Good in the world shines up in [Karl König's] words.

To this Barbara dedicated her life and being. Her last note read:

Thank you, all dear friends in Glencraig — in Camphill! God bless you, give you strength and conviction that the GOOD will be victorious!

With all my love, Barbara.

Anke Weihs-Nederhoed

(June 30, 1914 – August 27, 1987)

Marianne Sander

Childhood and Youth

Anke was born into unusual circumstances. Her parents had known each other for only three weeks when they married.

My father's father came from a long line of Friesian peasant nobility; my father's mother ... from the Prussian House of Brandenburg. My father was tall and fair ... and very good looking ... He had an air about him that made people want to spoil him ... and as a result of this and probably his own ambition, he was at the age of twenty three the managing director of an export-import firm with offices in Rotterdam, Shanghai, Tokyo, Melbourne, New York and Los Angeles. He traded mainly in jade. My mother was English, born in Melbourne of a father of obscure antecedents and a beautiful mother, who maintained her family after its move to Australia by making ladies' hats and painting rural scenes of bovine tranquillity ... because my grandfather could never reconcile himself with his move to Australia and became an alcoholic. My mother was entirely self-educated, musically highly sensitive, widely read, witty and fastidious in her tastes, but owing to the impecuniosity of the family circumstances ... she was both unschooled as well as untrained. She was tiny, dark, intense and imperious in manner. When my father met her while on his travels, he wrote to his mother in Holland: She just reaches up to my heart.

Even now I feel my long deceased parents ... in my make-up: my father in my body and physical reactivity, in a certain woodenness of common intelligence, in a basic passivity or indolence and there have been many who have wanted to spoil me as well. I feel my mother in ... my mind which tends to be restless ... fastidious, to all appearances imperious and equally untrained — and finally in my musical nerve. My self was not derived from parental sources, but had a different genesis and an own moment of emergence.[1]

Anke with O Yuki–San at a tea party in Yokohama

Anke was born in Melbourne, Australia on June 30, 1914, two days after the assassination in Sarajevo of the heir to the Austrian throne, which initiated the First World War. This fact remained significant for Anke throughout her life, as she in later years became increasingly aware of and interested in the situation of the present day world and of current affairs.

Her parents' marriage began to crumble with Anke's birth and the small family left Australia for good when Anke was eighteen months old. Already, as a small infant, Anke experienced both having all the comforts that money could buy and parents with no time for their one and only child. She was in the care of everchanging nannies in everchanging countries: Australia, Japan, Hawaii, America, Holland ...

Anke was a highly sensitive, intelligent and alert child, who was acutely aware in her young life that she was 'in the way' of her parents. There were many traumatic experiences of being without a permanent home. Discontinuity became a pattern, as the family moved between different houses, hotels and large steamships.

Anke quoted a stanza from the *Odyssey* to describe her situation:

No One is my name: for
everyone calls me No One,
my father and my mother
and all my companions ...[2]

She did not see much of her father, who was usually travelling, frequently

*Anke with her father
at Honolulu in 1915*

accompanied by her mother. Nevertheless, she did see her mother often in these first six years, with whom she had an uneasy relationship.

Anke wrote:

We stayed by the seaside at Yokohama, but my father had to leave on business. The day we were to sail for Los Angeles, I took ill with whooping cough and was not allowed on board ship nor could my mother accompany my father because of me. She was always inordinately gentle and intuitive when I was ill and was what I clung to when my mind wandered in fever; she was my motive for living. When I recovered from an illness, she would often say that I was not her child, but that she had picked me up somewhere. This made me howl with rage and smash things ... My mother did not wait for my full recovery but joined my father wherever he was, leaving me with my nanny O Yuki-San in Yokohama ... When my parents returned to Japan, they found me babbling uninhibitedly in Japanese, to which my mother reacted in disgust. We left Yokohama soon after and stayed for a while in California, although I did not know where that was. We occupied a big house standing in heavy, oppressive shade. Oranges grew in at the windows and outside there was a pool of huge forget-me-nots.[3]

Even as a very young child Anke experienced bright glaring lights and bright sunlight as traumatic.

Very early on I developed a preference for dimness, shade, coolness and the minor moments at the edge of the day, for the unseen, the long, slant shadows cast by the sinking sun, for mists and steel grey folds of cloud low over hills, for the andante of rain dripping from the eaves.[4]

During much of her life Anke was plagued by severe migraine attacks or 'sick headaches' as she called them, often lasting for several days. No doubt her over-sensitivity to bright light was linked to this.

Anke with her mother in Holland

On one of her sea journeys she experienced the sea burial of a crew member. A little later, she herself nearly drowned when clinging to her father's back while he was riding the waves on a surfboard. A splash of brine whipped across her eyes and she let go to rub them and sank into the dark depths of the water from which she was rescued only just in time. Of these experiences Anke writes:

I began to be morbid about ships and the sea. The ill omen was the appearance of our huge pigskin trunks in the hotel bedroom. While my mother and the maid packed our belongings, the pounding in my bloodstream thundered in the room even if my mother and the maid did as if they couldn't hear it. Choked down waves of terror at the impending journey to the docks would gather into a whirlpool of nausea and the bathroom door would come open only just in time. I was never seasick at sea — only on land. At the docks, I followed closely in the wake of my parents, who would be too preoccupied to take my hand through the long-drawn-out ritual of the passport and customs examination ... trying not to take in the broadside of our ship looming all down the wharf. Then at the foot of the gang plank, terror erupted. My father would put down his bags with an oath and carry me, screaming, onto the ship ... Up on deck I watched the tug-boat pilot the ship out of the harbour, which did not add to my peace of mind, for I supposed the ship was too stupid to find its way out by itself. Clinging to the railing, I waved my handkerchief enthusiastically to the crowd of people on the fading wharf, although there was never anyone we knew among them because we never came from anywhere where we knew anyone.... Interspersed between ships,

ports and cities, there were the interminable trans-continental train
journeys which not only made my body ache because of the constricted
space to move about in, but which made my very existence ache. With the
thud of the iron wheels along the tracks my life rubbed and thudded
along the bottom: Da-dum, da-dum, da-dum, da-dum, lum-da, dum-da-
lud, mud and blood, dadud — with nose pressed against the grimy
carriage window, I hummed this dirge over and over ...[5]

We can sense from these descriptions the loneliness and desolation in
the life of this small and vulnerable child, who had no playmates and
whose great and desperate yearning must have been for a 'normal' home
in a 'normal' family.

When Anke was six her parents' marriage finally broke up and her
father disappeared from her life. She was not to see him again. Her mother
was left more or less penniless and in order to make a living, she tried her
hand at secretarial work and journalism in New York and elsewhere.

One day when Anke was with her mother in a bookshop she was
allowed to choose three books for herself for reading on a forthcoming
boat journey, during which her mother was to be employed by a wealthy
actress. Anke chose nine books, all of which she wanted badly. However,
when her mother did not give in to her demands, Anke went up to a stout
woman in a green tweed suit standing nearby and said to her:

'Please help me! I need nine books and my mother will only let me
have three ...

I did not take in the answer the woman in the green tweed suit gave to
this untoward plea, but only perceived that all nine books were being
parcelled up ... Nor did I take in the fact that my mother and the woman
in green were deep in conversation ...[6]

On returning from this journey, Anke found herself in the care of the
woman in green. Eventually she understood that her mother had handed
her over to the woman on that day in the book shop. Anke herself says
about this:

The woman in the green tweed suit was now 'responsible' for me
and was going to 'support' me until I was eighteen provided my mother
would 'do her part.' These phrases ... were repeated daily. I tried hard
to embark on themes of conversation which allowed for no reference to
my person, but even the remotest themes had a way of veering round ...
It was not that I disliked her; only with her my life took a totally alien
course.

Yet, I was dimly aware ... that it was I who had singled her out. I
sensed I had an account to settle, the nature of which was buried deep in
Time ... I had delivered myself into her hands to clear an existential
debt, which was not a matter of a mere nine books; it was an
indisputable hurdle that had to be taken before life went on.[7]

And so Anke came to the house of Miss Tyler and her younger sister Dorothea. The two ladies were employed in a large orphanage, Miss Tyler as a house mother and Dorothea as a teacher. Anke was to stay with them from age six to eleven. Dorothea was an excellent, imaginative teacher, but the human relationship between Anke and the two sisters was extremely poor and would deteriorate drastically in time. However, these years also brought the experience of nature to Anke in a hitherto unknown way. The girls' orphanage was situated in the most exquisite, partly wild countryside in Pennsylvania which Anke often roamed for hours on end, getting to know and love plants and animals. She was invariably alone as Miss Tyler did not allow her to mix with the other girls outside the classroom, because they were 'of an inferior status' being proper orphans, whilst Anke's parents were both very much alive. Miss Tyler regarded Anke as her personal liability, and when the payments for her upkeep ceased after a time, she became increasingly possessive, even wanting to adopt her. All this was strongly resisted by Anke herself who was longing for her mother.

However, during these five and a half years she did not see her once. But her mother did send letters regularly and also books. Among these, given on Anke's eighth birthday were the *Iliad* and the *Odyssey* by Homer rewritten for children by Padraic Colum, with illustrations by Willy Pogany.

A little apprehensive of the Unknown, but trustful of my mother's guidance of my mind, I opened the Iliad *— and read the opening lines. — There was a thunderclap in my deeper existence as out of a hitherto undefined source, a rumbling rose up out of an agelong sleep accompanied by flashes of recognition: I knew the events told of in this book. This was whence I had gone forth. It was my schooling long before I was born, my legitimacy. The discovery of myself poured out over me in a flood of bliss and reunion. Yet, at the same time it was a new dawn and I strode away from my beloved beasts and Fairy Tales and towards a rising inner sun. Everything else was swept aside in the thundering roll of chariots, swallowed up in the blinding dust in their wake which, when it subsided, revealed the heroes who were gods and the gods who were men, whose striving was my striving, whose victories my victories, whose griefs my griefs and whose deaths I died over and over again and whose divinities filled the waiting shrines of my mind as a cloud-burst renews the spring. A veil rose from Olympus: my god was born. My parents, as well as Miss Tyler, were not religious. I had not been christened and had no experience of traditional religion. Now Zeus and Athene went before me. Thus the* Iliad *and the* Odyssey *became the breviary of my childhood, the rule by which to grow.*[8]

From quite early on Anke had learned to lead a double life. An inner, imaginative, rich and colourful one, full of hidden sadness, frustration and disappointment, but also joy. And an outer one, shy and withdrawn, yet she possessed great physical agility and enterprise. Many traumatic experiences left their imprint on her highly sensitive soul, and she suffered feelings of abandonment, insecurity and self doubt. At times, when the injustices inflicted upon her became unbearable, she displayed a severe temper. However, a strong determined will to cope with life, come what may, grew increasingly within her, giving her the endurance and capability to hold out and to grow independent in her thought life and pursuits. Already at a very early age her search for the truth and the meaning of life in all its manifestations, was outstanding.

At this stage in my childhood — I was now nine — I began to think about thinking and knew myself as one who thought, albeit my thinking was more imaginative than intellectual. I began to put questions rather to myself than to Dorothea, having formed the notion that there was nothing I could not understand if I thought strenuously enough about it and that only what I found out through my own efforts was really mine. — I began a process of discarding what was not mine, of testing my ideas according to my own experience. I thought about clay, the construction of looms, the flight of birds. I invented a safety pin, an egg beater, even a typewriter — in my bed at night.[9]

Time and time again, even as a child, Anke had 'out of body experiences.' She describes one here:

The room in which I slept was bare and cold. I spent no time in it during the day — all it contained was a narrow bed and a rickety wicker chair. — I sat down in the wicker chair. There was a presence in the room. I saw it; it sat on a similar chair. It was my Self. We looked at one another. Self: 'Do you know that you told a lie?' — 'Yes, I know I did' — 'It wasn't a mouse at all. Why did you blame a mouse?' — 'I was afraid' — 'Afraid of what?' The Other looked at me, and I bowed my head in shame. 'You are a coward' — 'Yes, I know I am' — 'You needn't be a coward' — 'I can't help it' — 'You must help it — you alone.'

Through communication with the Other it grew light in the room and the weight oppressing my existence began to lift.[10]

By the age of eleven, Anke's relationship with Miss Tyler had badly deteriorated. Both Tyler sisters had come under close scrutiny from the directors of the orphanage and Miss Tyler herself became an increasingly unbalanced and neurotic person, who directed her revenge at Anke. Domestic chores such as cleaning, mending, helping with cooking and laundry, were allocated to the girls. Anke was supervised by Miss Tyler personally, who took a sadistic pleasure in making her do certain tasks such as dusting the staircase banisters, over and over again, as it was seemingly never done to her satisfaction, Such situations often escalated

Growing up in America

into violent rows and Anke was punished by being placed either into a scalding or a freezing bath or by having her legs and feet lashed with a whip until they were bleeding, needing weeks to heal. Anke tried to hide all this from the teachers and others in the house, but soon the school doctor and some of the teachers became concerned. One day, after a scene of particular violence, Anke, with a pillow, pushed Miss Tyler down the stairs. Miss Tyler broke a leg and the result was that Anke was put on a train and sent back to her mother in New York.

The police were brought in, and both Miss Tyler and Dorothea were dismissed from the orphanage. Some months later, Miss Tyler, who was now living with her sister privately in a small house, chronically ill and in a wheelchair, asked Anke to visit her. Anke, against her mother's will, went to see them. Miss Tyler was apologetic and ashamed and Anke was relieved at having concluded this chapter in her life in a somewhat decent manner.

For a while Anke now stayed with her mother who lived a Bohemian life in a large squalid room in a back street of New York, trying to make a paltry living out of occasional journalistic work.

The relationship between mother and daughter was cool, yet they cared for each other's needs. Eventually another school was found for Anke in upstate New York which she called 'Freedom.' This school was housed on a big farm in a beautiful area.

Freedom had student government. Our teachers were there as experts in their respective academic fields, but not as representatives of

authority. Authority was vested in the school's Assembly which
comprised the pupils save the very little ones of whom there were few at
Freedom. Office bearers were drawn from the senior boys and girls.

We were fierce in our allegiance to the code of Freedom and the whole
school suffered when any one of us forgot, besmirched, misused or
violated it. Yet I myself was, from the beginning, compelled by an often
uncontrollable drive to challenge just the code I so loved, to test it to the
utmost in order to discover that its strength and virtue were stronger than
my own weakness. This was to lead to my downfall two years later ...

Freedom used the Dalton Plan in its education programme. By
means of this method, the pupil himself was made responsible for
achieving the appropriate knowledge and ability in the respective
subjects taught ...

This plan designed to release and foster initiative and responsibility
in children at school resulted in a very mixed harvest at Freedom. Even
with the integrity of the atmosphere there, the method of academic
education engendered unbalanced ambition at too early an age, fostered
opportunism as well as fatalism in many and in a few like myself, non-
co-operation ...

As far as I was concerned, my schooling at Freedom was a failure
from the start. I adored the freedom at Freedom but could not deal with
it. I could not get myself to attend lessons, not because I was too idle but
because I found so much else to do. In spite of the richness of experience
opened up to me by Dorothea, my house of learning was built on sand
and my self-education through reading, indiscriminate.

But Freedom was a school of another kind — a schooling in
enthusiasm and community spirit; it was a schooling in knighthood — in
brotherhood.[11]

In Freedom Anke found friendship, acceptance and acknowledgement
for the first time in her life. She loved the place and its people and spent
the most harmonious two years of her childhood there. She excelled in
horse riding and other physical pursuits together with some of the other
children. Farm work was a major activity at Freedom and she eagerly volunteered for a variety of jobs. She was also part of a debating club with
such topics as Plutarch's *Lives* or Plato's *Symposium.*

After two years at Freedom, at the age of thirteen, Anke once again
began to suffer from extremely confused emotions bordering on self-
destruction. She resorted to a form of anarchy and subversiveness that
would lead to her undoing.

To arm myself against the end, I drove a wedge between myself and
Freedom. Six younger children became my bondsmen. They followed me
blindly and were the unwitting instruments of my anarchy.[12]

Obsessional ideas drove her on. One wild, rainy and windy night, taking some lamps and biscuits with her, she led her little band of children up the nearby mountain, where she knew there were caves. The lamps were soon blown out and the shivering group was soaked to the skin. At last, inside the cave it was at least dry. After an hour or so of fitful dozing, snivelling and crying by some of the children, Anke heard the gong from the valley below. Soon a rescue party from Freedom arrived. The rest of the night and the following day were like a nightmare to Anke. A school assembly was called. The verdict was that Anke was to be expelled from Freedom and was to leave the next morning. She cried out silently: 'Oh, God wipe all this out and let me stay! I love this place!'

My departure was befitting to Freedom. No sentiment was shown, but everyone was there. I shook hands with them all. When Einar, the farmer who drove me to the railway station passed the gates to Freedom, I experienced grief like the blow of a sledge hammer.

I was thirteen; my childhood was at an end. What would I be able to make of it? Where would I go from here?[13]

In the meantime Anke's mother had climbed the professional ladder and had become the head of the advertising department of Cunard Ship Lines as well as the editor of *Town and Country,* a society magazine. She was now a wealthy woman who could afford a luxurious apartment in New York as well as a lovely country house. It was her wish that Anke should become a ballet dancer and so, during the three years that followed her dismissal from 'Freedom,' Anke was sent to various dancing schools. Among these schools there was one founded by Florence Noyes, based on Platonic ideas, which was to have a profound influence on Anke's dancing style.

When she was sixteen her mother decided to have a year off in Europe, taking Anke along with her. Unbeknown to her, this was Anke's final departure from America. From now on Europe became her home, although in 1959 Anke did spend some months in the United States, preparing for the development of the Camphill Movement on that continent.

Anke herself says: 'Meanwhile, however, the next eight years were to be strangely digressive and superficial.'[14]

The Austrian Years

From age sixteen to twenty-four (1930–38), Anke lived mainly in Vienna. She loved being in Austria, experiencing it as a homecoming. At first she was taken in by a circle of friends around Sigmund Freud, staying with one particular family known to her mother. She continued with her training in various ballet schools, chiefly in Vienna, but also for a time in Berlin. Friendships developed, some deep and lasting. The circles in which she moved were often Jewish in background and she met well-known people such as Erik Erikson, Sigmund Freud and later Max Reinhard. At one point, shortly before the annexation of Austria in 1938, she found herself as part of a group of dancers dining with Adolf Hitler in Berlin, much to her horror and embarrassment.

Anke's mother, after staying for a year in Italy, moved near to Budapest, where she rented a large villa. This now became the occasional backdrop to Anke's existence. Her mother, meanwhile began to drink more and more heavily.

Anke had achieved a certain modest success in the dance world and was invited to give a solo evening in one of Budapest's largest theatres. She worked hard at the programme and at designing her own costumes.

But now my big evening in Budapest drew near. I looked forward to it with almost religious feelings of responsibility. I wanted to dance the human saga of sorrow, joy and love, to make a statement. My mother came down to Budapest and for the evening sat in the audience in a prominent place. Less than halfway through the programme she rose to her feet and produced such a drunken scene that the curtain came down and the evening ended in disaster ... Back in Vienna I wrote a letter to my mother thanking her for what she had done for me, but stating I would henceforward live my own life and not accept a penny of her money ... I do not know if she was hurt. — She went to England, bought a beautiful Elizabethan house in Hertfordshire where she lived until her death in 1947. — Dr König insisted I maintain contact with her and so I visited her once a year from Camphill. She died penniless, abandoned by all her friends; I was the only one to walk behind her coffin.[15]

Now a time of real poverty and hardship followed for Anke. Having just returned from a long stay in Berlin, she had no work, no money and nowhere to stay.

I spent some months sleeping on a bench in a common wash house on the top floor of an apartment building. My diet was sour cocoa and stale buns which could be had for practically nothing. Had it not been that I was now and then invited by friends for a proper meal, these months would have been a greater ordeal.[16]

Eventually she found work as a model for a well-known Viennese woollen firm and could afford a more normal lifestyle again. Soon she was asked to join a group of eight dancers of the State Opera and with them went on frequent tours all over Europe, which she enjoyed very much. Anke was brought into contact with Grete Wiesenthal in Vienna, a famous dancer of that time. They found an immediate rapport and worked very fruitfully together. And then, through a friend, Anke met for the first time Thomas Weihs and his friend Peter Roth, both young medical students.

From then on I saw the two not infrequently as they were doing

Modelling in Vienna in the thirties

Anke in 1933 in Vienna

obstetrics in a hospital near my dancing studio. All three of us were twenty-two ... Before that, and quite independently, Carlo [Pietzner] and I had met at an artist's party and Alix Roth [Peter's sister] and I met when she worked as an assistant to a well-known photographer who did a series of photographs of me.[17]

Thomas and Peter were part of a youth group which studied anthroposophy with Dr Karl König. When Anke developed health problems, they recommended that she saw Dr König to get his medical advice. Reluctantly Anke went to his surgery. This meeting with Dr König became the turning point in her life. Anke describes it in this way.

At the desk in the centre [of the room] stood a very small man with a large — a lion's — head. His eyes were very big and grave. When they rested on you, they did not only see through you, they seemed to create you anew. Something dormant in yourself responded whether you wanted to or not; you seemed to become what you really were, beneath the layers of habit, inhibition and illusion. He not only saw what you were but what you were meant to be. In Dr König the gaze was a channel for the flow of warmth, it was in itself healing, for one felt one was seen in one's hidden truth, and always with respect and compassion.[18]

Anke had arrived at a moment in her life when everything she had experienced in her hitherto fragmented, tortuous and dramatic childhood and youth seemed as preparation for what was to come. She had learned to cope with life and to stand independently on her own feet. She had also gained an inner maturity, richness of soul and an insight into life, well beyond her years.

Anke was born under the zodiacal sign of Cancer or Crab. The symbol of Cancer is the vortex: which can be thought of as two intertwining spirals drawn in such a way that the two spirals do not touch.

There is a gap necessitating a leap to reach the other. This sign can characterize a certain type of event either physically or spiritually: to leave behind the old road and to go courageously through the crisis; to leap into the future which is as yet unknown and allow it to unfold.

As the group around Dr König studied anthroposophy together they began to realize that they must implement what they had learnt in a living way. They would do this together with and in the service of disabled children and young people who at that time were still 'outcasts.'

Nick Blitz writes:

Between 1938 and 1939, as the Second World War was about to break out, the majority of the group left Austria and made their way to the United Kingdom which was willing to offer asylum to victims of Nazi persecution and others fleeing the tyranny of National Socialism. — Out of this flux of idealism and darkness the Camphill Movement was born.[19]

Most of the group were of Jewish origin and literally had to flee to save their lives. Anke herself, as one of the few who were not Jewish, went to London in June 1938 with Peter Roth where they were married.

On March 30, 1939 the group gathered again in Kirkton House, a small manse in the north-east of Scotland where, in Anke's words: 'The saga of Camphill began.'

*Anke, modelling as
a dancer in Vienna*

Camphill

The story of the heroic fourteen months in the bleak little manse, which had no electricity or central heating, only open fires — and the beginning of the spiritual adventure that would become, in time, the Camphill Movement, has been vividly described by Anke in *Fragments from the Story of Camphill.*

Amongst the group that found themselves in Kirkton House, Anke was the only one who had mastered the English language and who knew how to tackle daily domestic chores under adverse circumstances. The others had mostly come from secure and comfortable Viennese homes and the load of hard practical work was new to them. Consequently, Anke not only had to take a major role in cooking, cleaning and doing laundry, using only an old copper, but was also frequently in demand to help liaise with the authorities and parents of prospective pupils.

After the move, on June 1, 1940, to Camphill Estate near Aberdeen, from which the Movement took its name, the 'Camphill way-of-life' gradually took shape as more children in need of special care were admitted. Community life slowly developed through the daily experiences of achievement and failure. In this intensive learning process Karl König and his wife Tilla led with their wise and firm guidance.

From the beginning Anke was in her element. Her remarkable life experiences had equipped her as few others for the tasks that lay ahead. The experiment that was Camphill encompassed all the ideals and aims that had grown in her over the years, some consciously and some unconsciously. The two years in Freedom had given her a direct experience of the potential as well as the struggles of community living. Anke's inborn spirituality and creativity could at last find an infinitely worthwhile challenge to which to apply themselves. She was ready to take on anything.

Karl König wrote:

Anke's personality was to play an important role in the building up of Camphill, although earlier on she had only occasionally taken part in our work. She brought with her a past of international colouring.[20]

The development and growth of the Camphill Movement during and after the Second World War has been very well described elsewhere. From the beginning, and throughout, Anke was involved in all its milestones. Often, through her innovative and original way of thinking, she could give a well-timed impulse for new steps to be taken. It can be said that Camphill owes much of its growth and development and indeed well-being to Anke. She in turn thrived as Camphill flourished. Her contributions were highly valued by Karl König whose own inspiration, vision and ingenuity she complemented.

Anke with Peter
Purser at Camphill
House 1940

Anke's marriage to Peter Roth did not last. In 1947 they separated and divorced some time later.

In 1951 Anke married Thomas Weihs, whose own marriage had not been successful. He brought four children into the marriage. Anke could not have children of her own but now Thomas's children came into her life. To begin with this was not easy. Although they were badly in need of a mother, Anke herself was not a motherly person. She was more than willing however, to become their older friend and as the children grew older strong bonds of lifelong friendship and love grew between them.

Christine Polyblank, one of the four children, describes her relationship with Anke:

I think I can truthfully say that Anke had little to do with us when we were younger. She was the first to admit and to apologize for the fact, that she was not maternal ...

We were aged between seven and eleven when she married Father

Anke and Thomas setting off on their honeymoon

and I have no memory of her looking after us. However, she did begin to
make up family photo albums which show us picnicking happily together
by lochs and pebbly rivers. It was only when we were teenagers, home
from the holidays, and when Father and Anke had moved into the first St
John's Cottage and one of the old St John's school huts had been divided
up into little rooms for us, that we really began to sit together as a
family and where a real warmth sprang up between us. There were
however no slothful lie-ins for us! Anke made sure that we were all up
and in time for the family breakfast at eight. We met again for supper. I
mention this because one of our favourite family traditions sprang from
these suppers. On the last day of the holidays we were allowed to choose
our favourite meal and once Anke had introduced us to corn-on-the-cob,
this typically American food as yet almost unknown in Britain, we chose
it every time. It sounds like a small event but the giving and receiving of
life's little pleasures can have a strongly binding effect. During the short
time that there was left for us at 'home,' we did not have much time to
develop a 'family language' but we did come to call each other by
affectionate names, which we used until her death in 1987. Chailean
became 'Big Miss,' I was 'Little Miss' and she became quite simply
'Mrs.'

Camphill women in those days mostly grew their hair long and tucked
it tightly into little buns on their necks, while clothing was long,

generally shapeless and coloured as naturally as the heather clad hills around. Anke too adopted Camphill's favoured style for quite some time: from a wide round yoke the body and sleeves fell in rich gathers to wrist and ankle and the resulting voluminous folds were gathered by a belt somewhere in the middle. Anke did the same, but no matter what she wore, she always looked amazingly lovely. Slim and graceful in build and movement, she was a joy to watch. On her tiny feet she moved with quick, purposeful steps, whether it was in her little kitchen or down the long drive to catch the bus to Aberdeen. Later on Anke took to wearing 'dirndls' (Austrian country dress) in which she looked quite ravishing and which Father clearly much preferred.

Anke's world was that of the great mythologies, fairy tales and gospels in which she was widely read and very knowledgeable. One could only listen, spellbound, as she drew parallels between them all with the utmost ease and clarity and then gave them modern relevance, linking them to the human psyche. She believed that mythologies are human experiences of which one's own soul is the child. To her the myths were highly subjective and alive and could provide children with points of reference and identification in their own ultimate search for meaning and identity.

Anke loved to write and she was a keen correspondent. She invariably wrote pages in her neat and regular, slightly sloping hand and her favourite turquoise ink. When I later spent some years in Africa, her frequent letters were a life-line for me.

Something over a year before her death, and knowing that she was terminally ill, she wrote about her illness in this way: 'As far as I am concerned, Brother Ass, who has been my faithful beast of burden is definitely failing and why not after a long, full, partly difficult, partly lovely and rich life. He began to fail after Papi's death. I myself am neither depressed nor worried by a failure in health but as such look forward to moving on into the future, so to speak. The one lung doesn't quite function anymore, but there is no definite date fixed for a departure, my dear Daughter, and I beg you not to worry or commiserate, but take things as they come.'

As a role-model she was important to me and influential in my life. She set very high standards in every aspect of her life. In personal appearance, table manners and correct speech habits she was exemplary, and she did not let us get away with much! She rose early and spent her days in purposeful activity. There were no sofas or armchairs around because one simply did not lounge about! The way the parents returned from holidays gives an idea of the pace at which they lived: arriving back in the late afternoon, after a very long, uninterrupted car journey from their holidays camping in Greece, they would appear barely two hours

*later scrubbed, tanned, beaming, brimful of impressions to share, at
Gisela's supper table.* In the meantime they had cleaned, repaired and
put back in place, ready for next year, everything that had been taken
along. They had their post opened and laid in piles on their desks for
immediate attention the following morning.*

*While there was something about her which kept one at arm's length,
Anke was also warm and loving — more so on paper, perhaps, than in
the flesh. She was both beautiful and intellectual — her lovely high brow
doing good service to both. As I experienced her she was self-
disciplined, sometimes distant, diffident and withdrawn. But she was
also expansive, outgoing, festive and funny. She had a wicked sense of
humour and loved to tell amusing anecdotes, as likely as not about
herself, and as she did so she would hoot with laughter so that she could
barely speak.*

*I am very grateful for the part she played in my life and when I think
of her, it is with the greatest affection.*

Anke always related to the inner core in the other. It was a meeting
from soul to soul, from ego to ego, disregarding rank or status. She
befriended people from all walks of life. Barbara Lipsker writes:

*In a tender way she reached out to people who did not stand in the
limelight of events, but served modestly in the background; approaching
them with trust, appreciation and friendship.*[21]

A good number of the younger co-workers in Camphill thrived and
developed because of her ongoing and sometimes challenging support
and understanding. Anke had a way of investing the other with meaning,
of recognizing their potential. But in these friendships there could be
stressful times, often lasting weeks, when someone near to her had, usually unknowingly, hurt her feelings. Julian Sleigh describes it in this
way:

*Like many of us, I have known the times of estrangement when one's
very presence seemed to inflict pain on Anke's sensitive soul.*

*How one suffered in those times! One then had to make the first step
towards finding one another again; this would lead to relating more
serenely and in a sense more gently, from then on.*

*For it seemed that with Anke one could never be gentle enough, so
deeply did she feel all things.*[22]

Anke had great understanding and true empathy for deprived and maladjusted adolescent youngsters. Having had a severely deprived childhood

---

* Gisela Schegel, a long-time member of staff in Camphill and neighbour of St
   John's Cottage, often had lunch or supper tables open to guests. Thomas and
   Anke regularly attended.

The house community of Murtle, 1951

herself, she had first hand knowledge of what it could be like. She became active in inaugurating the Child Guidance College in Camphill, which aimed at ways to a better understanding of the essential needs of childhood and the improvement of daily life practices with children. Later, in 1978, both Anke and Thomas became involved in the Youth Guidance Impulse seeking a better understanding of adolescence with an emphasis on deprivation and maladjustment. This led to the development of a new branch of the work in Camphill, with a number of new Camphill places springing up. These met the needs of disabled youngsters after leaving school and before entering adult life in, for instance, a Camphill Village. And towards the end of her life, Anke's concern for adolescents and adults who were psychiatrically ill and turning to Camphill for help, clearly showed that Camphill would have to become involved in this field of work as well. The beginnings were set in motion of what is now the well-established Mental Health Seminar. This has since grown well beyond Camphill.

During the years of her housemothership in Murtle (1949–52) and Newton Dee (1952–57) Anke wholeheartedly involved herself in every aspect of life. Cooking, cleaning, laundry, nursing and her enthusiasm and idealism inspired others to become involved. Hers was a lively, buoyant and harmonious house community, where one felt in the right place, ready to face challenging responsibilities.

Holiday domestics

Friedwart Bock tells us about the time in Murtle:
Anke had been asked to be the housemother of Murtle House, the largest of our houses.

She was also one of the class teachers of St John's School, which had just begun to pioneer Waldorf education within curative education and had spent some time in Stuttgart at the first Waldorf School to prepare for her teaching task.

The weekly Council meetings also took place in Murtle House with Dr König as chairman and Anke as secretary. Anke had an amazing ability to embrace the life of the children and adults of Murtle House and was a gracious hostess to the general activities for which the house had become a centre. How did Anke manage to create a home for all the children and co-workers in a house as vast as Murtle? She had her Class to teach and yet her spirit inspired certainty and clarity and called forth a feeling of home-coming for the children and for us young people, who were finding our chosen home. She taught us to become a house-community and showed us how to include the children in our lives. The house meeting in the afternoon (on Saturdays) was a time of planning, of being invested with tasks and a time for developing initiatives. Anke managed these situations with much grace and charm. But there was always the reality of a delicate woman suffering from crippling

Carnival (Thomas, Anke, Hans van der Stok, Leonie van der Stok, Richard Poole)

*migraines, who outshone everyone with her energy and spiritual
strength. Anke brought a singular quality to her work with the children
and a profound knowledge of the forces of childhood and youth.
Celebrations and seasonal festivals, Sundays and the daily meals, the
opening and close of the day were all ennobled by Anke's touch, by the
way she would introduce imagery and elements of beauty and
meaning.[23]*

And about Anke's housemothership in Newton Dee House (from 1952
until 1957) Michael Lauppe writes:

*The house community numbered about nine to twelve co-workers
and teachers, plus over thirty boys. The guidance, imperceptible
leadership and understanding of the task at hand that Anke had were
astonishing.*

*The co-workers met before breakfast and Anke would speak the verse:
'The Stones are Dumb ...' Then the most urgent arrangements for the day
were discussed as well as problems described. I always came away from
these meetings feeling that through Anke's presence and brief words
most problems were dealt with smoothly and efficiently.[24]*

Anke was an ardent reader, and through her reading and studying
amply augmented her scanty formal education. She had a wide range of
interests, yet these were focussed. Mythologies, especially Greek but

As Viola in
Twelfth Night

also Nordic and Teutonic and those from further afield, had entered her
life early on. Anke had collected Fairy Tales from all over the world and
made comparative studies of these. This interest led into history proper
in which she was widely read. Combined with her exceptional and vivid
powers of memory, she was capable of far-reaching historical
overviews and interpretations. This knowledge merged with the immediate present and Anke's vital interest in current affairs was well
known.

Another interest of hers was the world of animals. As a young girl in
Pennsylvania she had lived in close proximity with animals in the wild
and had developed a deep empathy for 'the creature' as she called it. The
feline species, lions and cats, were her absolute favourites and she always
had in later life, in St John's Cottage, one or two adored cats. Books on
zoology and animal stories could always be found on her bedside table.
Anke, who occasionally experienced insomnia, used at times the early
hours, between two and five for reading.

She was interested in the development of modern psychiatry and in
social enterprises. She also avidly read the works of some of the great nov-
elists of recent times such as Leo Tolstoy, Franz Werfel and Nikos
Kazantzakis. With Tolstoy she had such an inner connection that she had
several vivid dreams about meeting him. All these interests were pursued
next to an ongoing and extensive study of anthroposophy.

Although from the moment she entered Camphill Anke did not dance
ballet again, for her the joy and meaning of dance were rediscovered in
1967 when she began to appreciate the immense therapeutic value of folk
dancing for the work in Camphill. Andrene Saile (now Thompson) writes:

Folk dancing

Anke used folk dancing in a therapeutic way with teenagers suffering from emotional disturbance. She believed that purposeful movement of the feet, in archetypal patterns worked beneficially and directly back onto the clarity of one's mind and she devised a sequence of exercises to foster this. She furthered this work in Seminar courses.

Culturally and artistically Anke was enormously active and capable. It was her initiative to create a regular puppet theatre for contact disturbed children, who responded wonderfully. Her story telling, mainly of Greek myths but also other epics, delighted audiences of adolescent, often maladjusted youngsters, who listened spellbound. Anke had an intimate relationship to the word, to language, and it was always very stimulating to listen to her rich, melodious voice. Every word was well chosen and consciously placed. This was very evident in her many stage productions of Karl König's and other plays. Reg Bould writes:

Most of us had almost semi-permanent roles. Anke was the Virgin in the Michaelmas Play and the Woman of Samaria in the Easter Saturday Play, both definitive and wonderful performances. Coming together for rehearsals were indeed some of the happiest times.

And Barbara Lipsker says about Anke's performance as the Woman of Samaria that it was: '... so soul-filled that one actually became a participant in that experience.'

There was Anke's wonderful sense of fun, the ability to see the comical side in things. It was contagious and helped one to be 'on top' of events. At Carnival time she was in the midst of everything, writing and producing

hilarious skits such as the famous 'Larder Key' which, as Reg Bould says, was:

> *... made up out of words and tunes from all the Camphill and Oberufer plays. We invariably based our Carnival skits on current happenings within our work and life. Anke was a great contributor in this ... treating them with wit and humour.*[25]

Anke became the editor of *The Cresset,* the journal of the Camphill Movement, which existed from 1954 until 1972. The journal contained articles of fundamental and lasting importance by Karl König, Thomas Weihs, Lotte Sahlmann and many others in Camphill including Anke herself, which are still referred to today.

Anke and Thomas led a simple yet gracious life. After 1957 they moved to a small house, built for them on Murtle Estate: St John's Cottage. From here they conducted their many further activities and involvements in and with Camphill, both at home and in the world wide Camphill Movement. They welcomed guests and visitors from near and far who enjoyed the cultured, warm and hospitable atmosphere of their home. Anke and Thomas were a good team. When they entered a room, the mood became festive.

Barbara Lipsker wrote about Anke: 'Hers was a unique mixture of modesty and regality.'

In daily life Anke together with Thomas radiated positive attitudes such as: one should be philosophical about life, one should not make a fuss, one could always adapt to any circumstance, and concerning work: work well done does not make one tired. Tiredness is the result of deeds only half or half-heartedly done. Thomas and Anke certainly lived up to these ideals. They loved their work and would give themselves fully to the tasks in hand. They could equally well relax and enjoy other pursuits. One of their great joys was to explore western Scotland in their little caravan or to drive down to Greece where they pitched their tent in the wildest places and lived off bread, goats cheese, honey and coffee. In these two places they felt totally at home.

Both Anke and Thomas lived in Camphill, Aberdeen until their deaths. The other founder members of Camphill had sooner or later gone out to initiate Camphill places in other countries and on other continents. It was in the 1970s that Anke increasingly felt the urge to venture out with a somewhat different concept of Camphill. Eventually she became instrumental in the founding of three further places in Scotland. Templehill in 1972, Camphill Blair Drummond in 1975 and Corbenic in 1978. Although there was to be a gradual metamorphosis of the initial concept, there was to begin with the strong impulse to create places for direct mutual help between all who lived in the place. Templehill started out with older psychiatric or maladjusted youngsters, who helped throughout the day with the care of very young, severely disabled children. The motto was: By giv-

During the Easter conference of 1983 in Camphill Hall with Rudiger Janisch and Imgard Lazarus

ing help you receive help. For a time this was an exceedingly courageous and most positive venture, which however had to be modified after it proved too much of a strain for all concerned.

The last years

In June 1983 Thomas died of cancer. Anke suffered the loss profoundly. She said: 'I do not want to overcome my grief for Thomas, but I want to learn to live with it.'

During the few years that were left to Anke she continued to travel widely all over the Movement and, as before, held lectures and seminar courses, had countless personal talks as well as maintaining a large personal correspondence.

Her concern for the further developments of Camphill in all its aspects was always in evidence in meetings, conferences and talks. Her addresses over several years, to large audiences, on Community Day, November 30, are an example. Through her ability to think clearly, and through her inherent sense of morality, Anke often acted as the moral conscience for the community and clearly put into words what others only vaguely felt. With courage she went for what she recognized as the truth: which was not always comfortable for everyone.

Kate Roth wrote:

During the years since Thomas's death, when Anke travelled throughout the Movement, there was a great wish in her heart: to try to kindle the essence of Camphill in those who sought it but felt lost and bewildered, and to encourage the individual connections within Camphill across the countries and continents, to hold hands firmly in order to meet the demands with inner strength and fortitude.[26]

Many who met Anke during this time remarked on how she had changed. Gisela Schlegel writes:

During the four years after Thomas's death, Anke changed; becoming more open, free and warm. Perhaps one could say that wonderful qualities, which she had always had, became unlocked. Many experienced this.[27]

Anke was able to transform her grief in an amazing way. She became ever more giving and radiant, inspired by new aims and resolves for a future beyond her own death. A half dormant cancer, which she had harboured for many years, finally consumed her body, setting her spirit ever more free. She looked forward to dying. Her own words were '... it is a festival.' And so, on August 27, 1987, light-footed as the dancer she had been and fully conscious, Anke crossed the threshold.

Thomas Johannes Weihs

(April 30, 1914 – June 19, 1983)

Christine Polyblank, née Weihs

We must not be content with the way things are. As Camphill we have a message, something to formulate and to convey through the way we live, through the way we speak, and in ways we do not yet know. With every year, every month, every passing day, the urgency and the need for this message increases. We must endeavour to equip all those who stay here and who leave us with powerful and intense enthusiasm for the good, for the dignity, the divinity of human existence on earth. Thus we may live up to the task that is laid upon us.

These were the closing words spoken by Thomas in his Annual Report at the Camphill Rudolf Steiner School, Aberdeen in 1975. He opened this address by placing the work of Camphill in a wider setting.

The impulse of Camphill, which Dr König started here, rooted here, has spread over the whole world. This impulse, so intimately linked to Caspar Hauser, is one of concern for the sanctity, for the divinity of man as it appears in every child coming into the world anew. We are committed to this impulse; Camphill is part of the greater movement springing from the words and deeds of Rudolf Steiner. It is part of the Christian impulse of the last two thousand years, and beyond that, of the inner moral striving of man throughout the ages ...[1]

Childhood and youth

Thomas was born in the spring before the outbreak of the First World War. He was the second child of Gertrude and Richard Weiss (the spelling of this surname was later changed), who lived on the third floor of an apartment block at No.10 Gerlgasse, in the 3rd District of Vienna. His father's family had come from Brodi, a town then on the Russian-Polish border. His mother's father was also from Brodi, and her mother from Czechoslovakia. Along with many other Jewish people, both families had

Gertrude and Richard in the early days of their marriage

escaped from recurrent pogroms and persecution and, in the 1870s and 80s, had arrived, full of hope for a new life in Vienna. Here, under the liberal Kaiser Franz Joseph, laws regarding Jews were less rigid, and here they believed they could surely achieve a better standard of living and enter the professions. Richard was able to work his way up from clerk to one of two directors of AGCI, a major chemical firm, and Hans Kelson, one of Gertrude's brothers, became a jurist of International Law who drafted the new Austrian Constitution in 1919, and was later to receive eleven honorary doctorates from countries around the world. For Gertrude and Richard's children the future was theirs to shape. Thomas became a doctor, his brother Ernst, an engineer, and his sister Karin, a teacher.

Shortly before getting married both Richard and Gertrude had themselves baptized, and outwardly adopted the Protestant faith. This was not done for religious reasons, for they were not religious people, but 'free-thinking' and with a strong social conscience. It was more to help with integration, perhaps also a gesture of appreciation towards this benevolent regime, and to realize their hopes in this new country in which they had such great faith. It was certainly also to protect their future children. Although both parents must have lived with an underlying anxiety, nothing of the past was ever spoken to the children who were protected from every hint of discrimination. It was therefore in an atmosphere of comfort, confidence and open-mindedness that Thomas, his elder brother Ernst and his younger sister Karin grew up as part of what became known as *la jeunesse dorée*.

Thomas's early childhood was, in his own words, exquisitely happy and sheltered. His mother was loving and most particularly fond of him. His father was a kindly, humble man, who had no wish to show off what he had. Although he had bought two apartments and knocked them into one

Thomas (left) with his mother, and brother Ernst

larger but unostentatiously furnished flat for his growing family, (which included an orphan cousin), they were in a fairly modest district. There was a live-in maid, and a cook who came in twice a day, but Richard was anxious about money and saved and invested much of his earnings, while his partner in AGCI lived in a luxurious fashion in a splendid baroque-style building with balconies overlooking the Botanical Gardens. However, Richard and Gertrude did have one indulgence, namely their own box at the Opera. While courting Gertrude, Richard had sung Schubert lieder to her piano accompaniment and this love of music, along with painting and sculpture, surrounded the three children as they grew up. Sunday visits to picture auctions were as much a part of life as visits to the museums, the zoo or the Botanical Gardens. Their apartment was full of original paintings and sculptures — they particularly admired Gustinus Ambrosi — and books. They had a subscription to *The Geographical Magazine*, which is still published today, as they wanted to know what went on in the world, and it was in this magazine that Thomas first began to discover a fascination for India. Over the years he would spend hours with his little sister Karin, pouring over the pictures of India and planning how he would become a doctor and work there among the poor.

Richard's sister Hermine, (the mother of Walter Johannes Stein, a well-known anthroposophist) was the children's favourite aunt: she seemed to have a never ending supply of fairy tales to tell, and when she began with the magical words *'Es war einmal — na, wann war es denn? ... wo war es denn? ...* [Once upon a time, ... now, when could it have been? ... where could it have been? ...]' with weighty pauses in between, the children were truly spellbound. The family often went on long summer holidays to Yugoslavia and other places in the mountainous regions of Kärnten and Salzburg, taking huge baskets of linen and cutlery and household things with them as they travelled by train. Once there they were joined by other members of the family. These were enjoyable, sociable occasions.

Thomas enjoyed playing boisterous games with his brother Ernst: an absolute favourite was to race around the apartment in a *Graf und Stift* — the little round table in their room turned on its side became the perfect vehicle, and the smaller circular shelf underneath made for particularly exciting cornering. But it was to his little sister Karin, five years younger than himself, that he was most close. With her he played patiently and lovingly for many hours. For her he made toys, furniture for her dolls, even little coat-hangers. Karin was totally devoted to him. She writes:

As far back as I can remember I adored him. Throughout my childhood I depended on him to set up an ethical code for me to act upon. He never scolded or reprimanded me nor did he need to pass moral judgements, except in cases of injustice. I remember him coming home from school ... he must have been seven years old — sobbing inconsolably. The teacher had banged a child's head against the blackboard when the child was not culpable of any offence other than not knowing the answer to the teacher's question. His rage at such unfairness and his distress over his impotence to alter the course of events made a great impression on me ...

Thomas had the ability to make me see what I was like and make me change my course of action. I recall one incident in particular. I must have been eight years old. I had no idea why it made one of my classmates cry when one called her by her new surname of Horn instead of Benesch ... I merely thought it funny how easy it was to make her tears roll down ... and frequently amused myself by calling her Horn.

When I told Thomas of this exploit he looked at me in disbelief: 'But

*you are making her unhappy,' was what he said. It was the first time I
realized that there was evil in me ...*

From an early age his fine, sensitive feelings led him to experience
things very deeply and he seems to have felt injustice, and the suffering of
others in quite a conscious way. Compassion, an ability to inspire change
and to bring out the best in others are characteristics we can see throughout Thomas's life.

There was another side to Thomas to which he sometimes referred.

*I had been a very violent child, with a terrible temper, so much so
that I had twice nearly injured my brother who was stronger and much
more agile than I. My parents had even considered sending me to
boarding school.*

He then describes how he took hold of this temper one day in a quite
remarkable way:

*I owed to my first English teacher a neurosis that lasted for six
incredibly burdened years. He came into the classroom and told us
about the English people ... He described how very controlled the
English were, how well mannered, how they kept to certain forms and
laws of conduct, and I was greatly impressed. On the second day he
spoke of one obstacle to learning English, and that was just one sound.
It was the 'th' and we roared with laughter. He got quite red in the face,
his neck swelled up, and he tried to explain to us that the 'th' was so
very important, and we thought it was fantastically funny and couldn't
understand what was the matter with him. He went into such a violent
temper that I had a dream that night: I was playing chess, and the chess
figures were my brother, my sister, my father and my mother, and I was
shifting them quite coolly from one square to the next ... And from that
moment on, I had a self-control with which I could drive every member
of my family, and anybody else, completely up the wall. I did this,
although I was not completely happy with myself.* [2]

Much later in his life he was to say of these rages: 'When I was fighting with my brother I was really fighting with myself.'[3] His relationship
with his brother was, however, fundamentally good. In later years, he and
Ernst were often to be seen setting off on long hiking and canoeing trips
to the mountains and down the Danube. Karin remembers their mother
frequently holding her brothers up as examples of good behaviour.
Certainly Thomas was normally most considerate. However, his deeply
feeling, passionate nature lived on throughout his life and could be seen in
the way he espoused causes in which he had come sincerely to believe.
Many have spoken of the deep despair he experienced when he failed in
putting these over to others.

From the moment he entered school things changed for Thomas. He
has described his whole school experience as a negative one.

I remember well the experiences of my first three school days. Having had an exquisitely happy and sheltered childhood, I went to school in a fairly dark, dismal building, an elderly gentleman in dark clothes talked to all of us. We were quite a large group of children. What he said was strange, and he asked us questions. I usually knew the answers, so I told him, and he was pleased. This gave me a bit of confidence, so I went the next day! He again told us things, and again asked us questions, and I again knew the answers, so I told him, and he was not pleased, which left me puzzled. Then I realized that he had a quite peculiar habit — he wanted one to put up one's hand before one gave the answer.

Now, we had never done that at home, but I thought 'He's old, maybe he needs that.' So the next time I put up my hand and answered, and he was pleased. But, on the third day, when the same thing happened, he was not pleased. Then I was very *puzzled. He asked, I knew the answer, I put up my hand, and spoke, and he was cross. I did find out in the end that he wanted those to answer who didn't know the answer, and then I gave up.*[4]

Thomas was a bright and intelligent child who had responded with warmth to the colourful, nourishing tales told by Aunt Hermine. Now the dry nature of the subjects taught and the methods used, coupled with the lack of enthusiasm of his teachers, left him unmoved and uninspired. Compared to his brother Ernst, whom Karin used to watch from the window as he set off for school every morning, head held high and brief case packed with work tucked securely under his arm like a veritable professor, Thomas did only the work he had to do, always just getting the grades he needed, remaining somewhat aloof, and dreaming his way through school life.

One day, when he was twelve years old, Thomas was sitting at table with his family when he observed his father spill some soup on his tie. He saw his mother's face, first irritated, then loving, as she wiped it off for him. Although this had often happened before, Thomas noticed it for the first time and was shocked. 'How can this be my father?' he thought. But then: 'I must behave in such a way that he can be a worthy father.'

His mother and father were no longer simply his parents but were now people in their own right. This marked a step in the birth of personal identity, but was also experienced as a moment of intense loss.

Thomas now entered secondary school, where he began to develop a keen interest in science. He found he could not help but bring his scientific thinking to bear on the compulsory religion lessons. At first he had to attend the Catholic lessons and later the Protestant ones. This brought up the powerful question as to whether there were two Gods, a Catholic God and a Protestant God, and was quite a dilemma for him. Later, in his confirmation classes, Christ's death and resurrection were likened to a butterfly rising from a cocoon. 'But the butterfly was not dead!' thought

Thomas at 12 years of age

Thomas. Trying to grasp the resurrection with his thinking, he argued with the priest, but when his questions were not answered, he refused to be confirmed. In a talk she gave after his death, his wife Anke described the awakening of his conscious thinking in the following way:

When he was about fifteen or so he began to search for the truth. He looked at many of his teachers and felt that they were pretending things; that they were saying things that they didn't really believe and which they didn't live up to. Through this he often got into trouble.

It was about this time that Thomas also became politically aware and he soon pronounced himself a Social Democrat, earning for a while the name of 'Red Thomas.'

A moment of despair

At the age of eighteen Thomas became depressed. Questions about his life and the world troubled and disillusioned him. He was still close to his sister Karin, and he was now in the habit of introducing novels and poetry to her — Rilke and Cocteau — and they were both much influenced by the despondent, melancholy atmosphere these created in them. Often he sat by Karin's bed in the evenings and discussed his plans with her. At that time he still wanted to be a doctor in India. Then one evening, as he was reading Turgenev to her, he suddenly said: 'Life is not worth living.'

When she reminded him of his plans to go to India he replied that it was not worth while ... everything was meaningless and that he was going to take his own life. When she returned from school the next day she found that he had made such an attempt, and for the rest of his life he had a lead bullet wedged at the back of his neck. Thomas never referred to this and when questioned always said that it was of no real significance — a brief episode of no great importance. Like a rage perhaps, overwhelming, then over and forgotten. Karl König too suffered from depression at this age and also toyed with thoughts of suicide,[5] as did Hans Schauder.[6] Thomas, as with so much else in his life, took it to the extreme. Rudolf Steiner writes about the suicide of young people[7] describing how an early childhood injustice can, over time, be covered up by many layers of the soul, and when a similar injustice occurs many years later: 'that which has lain dormant below in the surging waves of his soul begins to stir and becomes active ...'

But we can also consider this, spoken by Thomas in a lecture in 1969:

While we are children we are right to live in our wishes, to say what I so long to be is my true nature; but when we leave childhood behind and enter maturity we have to learn to face ourselves. The moment of shame has to be accepted and endured.[8]

Throughout his life, he did frequently refer to the 'problematic and burdened nature of the human being.'

In order to protect their three children from all discrimination, Thomas's parents had thought it best to bring them up in ignorance of their Jewishness. But as anti-Semitism began to spread, each learnt individually of his roots. Thomas immediately expressed pride in his heritage; it was a positive experience for him and seemed to come almost as a relief.

Thomas, on the right, with Ernst, his mother and Karin

When he was eighteen Thomas entered the University of Vienna to begin medical studies. No doubt he hoped to find teachers who would offer real leadership and inspiration, but this was not to be and he continued to do only the work he had to, and thus to scrape through, just as he had at school. The barren, soul-destroying atmosphere at the University drove many students to the coffee houses, where they did much of their work, alone or in groups.[9]

Meeting the future

It was possibly on his very first day at the university that he met Peter Roth, who was also in his first term of medicine. They became inseparable friends and went everywhere together. Peter describes how they participated fully in the cultural life of Vienna, and how, while he and many of their friends 'burnt for this or that painter or musician or actor ... Thomas went about with a great amount of aloofness ... he had ... a decent detachment which valued the ideals and deeds of a road-sweeper ...' as much as those of a high-class opera performer.[10]

Vienna nonetheless held many distractions for Thomas. With his charm and exceptional good looks he had a wide circle of friends, and he led a busy social life visiting the coffee houses and ice-cream parlours. His life-long love of the cinema began at this time. Dancing was done in people's homes rather than in dance halls, and he spent hours walking in the park and along the Danube. An important activity for any cultured Viennese was the art of talking. During this period he met many interesting people in the art world. Dr König's perception of him as 'living in style, enjoying life and with a good amount of savoir vivre'[11] was accurate. So it is not surprising that Thomas continued to get only the grades he needed to continue his studies. There were, however, two areas in which he excelled. One was obstetrics; he had an affinity with babies which lasted all his life. The other was his bedside care of patients — they seemed to feel secure with him, somehow encouraged by his warm, listening presence. This ability to give his full attention to another, to enter empathetically into the concerns of the other, was a quality he clearly already had as a young man, but one he developed ever more consciously throughout his life, and of which he frequently spoke in his lectures in later years. His friend and colleague of many years, Morwenna Bucknall, referred to her experience of this at the Memorial Evening for Thomas in this way:

> However darkened and disarrayed a person might appear, whatever their 'outer garb' of appearance or habit, it was important to remain faithful to the potential in that person, and to let nothing get in the way of this.

Thomas and Peter were always on the lookout for new and interesting things and one day in the autumn of 1936 they heard of a doctor who was giving a series of rather unusual lectures on zoology in the Town Hall. They went — but at the end they looked at each other and said: 'This is not for me!' So it was with some astonishment that they met at the next lecture. These lectures were given by Dr Karl König. The story goes on to relate that as they left the hall Mrs König saw them and said to her husband, 'There goes our future!'[12]

At the second lecture they actually met and spoke with Dr König and it was not long before he invited them to join his study group, which became known as the Youth Group, which met weekly in his beautiful family home. What Thomas found here as he joined this questing group of young people, under the leadership of a small but inspiring man, was radically new and modern. It demanded a complete break with the old, meaningless, superficial life he had led as one of the privileged *jeunesse dorée*. Thomas was captivated. Had he not taken this step he could well have

*Thomas as a
young medical
student*

spent the rest of his life doing no more than was necessary. He could have become wealthy and, following in his father's footsteps, become a collector of sculptures. Now he was to become, in a sense, a sculptor.

Asked for his first impression of Thomas when he arrived to join the Youth Group, Rudi Lissau, a long-standing member, responded warmly with: 'A man! ... with a lovely masculinity ... confident ... and exceptionally handsome.' Hans Schauder, another member of the group described him as: 'a truly handsome man. He had a very attractive personality and was easily able to overcome any difficulties. He had no fear. There was something of the adventurer in him. He was capable of coping in every situation. He was kind by nature ... But there were also problematic traits in him. In this respect he was a typical Viennese ...'

Dr König was soon describing Thomas and Peter as 'Castor and Pollux, the heavenly twins' and while this may have been in no small measure due to their good looks, it also reflected the exceptional qualities he recognized in them, qualities that they brought to the group and that they would later bring to Camphill. Of his early attitude to the Youth Group studies, Rudi adds that: 'While Peter was more inclined to embrace what came towards him, Thomas was slightly more wondering, probing ... but in a gentle and mature manner.' He was to wrestle with König's ideas, with Steiner's ideas and with the whole of Christianity, trying to find what was true for him. Throughout his life 'I believe ...' was a phrase he frequently used; he would only speak about anthroposophical ideas when he had made them his own even when this created rifts between himself and his colleagues in later years. In an obituary for Thomas, the Christian Community priest, Michael Tapp wrote:

His roving and questioning soul may make one feel that he received a very appropriate name. Like his apostolic predecessor he seemed to combine doubt and affirmation to a mutually creative tension which made him a person both of the here-and-now and of the future.[13]

What was it about Dr König that enabled him to draw such a gifted, brilliant group of young people around him, and later take a group of them to the bleakest north of Scotland, and get them to devote the rest of their lives to his project? Rudi Lissau explains:

As a man and a doctor he could see much more than others ... he had faculties that went beyond the ordinary ... a fascinating person ... inspiring in a quiet way without doing anything consciously ... and he was funny.

Barbara Lipsker in her autobiographical notes writes:

Although Dr König was just ten years older than the group, one could have the impression that he had never been 'young,' but that he was born into this world wrapped in wisdom, the stars of his earthly realm around him increasing in strength and clarity beneath the layers of habit, inhibition and illusion.

In her autobiography Anke Weihs described him:

In Dr König, the gaze was a channel for the flow of warmth, it was in itself healing, for one felt one was seen in one's hidden truth, and always with respect and compassion.

Alongside this it must also be said that he could be extremely unpleasant and temperamental; he could dominate, and inspire fear.

He was a king ... at 3 p.m. in Camphill House there was complete silence, no-one moved for Dr König was meditating.[14]

Whatever it was that Thomas met in Dr König, it aroused his deepest interest, engaged him fully and rekindled his enthusiasm for life. His whole being seemed to come awake and unfold. He had met Dr König and through him, Christianity and anthroposophy, and as his understanding of the existence of the spiritual world became more real, he began to find meaning and direction in his life. Together with the group, he would *live* anthroposophy.

Shortly before meeting König and the Youth Group, but most likely in the spring of the same year, Thomas and his sister Karin were walking out one Sunday morning as was the custom for Viennese Society, when their eyes fell upon a particularly attractive and vivacious young woman walking in their direction. Thomas's response was an immediate 'That's the girl I'm going to marry!'

A short while later Karin went on a summer holiday to Flims in the Swiss Alps, and she bumped into Henny, this same striking girl. Henny and Karin immediately became the closest of friends. All this was to change soon after their return to Vienna, where Henny attended the Schule Hellerau. At Henny's request, and much against her own better judgement, Karin took her home, though she had no doubt that she would lose this girl, whom she now regarded as her very own friend, the moment Thomas set eyes on her. As Henny entered the flat, she tripped and fell headlong into the hall, the contents of her handbag spilling out. Thomas was there to gather them up. With this dramatic gesture Henny entered Thomas's life, and it was only a short time before Karin's fears were borne out: Thomas and Henny found a small apartment in the 3rd District, Neulinggasse 53/24, where they set up home together.

Henny — Helen Ida Emma Stoll — came from a wealthy Swiss family whose home was in Flims. Her father had made his fortune trading in India where he had met and married Emma Bechtler, and where Henny was born on February 26, 1919. When he became ill with tuberculosis and malaria the young family returned home where, to Henny's deep distress, her father died, leaving her in the care of nannies, nurses and her rather distant mother whom she believed throughout her life to favour her younger sister Beatrice — 'the smiling one.'

Henny had everything money could buy yet she grew up dissatisfied, with little self confidence and less self esteem, forever seeking recognition and affection. The effect of being both spoilt and neglected on a wilful, spirited, beautiful girl resulted in her growing up to be charmingly child-like but immature and self-centred with some almost delinquent behaviour. The combination was potent and throughout her life she left a trail of chaos behind her.

News of Henny's new living arrangements soon reached her mother who, armed with her lawyer, hurried to Vienna to collect her wayward daughter. But the birds had flown, and sought refuge at Peter's house. Her mother now made her way to Thomas's parents in the Gerlgasse; an agreement was reached and Thomas and Henny were married on February 24, 1938, in a quiet ceremony surrounded by their two reluctant families.

The moment of decision

As Thomas entered his final year of medical studies, life for Jewish people in Vienna was becoming daily more unpleasant, even dangerous, due to anti-semitic activities. Well before Hitler arrived there was rioting on

The newly-weds Thomas and Henny

the campus so that the whole of his last year was disrupted and neither he
nor Peter were able to sit their final exams. Then, in March 1938 Hitler
crossed the border into Austria and occupied the country.

Thomas and Henny finally left on October 1 and settled in Basle where
he was able to repeat his final year and receive his medical degree. They
lived extremely comfortably in a lovely rented apartment, and during this
year Thomas had the great privilege to work with Dr Ita Wegman, the
medical collaborator of Steiner. It was also during this year that letters
came from Dr König inviting him to join the community which had by
now found a home in Scotland. Thomas stood facing one of life's cross-
roads. India, the place of his youthful dreams, was now also where
Henny's family were keen that he should establish himself as a surgeon.
There he could certainly do much good work and he and Henny could live
in considerable comfort. Or he could follow Dr König into a startlingly
new life, *living* anthroposophy, in community, and with children with special needs. The two of them must have struggled with this question and it
has gone down in family folklore that it was, astonishingly, Henny who
made the decision: 'Let's go to Scotland!'

They were able to get places on the last civilian boat across the Channel
just a week before Britain declared war on Germany, and they made
straight for Kirkton House. Henny describes how they arrived 'hand in
hand,' both of them full of goodwill for this new venture. As they entered
the front hall of the bleak manse they were greeted by 'Little Peter' (Peter
Bergel) who was leaping about fluttering his arms as he muttered: 'nice
and friendly, nice and friendly, the box, the box, this and this ...'

This was the first person with special needs she, and possibly he, had met.

From a life of privilege, they settled into the primitive conditions of the
draughty old manse, without heating or electricity and with one bathroom
for the whole community. What were to be their tasks here? Entering
immediately into the spirit of the venture, Henny bought some chickens,
and Thomas set about making a hen house. There was much maintenance
to be done, and work on the land was needed. Thomas threw himself headlong into these tasks. Always the scientist, he first studied books on joinery and farming, and then, together with Peter, he began the routine of
spraying the fields with life-giving biodynamic preparations, as though he
had been doing it all his life.

Things were not going so well for Henny. Her memories of this time
are of the dark wood between Kirkton House and Williamston House and
of an ancient druid altar she had to pass when she went from one house to
the other. It rained constantly and as the November winds howled around
the bleak manse, it seemed to her that they were joined by the voices of
the dead which rose up from the tombstones in the graveyard below their
bedroom window.

On Whitsunday, May 12, as the community sat down together to enjoy a fine, celebratory dinner, the police arrived to take the men away to be interned as enemy aliens. Henny was distraught and, although she was pregnant, she sensed that this was the beginning of the end for her and Thomas. Where she went then is not clear but it is likely that she moved to Williamston House to be cared for by the Haughtons. When the move to Camphill took place, Henny rented a property nearby, Durris Cottage, where, on July 12, 1940 she gave birth to Thomas's first child, a daughter, Chailean — known throughout her childhood as Anne, or Anny.

Thomas, meanwhile, was interned with the other married men on the Isle of Man where they were placed in boarding houses and left to do more or less as they pleased. They were thus able to devote themselves intensively to spiritual research together with other inspiring anthroposophists such as Dr Ernst Lehrs whom they met there. In October 1940, Dr König (who had been released somewhat earlier) was overjoyed to receive a letter from Thomas reaffirming his commitment to join the community, the last of the group to do so. When the rest of them returned to the womenfolk — Thomas was released in November — the move from Kirkton to Camphill had been accomplished. Thomas now found himself in a difficult situation. Henny, with their newborn child, was living just a few miles away, while his life's work, for which he now felt more prepared than ever, and eager to begin, lay in Camphill with Dr König and the new community. Some remember the incessant ringing of the telephone during the evening meetings and the sound of his motorbike roaring off late at night, only to return early the next morning. When Henny then moved into Camphill House the relationship was tempestuous. Thomas had an intriguing scar on the palm of his right hand. When his children asked him how he got it, he told them this story: Henny had asked the community whether she could buy some chickens and keep them in the grounds somewhere. When the answer was no, she went ahead and got them anyway — a dozen hens and a fine cockerel — and had them delivered straight to their bedroom upstairs in Camphill House. It was while trying to catch the cockerel that he got the scar.

Since the earliest times of the Youth Group in Vienna the practice of acting the Oberufer Christmas plays had always been seen as an essential part of community building. This practice continued, and one year, Henny took the part of the young shepherd. It was to be perhaps the only moment that Dr König really noticed her and felt touched by her struggling being. He spoke with her afterwards and it was a moment she occasionally mentioned even into old age — for the length of one performance she had been seen and valued by Dr König. The only person in the community she remembered as having been consistently kind to her was 'Frau Doktor' Tilla König.

Henny, Thomas and baby 'Anny'

Anke described Thomas's move into Camphill in the following way:

From the time when the men came out of internment camp, life in Camphill really began. Thomas's life and Camphill's life became one from then on ... Thomas never wanted to be a leader, but he was no doubt an example, because he had a power of endurance which was very, very rare. Thomas in his early days had very broad shoulders, and wherever one saw this pair of shoulders one knew it was alright, nothing could really go wrong. We relied heavily on him. He had a very sharp mind and he was the one of us who stood very freely at Dr König's side and helped Dr König. He was really the right hand man of Dr König for quite a while, taking him for drives, standing in when Dr König couldn't give a lecture ...

There was nothing that Thomas wasn't willing to do. Never did he say no to anything. Some of us once talked about these early days of Camphill and came to the conclusion that Thomas was really the midwife who brought Camphill, Dr König's baby, through the birth passage. I think it was so, in a way.[14]

And how did Thomas experience those early days? Speaking in 1979 about the phases of Camphill he said:

Nineteen thirty-nine to forty-nine was the phase of absoluteness and intolerance. We saw our task in standing against the whole world, the Nazi regime, from which we had set ourselves off. We were also fighting as enemy aliens against hostile suspicion, we were set off against the Anthroposophical world. We wanted to live, not study Anthroposophy. There was the intense, determined leadership of one who was aware of his mission but antagonized others. We lived, convinced of our task, certain of our mission and spiritual intention. This phase also saw the birth of our Spiritual Community ...

It was strenuous but triumphant. It was easier than any later time.[15]

There was clearly no place for Henny here. She had in the meantime bought Eidda House, some two miles away in Culter, where she and Thomas lived with little Chailean. Thomas continued to struggle to live two lives, but in the summer of 1942 he left Henny to move fully into the community. Marie Blitz, a young Viennese woman who was a member of the community, now fell suddenly and deeply in love with him, and over the summer months they had a brief affair. Marie's despair was great when this came to a sudden end, and when she then discovered that she was carrying Thomas's child. But Henny, too, was expecting a child. Marie's son Nicolas Martin arrived on March 30, while Henny's daughter Johanna Christina (Christine) followed on June 26, after which Thomas and Henny moved into Camphill Lodge. Here Henny became 'Lodge-mother' and took on the running of the house with a dormitory of difficult teenage boys, several suffering from epilepsy, in addition to her two children, and she was soon pregnant with her third child.

Thomas with his son Nicolas

It became ever more clear that she could not be part of this venture although many aspects of it had deeply touched and also changed her. For the rest of her life she used health foods and homoeopathic medicines, and believed in living in the present and trusting in the future — therefore there was no need to save, invest or insure, an attitude which left her in her last year on this earth with the shell of an uninsured, burnt-out cottage for her home. She could not interest herself in any meaningful way in the spiritual life, the constant study, the lectures, the reading and meditation. Nor could she tolerate sharing her husband with Dr König and the community, nor living with the deeply disturbed children, nor the constant hard work and the drabness and poverty of the whole venture. When not with Dr König, Thomas was dressed in his blue and grey 'weatheralls,' devoting his days to maintenance and land work, while she longed to wear beautiful clothes and live the life of a doctor's wife. Sometime after the birth of her third child, Lucas Francis, she moved out again, this time for good. For the first of the two children she had with a new partner, Thomas signed the birth certificates. But with the arrival of the third one, a turning point had been reached. They were divorced in 1950. Very much later in his life Thomas told me that he was somewhat burdened by the fact that he had let her go. He was well aware how difficult her life continued to be.

To conclude Henny's story: when she had brought her six children into the world she parcelled them all out and went to drama school in London, and for many years after that she struggled to recoup the fortune she had by then all but lost, by treading the boards as actress and singer first in London, and later in Paris. Fame was surely just around the corner!

Eventually she withdrew to her bolt-hole, a simple peasant's cottage without bathroom or hot water, the sort of place French actors and intellectuals bought for their 'resting' moments, and here she spent her last years, alone with her books and her collection of stray dogs and cats, until her death in 1995, aged seventy-six. She died poor but not chastened, inveighing against almost everyone. Everyone, that is, except Thomas.

Principal, teacher and general handyman

One of the early lessons for individuals in the community was that each was responsible for everyone and everything. Early rising was essential if all the work was to be accomplished, and every task was sacred and was to be undertaken with devotion. Personal interests and hobbies must give way to the needs of the community. And so the elegant young Viennese doctor, whose main interest had been neurology, and who had come to help set up a medical clinic — although he now carried the title of Principal of Camphill House — in fact spent his time repairing whatever was broken, helping out wherever there was a need, teaching and working with delinquent boys on the land. Angela Carpos, later a Waldorf kindergarten teacher, describes how she and three other young adolescent refugees who had found their way to Camphill had lessons in science and Greek mythology with Thomas; their classroom was the kitchen in the Lodge. When she was just seventeen years old, in 1945, Valerie Daniels, later a curative eurythmist, came to Camphill, to work on 'the farm.' This consisted of two cows with a modest byre, and four or five Shetland ponies. These stout small beasts could be seen pulling their little blue two-wheel carts around the estate, full of dead leaves, or compost. The delinquent boys stood in the carts and, looking not unlike the Indian God Arjuna's warriors riding jubilantly into battle, encouraged the little ponies onwards. Some of the land that sloped down between Camphill House and the River Dee was put down to hay and some to corn, and the ponies were also used to pull the plough and harrow.

On a fine day during the harvest season the whole community would down tools to come out and help in the fields, gathering the corn and binding it into stooks, the women dressed in their beautiful Austrian dirndl dresses. The atmosphere was festive, spontaneous and positively Viennese. During the day Thomas was in charge of all this activity and took full part in it, with rarely a still moment. Then, at five-thirty in the evening, he gathered the boys together for their story lesson. Valerie describes how she was constantly and irresistibly drawn to listen as, with the greatest gentleness, he told the life story of Buddha.

Planning and budgeting were in their infancy then so that one day, when Valerie went to collect her five shillings pocket money from petty cash, she was told that Thomas had taken it all to buy a new cow.

One thing was becoming increasingly clear: they were running out of space for the work with the growing numbers of behaviourally disturbed boys who were coming into their care. So a search began for a new property to rent or to buy and towards the end of 1945, Newton Dee, a large estate with an eighty-four-acre farm, came on the market. A new era in Thomas's life began.

The farmer

The new farm was to be run biodynamically and was expected to provide a measure of self-sufficiency for the community. For the boys, running the farm was to be their lifeline. 'The mere taking part in certain chosen activities, while the rough work was done by others, would ... not be good enough'; only 'the actual work' could bring about the healing that was needed. In other words, together with the farmer, the delinquent boys had to take responsibility for the farm and know that its success lay with them. The boys were aged between fifteen and eighteen years, and had all come through the Juvenile Courts. The task of farmer fell to Thomas who took to it, as he did to every new task, with huge enthusiasm. In a detailed and thorough Farm Report written after only a year of this work, he was able to note:

On the day we took possession of the farm, two boys were already drawing their first furrows with a horse-drawn plough through the stubble. Since then ... the boys have not only learned to plough and to cultivate, to sow and to harrow, to harvest and to load, but also to handle horses, to milk and feed cattle, to rear calves, and a great number of manifold other activities.

He had managed to start up and run the farm using just over half the estimated necessary capital, and the £700 profit made was absorbed into capital outlay. Within five years the whole farm had been completely transformed, the fertility of the land hugely improved and many of the boys had been able to take up successful employment on other farms.

Anke takes up the story:

Thomas had never farmed before but he had an enormous amount of farming books ... and he went around talking to all the farmers in the area asking questions and in the end he managed ... as though he had been a farmer all his life. We had no tractor, we farmed it with six ponies, we had twenty three cows, all hand milked, and Thomas ran this farm with these delinquent boys. I used to have story lesson in the afternoon with these boys and I told them for instance the two marvellous sagas from Homer, the Iliad and the Odyssey ... Although he

Thomas with two of the boys on Newton Dee farm in 1948

*was king, Odysseus himself put his hand to the plough and did all the
work that was necessary there and these boys got the idea that Thomas
was the reincarnated Odysseus!*

*There was something in this, ... because this hero Odysseus was also
the hero of endurance ...This incredible endurance was a quality which
Thomas always had.*[16]

Friedwart Bock, who joined the team at Newton Dee in 1949, remembers:

*Thomas was worshipped by the lads, but he was always forthright
with them. Occasionally they would run away. Then the work on the*

*farm suffered. Following one of these episodes Thomas got up in the
dining-room and made a blazing row. This was followed by a remorseful
silence. Then into this quiet one of my 'non-speaking' boys said loudly:
'Damn you, Dr Weihs!' Everyone burst out laughing, including Thomas,
and they were able to go on with the meal.*

Thomas could be impatient and it is clear that traces of the fiery temper of his childhood remained. Although he would eventually think of
ways to help his colleagues when they were struggling, his immediate
response could be sharp. To a co-worker who was complaining about
someone, he was heard to snap: 'Well, you can't dissolve him in sulphuric
acid!' Generally, however, he was always ready to offer his support to
those who needed it.

Valerie would sometimes ride over on her horse to visit a friend in the
evening, and describes not only how hard Thomas worked, but how full
of care, wonder and understanding he was for the most unlikely creature,
and how full of empathy in social situations.

*As I came over the fields, I'd see Thomas ploughing. It was late in the
evening, he'd be ploughing the fields with a horse. Late one particular
evening, as I was saddling up in the stable for the return journey,
Thomas and Anke came to the door of the stable. Not wanting to be
seen, we scurried up into the loft. They came in to have a look at the
horses and cows, moving from one to the other, to make sure they were
all right. And we were peering down from above, from the hay loft!*

Once, she remembers, he described how he had pursued and cornered
a rat in one of the barns. What he spoke of was his admiration for the
courage of the rat which, when it realized it had no way out, turned to face
him. And again:

*At the festivals the boys were allowed to have horse races. Ginny and
Mora were powerful garrons, Ginny being the faster. June was a smaller
grey Sheltie and, as the only girl, I chose to ride her. Thomas was so
pleased when June won instead of Ginny.*

*'It doesn't depend on the horse but on the person riding it,' he told
the boys, and he thought it was a good thing for them to see this.*

From very early on in his life he had shown strong heart forces,
although he was also clearly a person of will. On one occasion, Valerie,
who was the only girl, insisted on joining the boys in jumping over the St
John's fire. 'I didn't quite make it and landed in hot ashes. As quick as
lightning, Thomas leapt forward and carried me to safety.'

He lived his work on the land so fully that themes from nature entered
into other areas of his work. When, as a service holder, he took the Youth
Service on Sundays, he would describe in evocative pictures, for example,
the purity of the snowflake, and how the earth is transformed when the
snow falls.

Holding the lay Sunday services, taking religion lessons and attending the Saturday Bible Evenings were activities in which more or less all the founding group members took part. Camphill's destiny was strongly bound up with Christianity. But many of these young Viennese, including Thomas, had had no relationship to Christianity before meeting Dr König and joining the Youth Group. Thomas describes how developing his own individual connection to Christianity had been a tremendous experience for him. It had taken four years of the most intense wrestling and groping through darkness, but it finally led to a true relation to the Christ. True, deep and lasting. Sometimes, in the corner of a photograph taken while holidaying in the wilderness of the west coast of Scotland, or in the mountains of Austria, it is just possible to see the Bible Evening paraphernalia laid out on some simple surface — Bible, candle and snuffer.

Challenges are always present, and a great and unexpected one loomed as the outside world began encroaching on the life of Camphill, a challenge which proved to be a real testing case for Thomas: high-power electricity pylons were to be built over the fields at Newton Dee, the sort of structures which simply begged to be climbed by maladjusted boys. Thomas, single-handedly, fought all the way to the House of Commons, but to his great despair, was unable to stop them being built.

The family man

On and off over this period and the next ten years, Thomas had care and responsibility for various combinations of his four children. The question of who his family was, and where his loyalties lay must have been quite a dilemma for him. When Thomas died, he lay in the chapel of Camphill Hall. During the funeral service it was customary to have the family sitting close to the coffin in the chapel, and the Community down in the hall. The question then arose: who was his family? It was finally settled that his immediate family, sister, children and grandchildren should sit on one side, and his community family, Carlo Pietzner, Alix and Peter Roth, Barbara Lipsker and others from the earliest Camphill days, should sit on the other. Anke belonged on both sides.

The experience of Thomas's children was that his time was very much taken up by the Community. In their early years the Weihs children were mostly in nurseries or dormitories, often together with special needs children, as well as other staff children. They were looked after by a series of nursery mothers and moved about between estates, houses and nurseries, shadowing their father's movements. Only in their last years while at boarding school did they come back to spend holidays in their own rooms in the old St John's school huts, next to old St John's Cottage, and have breakfasts and suppers together, and even a family Christmas one year. When, as young adults, they reminded him that he had omitted to invite them to the wedding breakfast of his marriage to Anke, he was truly penitent and did not know how this could have come about. But, for Christine, Thomas's second daughter, from the moment she arrived back in Camphill, a small, motherless four-year-old in a community of strangers, and he knelt beside her to tell her, 'I'm your father,' she sensed that she had come home. Throughout the turbulent movement, growth and change of Camphill in those early pioneering days, he was their anchor.

When Lucas was just one year old, he was given over to Thomas by Henny. He was cared for by Mrs König, then by Morwenna Bucknall, also spending short periods with his father. By 1949 at least three of his children lived with him in Newton Dee House.

Thomas was a tolerant, patient and kind father, though the many demands on his time meant that they saw comparatively little of him. But there were star-points in the week. Every Saturday morning, the children knocked on the door of his room and waited in high excitement for his 'Come in!' They had come to claim their pocket money, and every time he showed the same surprise as they trooped in, cupped hands outstretched. He would fumble around in various pockets in his waistcoat and jacket before bringing out a handful of coins and sorting out the thrupenny pieces. They were always delighted with this ritual and rushed off to the sweet

Thomas sawing logs on a family holiday

*Thomas with Christine, 'Anne' &
Lucas on a rare family
holiday in a croft in Dingwall*

shop in Bieldside to spend the handout on Highland Toffee, liquorice or sherbet.

The children did have some memorable family holidays when Thomas rented a cottage — a simple Highland croft — in Tomintoul or Dingwall. There they spent the time in leisurely daily rambles in the hills where the greatest excitement, when Anke was with them, was the imminent sighting of a warlock. Or, they would paddle or swim in mountain brooks and rivers. While their father sawed logs outside, they prepared the supper, and then, eating together round a small table, they had his full attention and the experience of being a family.

He never raised his voice to his children. When two of them, aged about fifteen or sixteen, were boarding at Wynstones School, they were asked by inexperienced hostel parents one Saturday morning, how much pocket money they wanted. This was a new situation for them and, without hesitation they upped the sum they usually received (five shillings and six pence) by a couple of shillings. This worked so well that the following week they upped it by a couple more. It wasn't long before they were getting one, then two pounds a week, joining record clubs, going to the cinema, even buying clothes, until the holidays came round and they hopped on the train for home, unaware of any wrong-doing. One morning Thomas quietly said to them: 'I'd like to talk to you both in my room.' He informed them that the extras bill had just arrived, that it was unusually high and then asked quietly but quite firmly what the money had been spent on and why they had done it. They hung their heads. He simply said that it must not happen again — and so the new lifestyle came to an abrupt end, the lesson was learned and the episode was never referred to again.

As the children grew up they lived with his astonishing sense of purpose, with the earnest way he devoted his life to his chosen paths —
anthroposophy, community life, and Anke. They observed how he worked
tirelessly to bring balance into his life: being naturally intellectual, he
worked on his artistic abilities; being naturally intense, with an underlying restless, even fiery nature (his fast driving and apparent disregard for
the rules of the road showed a daring they much admired) he worked to
develop in himself a calmness and unflappability and it is remembered by
his family that he could allow a daddy-long-legs to fly all round his face
while he was peacefully reading without the slightest urge to flick it away.
He expressed admiration for things beautiful or well done, and gave praise
and encouragement freely.

Although he was such an absentee father, with so little time and space
for his children, they nonetheless held him in the highest and warmest
regard. In his book *Children in Need of Special Care* Thomas likens the
handicapped child to a musician playing on a faulty instrument.
However great a musician he may be, if the instrument is faulty, the
music will seem poor. He describes how the onus is on the audience, on
the quality of listening, the reception. A sensitive listener will know
from the phrasing and the intonation that this is indeed a fine musician
and will applaud, smile and rejoice. And when the musician sees how his
playing is received, he is content and happy, and goes on to try even
harder, to excel. During the relatively short periods that his children had
with him, they remember that he seemed to hear and see only their good
intentions, and this expectation of the good made them feel both
included and loved.

The doctor

In 1954 a third phase in Thomas's life in Camphill began. Dr König
became seriously ill and handed over much of his medical and adminis-
trative work to him. It also meant that he finally began the work for which
he thought he had come in the first place. 'Farmer Thomas' now became
'Doctor Thomas' and the tasks of the medical care of all the children,
interviewing all the applicants for places in the schools, as well as leading
the child-clinics and working with therapies and therapists now fell to
him.

Dr König had established the practice of regular clinics for each child
and these were attended by all those who had immediate care of the child:
the nursery-mother, teacher, therapist and the doctor. In the year 1949,
Gisela Schlegel, whose father had been a doctor, and who had some years'
experience as a nurse in Germany, joined the community. She regularly

experienced Thomas with the very ill children and felt immediately that he answered her idea of the ideal doctor. She described his immense tact when dealing with the most withdrawn and unresponsive children: when an autistic child attended the clinic, Thomas would sit him on his lap, facing outwards, and speak to him softly from behind and the child was able to listen and respond. He always spoke with the children, and only later shared his thoughts with the group. At one time, a Down's syndrome child was very ill with pneumonia, and although he died, 'Thomas's presence throughout the illness brought a remarkable warmth and security; all anxiety melted away and one had the strong feeling that karma would work itself out.' On another occasion a small boy was lost in the fast-flowing Dee and after a search that lasted three days and nights there was an evening gathering, attended by the child's father and other family members. He had had no mother. Thomas gave a moving image of the child 'wandering off — searching for his mother.' As the relatives left, they commented on what a wonderful place this was and hoped that many more children would be able to come. The feeling of deep love and respect in their working together, between nurse and doctor, grew over the years. It was Gisela who was to nurse Thomas through his final illness some thirty years later.

Many parents met Thomas as he interviewed children for admission over the years and many have spoken or written of their impressions of him. This letter was written by Dr Denis Durno and refers to his first meeting with Thomas:

It was the late 1960s when as a family we were exploring all possibilities for our oldest son's education. We had been singularly unsuccessful with representatives of the local education authority, who seemed to leave us all downhearted and dispirited after each interview. Feeling desperate and without real knowledge of Camphill we decided to write and request an appointment to discuss what Camphill had to offer.

We were sent an appointment to attend Dr Weihs's office in the basement of Murtle House on a Saturday afternoon. We were also asked to come as a family. Although our concern was for our oldest son, our third son also had learning disability and it would be an opportunity to introduce him to Dr Weihs. The drive from the main road to Murtle House was to be the first of many future visits. We were immediately struck by the peace and tranquillity of the estate. My reaction as we turned into the drive was to switch off the car radio. This became a habit for many years.

It will come as no surprise to those who have experienced a meeting with Thomas that after saying hello and the formal introductions we were already beginning to feel better. For the first time we were speaking with

*someone who heard what we were saying, understood what we said, and
had a clear view of how he might help. No judgements were being
imposed upon us; our sons, indeed our whole family were being
respected in a way which to that time we had not experienced. We were
offered help and we felt we could accept this without qualification, a sort
of leap of faith requiring no further evidence.*

*There are a number of obvious reasons why our first meeting was so
successful. Thomas had a natural charm, good looks, a mellow voice, a
command of language such that his words floated from his lips and
landed somewhere inside your head like feathers or silk. These first
impressions are too easy to offer as a final explanation of his skills.
They have more profound roots in the birth of Camphill and all that
means. I believe they come from Camphill's spiritual origins, they come
from the hardships of working with the struggle of establishing
communities, but most important of all from a deep personal knowledge
of living, working and learning from every individual whose disability
had challenged him.*

*Thomas helped us to help our sons, he also helped us to help
ourselves in our marriage and I have no doubt much of what he taught
me helped in my role as a doctor.*

Over the years children who attended the Camphill Rudolf Steiner
Schools often returned to revisit the place where they had spent much of
their childhood, and many wanted to meet Thomas again. Some kept in
contact more or less from the moment they left and one of these is Jenny
Bradley. In her book *One More Turn* she describes Thomas as a fatherly
figure who did not experience himself as in any way superior to her, and
how this simple fact had helped her to accept that she needed help. He was,
until his death, a true friend to her, and brought meaning into what she
experienced as an impossible and meaningless life. About his experience of
living and working with people with special needs, he wrote: 'What has
helped me to mature and to live without fear and anxiety and with an
unusual degree of fulfilment and happiness I owe to the 'handicapped.'

Remedial work

In the spring of 1971 Thomas completed his first book, *Children in Need
of Special Care*, which he described as being the fruit of thirty years of living and working closely with special needs children. (This book, in 2004,
has been in print for thirty-three years and has been translated into twelve
languages.) In the preface a special thanks is offered to 'my friend Graham
Calderwood, whose untiring help made the book possible.' On the writing
and the content of the book Graham writes:

Thomas always found it hard to write. I suppose it was too sluggish a medium for him — indeed, he once told me that the effort of 'proper composition' got seriously in the way of his thinking. Speaking, however, was quite a different matter. So it fell out that, when he came to produce his book, Children in Need of Special Care, *he did not write it. He spoke it. He spoke it into a tape recorder, and Anke transcribed his recorded words on to paper, double spaced, for editing. The manuscript grew and grew, then was retyped, and typed yet again, as it was slowly converted into something approaching standard, written English.*

Eventually, this great, sprawling interlinear came to me. Now, English is my mother tongue, and by that time in Camphill I had acquired a reputation for being able to use it. It was probably undeserved: it was simply that I was one of rather few native English speakers around at the time! But both Thomas and Anke thought that I could put the finishing touches to the language of the book, and invited me to do so. Thus began a most interesting interaction between the three of us.

I for my part was most anxious that Thomas's inimitable style be preserved. Anke, for her sake, wanted the English to abide by the rules (her own had a precise, crystalline quality which I would say belonged to an earlier age). Thomas's English was — his own. As might be imagined, discussion developed at once, some of it quite heated, but none of it (let me say immediately) unfriendly. Indeed sometimes our discussions left us helpless with mirth as we all at once saw the comic absurdities of our joint efforts. There is a saying — it may come from India, I don't know: 'A camel is a horse designed by a committee.' I think that, at the start, our camels comfortably outnumbered our horses. We found a fairly efficient way to work together in the end.

Of the many fond memories I have of that co-operation, I especially remember Thomas's modesty. If we were to want, for some reason, to draw a comparison between Dr König and Thomas, we would find one here. I had, on occasion before this, 'corrected' the English of Dr König's lectures for transcription into print, only to have the heavens fall on me when he saw my efforts. Dr König left me in no doubt that English as he spoke it, and no other, would do to express his thoughts, never mind what native speakers thought. Thomas, by contrast, rarely ventured more than gentle query of my syntax, and almost always deferred to my views, or to Anke's. We had often to encourage him to be more severe with us.

And I remember how it all brought me to appreciate the manner of Thomas's thinking. Now, this is a little difficult to convey exactly. I think

I had, in common with others, nearly always grasped intellectually what he had to say. He was, after all, a lucid and logical thinker, and lucid and logical thinking is, by these very virtues, relatively easy to follow. But there was more to his thinking than mere intellect. At the very least, it was also informed by qualities of imagination and intuition, and sometimes by inspiration. There was more even than this. Perhaps it was artistry.

It is said of Thomas that he had a scanty relationship to music, and, as far as playing it, or singing it were concerned, that may have been true. He was certainly diffident about doing either, and was only with difficulty persuaded to attempt them. But when he thought, or spoke his thoughts, I think that all the elements of musical composition were there. I risk hyperbole, but I do not think it wholly absurd to suggest that Thomas thought as others sing.

This was the style or quality that I was keen should survive our often rather precious concerns with 'proper' English form as we tinkered with his book. I hope it did.

About Thomas's contribution to curative education, Graham writes:

The idea of developmental handicap is not unique to Thomas, and is found wherever remedial education is practiced in an Anthroposophical context. The idea probably originated with Rudolf Steiner, and it was certainly promoted by Dr König, but Thomas espoused it strongly, and took it far.

Lying at the heart of the developmental view is a kind of central dogma. It is that whatever bodily equipment may fall to the lot of a person, its owner is a person: that person is a Spirit — and Spirit is perfect.

A circle drawn on paper with a set of compasses, no matter how exquisitely, is not a circle. The notion which it attempts to 'incarnate,' however, is. By the mere act of becoming visible, the drawn circle fails. A true circle is necessarily supersensible. Rudolf Steiner said that the major part of a human being is invisible. We can see why.

Whatever we have become, we did not become it all at once. It took time: our childhood. But some of us are hampered, and do not get to take some one or several steps in our development. Though each of us is different, there are patterns to misdevelopment, just as there are to development that goes well. This is both astonishing and important. It need not have been like this. Departure from expected routes could entail descent into mere chaos, but it does not. It is as if the world, at least insofar as Life is concerned, gives in to disorder with great reluctance.

Thomas, with others, explored these patterns. Perhaps the most important thing that he brought to our amazed attention is that disability is not always, or indeed wholly, a one-off singular event, and even these (such as accidental brain injury) will have developmental consequences.

In Steiner's *Curative Course*, several polarities in childhood disability are described. Dr König developed this theme, describing a twelvefold Curative Clock with six polarities. Thomas now worked intensively with these six, developing and applying them in his medical and teaching work. For example, a better understanding of both Down's syndrome and autism can be gained through contrasting them. Thomas described the Down's syndrome child as having an immediately recognizable appearance which retains certain features of an early phase of embryonic development. This is coupled with special soul qualities, being usually loving, cheerful and trusting, but also unpractical, generally lacking in intellectual ability and cunning, and with a lack of awareness of sexuality. The autistic child, by contrast, is physically fine featured, often strangely beautiful, alert and masterly in handling mechanical objects, but withdrawn, fearful and uncommunicative, avoiding human relationships. By allowing them to live and learn side by side, he described how these children helped and complemented one another to the benefit of both.

Thomas was keen that there should be as little distinction as possible made between the special needs children and the co-worker children. They should grow up together, as brothers and sisters, sharing home and school. Thomas put this into practice with his own children who remember even sharing a nursery. Friedwart Bock recalls a Principals' Meeting when Thomas brought, in the strongest possible terms, a concern he had, namely that distinctions were being made, saying that co-workers must work to achieve a more equal relationship.

Thomas often spoke with great warmth about the 'mission' of special needs children; they were *never* an unfortunate lot or a mistake or an irrelevence. For example, he noted that Down's syndrome children were not described before about 1860, and within the last one hundred years they were being born in increasing numbers all over the world. At a time when 'sex and intelligence have so moved into the limelight,' when it is almost impossible to go anywhere without being confronted by sexual images, and the measure of a person's intellect has become the measure of their worth, suddenly there appear a host of Down's syndrome children: gentle, helpless, unpractical, and lacking in intellectual and sexual interest or ability. What could be the meaning of this?

Graham continues:

Empathy — its existence, and the understanding of it — came to figure largely in Thomas's outlook. He came to consider it the most important force in curative or remedial education. He traced it in both the works of Rudolf Steiner and in the publications of R.D. Laing. What is perhaps unique in Thomas's approach to empathy is that he identified it as a force, a force in the same sense that gravity, or electromotive force, are forces.

The importance of this approach lies in the recognition of the universality of empathy. Empathy is not a subjective, personal emotion, but something objective, which, though tied to consciousness and to a person, is not personal, in the sense that it is free of ego. The prerequisite condition for the success of empathy is a kind of selfless compassion in the practitioner.

A strictly scientific outlook can lead to a certain kind of fatalism: we can come to believe that some sorts of events have consequences about which nothing can be done, because they lie in universal domains outside our control. For example, the force of gravity is controlled by a universal constant, the so-called 'big G' and we may not alter this constant one whit, no matter how we try. In the past some disabilities were seen to fall into this category, and nothing could be done about them, or to cure or reverse them. Sometimes this view became the official view. Professionals and administrators espoused it. When they did, the outlook for the person with disability became bleak, especially if the disabled came to believe it themselves. Thomas fought long and hard against this view in the public and professional domains.

The antidote for all this, said Thomas, is empathy, for it preserves objectivity: it may be so that some or perhaps all of the aspects of a disability are, indeed, not to be corrected or changed, and empathy, properly exercised, can lead to the proper recognition — and the calm acceptance — of the truth of this. But empathy, with its embedded compassion, does not direct us to abandon the handicapped person to a seemingly brutal and inescapable fate. Rather, it enables us to perceive just how the handicapped person copes now with his or her predicament, and how he or she may be helped to cope with it in the future. Empathy, properly deployed, might be described as 'practical destiny management,' which, at worst, would just be making the best of a bad job, but at best could lead to a valid perception of the meaning, or point — indeed, the worth — of a person's destiny. In this, Thomas excelled.

Clearly, the significance to the handicapped person of the success of this empathetic approach increases with the severity and apparent hopelessness of the handicap.

Thomas led us to understand that love and compassion are universal forces. He told us that empathy yields the best of both worlds: it combines the rigour of scientific enquiry with the healing forces of love and compassion. Thomas may be said to have begun in the first of these worlds, but to have ended by spanning both. There is no doubt that he became adept at the practice of empathy.

Community building

Bernard Graves, who worked with him during this period, reflects on the strong community building impulse Thomas carried:

In his professional life within Camphill, Thomas is remembered as the Camphill Schools' Superintendent and Medical Consultant. Inspired medical doctor he was, but in his earlier years at Newton Dee, Thomas was a biodynamic farmer, healing the land. Perhaps it was his love of nature, his dedication as a farmer and his mastery as a physician that enabled him also to be a truly inspired educator and healer. His deep insights into what sustains each individual in body, soul and spirit, and his interest in whoever he was talking with gave one the experience of being met in the present by a faithful brother. Thomas could be referred to as a modern man who combined the dignified qualities of Medieval Knighthood and the Nobleman with the virtues of Monkhood.

Throughout his life he dedicated his professional life and personal striving to the service of healing through agriculture, medicine and education. Along with other founding members of the Camphill Community, Thomas was challenged by Dr König to bring alive those impulses that are depicted within the images of the stained glass windows of the Goetheanum (the Anthroposophical Centre in Dornach, Switzerland). This work was undertaken as an inner path of study and contemplation, providing both inspiration and substance for community building.

We can see reflected in Thomas's biography as farmer, doctor and educator, historic impulses transformed and individualized. On behalf of the Camphill Community, Thomas intensely concerned himself with the Knights Templar, an organization of the early middle ages that upheld certain ideals of brotherhood, that worked to form communities that would 'serve the good' of the land and the good of the people in body, soul and spirit. This community of brothers fought outwardly and inwardly to resist those forces that wish to either entice us away from freely serving the good, with promises of greater power over our neighbour, or to imprison men's spirits with the lure of gold and materialistic values. Central to the brother knights' striving to serve the 'good spirit of our time,' the Christ impulse was the recognition that as individuals we sometimes 'err,' but through brotherhood and community, where we adopt the attitude that 'we are each other's brother and keeper,' human error and imperfection can be transformed.

Thomas was one of those who recognized and responded to the call and challenge made to all humanity in the last speech of Jacques de

*Molay, March 18, 1314 (the last Grandmaster of the Knights Templar
1295–1314) before he embraced death by being burned at the stake at
the instigation of Philip the Fair of France. This was a speech in which
the Grandmaster took responsibility by publicly speaking out the
'truth,' knowing full well that this would seal his execution and bring
about the demise of the Knights Templar. He spoke out of a new
consciousness, one that acknowledged that the very fragility of
humanity, in its potential to do the wrong thing, could be transformed
through 'free will' to do the good and so become a strength rather than
a weakness of his humanity.*

*Behind the scenes of history, then as now, Luciferic temptations and
Ahrimanic imprisonment — as personified by Philip the Fair — continue
to challenge us as individuals and communities.*

*To counter and harmonize this archetypal duality, better known as
'dualism,' Thomas strove to bring about a 'middle way.' This middle way
that he advocated is based on qualities of 'empathetic recognition' that
embraces polarities and rejoices in the diversity of ideas and of
individuals.*

*Thomas recognized the deep Christian impulses of the Knights
Templar, though perhaps as an organization ahead of its time, to bring
about the Good on Earth. In his life Thomas lived out of this impulse, to
bring about the good on earth, and he empowered others to do the same.
Perhaps one can also recognize in him the figure in the North Green
Window of the Goetheanum, the modern man that walks with the Moon
at his back towards the new Sun, accompanied by the stars above,
uniting 'his will' in the service of the world being 'the Christ in all.'*

Over the years Thomas gave many lectures on community and community building that were of great support and value, and that are still
referred to today.

Reaching out beyond Camphill

During the 1950s Camphill spread to England, Ireland and abroad, and
consequently Thomas began to travel more widely as his medical, teaching
and lecturing work grew. In 1957 Thomas accepted an invitation from the
Hopeland's Trust to travel to Zimbabwe (then known as Rhodesia) on a
lecture tour and this was followed by similar invitations to Downingtown
and Lancaster in Pennsylvania. In the same year, with Anke as his Deputy,
he became Superintendent of the Camphill Rudolf Steiner Schools, a position which gave him overall responsibility for the work in Scotland. For
someone who was not ambitious, but whose whole aim was to work out of
true brotherliness, becoming Superintendent was an onerous task.

During this period his professional reading led him beyond the works of Steiner, König and other anthroposophical writers, and although he unquestionably never wavered from the path of anthroposophy, he became a keen student of R.D Laing, Freud, Jung and others. He also began to make contacts with child psychiatrists outside Camphill. It is possible that some of this wide-ranging research went beyond what the community considered appropriate, and some colleagues felt that he was allowing himself to be distracted from his central task. But from the moment that his own personal thinking life had begun to stir in the twelve-year-old Thomas, he had experienced his life as an earnest quest for truth and knowledge. Karl König, anthroposophy and Camphill had all helped him on his way. His reading of Steiner, who spoke most helpfully of all, prompted him to be interested in everyone and everything, and it was this which led him to reach out beyond Camphill and into the greater world. Here, he wanted to rouse people from the lethargy of the unquestioning, conventional thinking he experienced in young and old all around, and he wanted to share the life-giving soul nourishment he had received from both anthroposophy and life within the community. He invited many people to Camphill where they could experience at first hand the unique gifts Camphill community life had to offer, and he spoke about this often.

Responding to invitations, Thomas began to spend more time lecturing, and wherever he went within the anthroposophical movement, his lectures to teachers, doctors, farmers or artists were always accompanied by the caveat that Steiner's words should be taken as indications and not as dogma. When listening to him one sensed that everything he spoke of he had fully digested and made his own. He frequently gave examples from his own life's experience to illustrate the point he was making. Though deeply influenced by Steiner, Thomas was not starry-eyed and was aware that due to a certain degree of fanaticism in some adherents, anthroposophy was often seen as a cult. This led some to feel that he was somewhat heretical, and it is true that he could say quite provocative things. On one occasion, he was one of three speakers on a panel discussing abortion. The general feeling in the hall was that this was *never* acceptable. Thomas spoke about the human predicament; how there is not a right and wrong written in stone, how every situation has to be decided in the moment. We ourselves are becoming Godlike and as every unique situation arises, we have to find a unique response. He then described how, as a young Jewish student in Vienna, a city riddled with violent anti-Semitism, he and his young wife had realized that it could not be right to bring into this appalling situation the child she was expecting. They had to do whatever was necessary to prevent the birth. This was received in silence, and the discussion came to an end.

The subjects of his talks and lectures were wide-ranging. He was regularly asked by the community to bring fresh, imaginative and meaningful insights into the cycle of the year and its festivals, both to the children's assemblies, and in evening lectures to the co-workers: new arrivals, and those who had been there for many years. He lectured as a doctor on the diagnoses of special needs children, on Down's syndrome, childhood psychosis, childhood schizophrenia, and curative education. He also spoke on subjects and themes chosen more freely out of himself: farming and crafts, the Buddha Impulse, the Holy Grail, reincarnation, meditation, empathy, morality, and much more. Wherever he was to talk, there was a keen audience waiting. During the years that Rudi Lissau was in charge of booking speakers for Steiner House in London, the hall was always full to capacity when Thomas was to speak. Rudi described why he thought this was so:

The greatest danger to global society are the 'people who know,' who are so convinced of what they know, who are so certain of themselves that they don't ask questions. Among these are religious fanatics throughout the world. Thomas's talks would be constantly backed by references to people in different streams of life. He would say: 'See, there are other examples; you need not go my way, nor the way of König nor Steiner.'

Personal aspects

Thomas's companion in his life and work was Anke. There had been an unspoken moment of recognition between them at the time they house-parented together in Camphill Cottage in the early days. They had, of course, known each other since Vienna although they had not always got on so well, each accusing the other of being proud. A story he enjoyed telling his children in later years, always in the hearing of Anke, was how he had gone to Dr König one day in a fury demanding that he and Anke be given different houses to run as working together was simply impossible. König had said no, they should manage, and that Thomas should 'go back and learn to love her,' adding jubilantly: 'which I did!' But it was not until 1951 that they were married.

Over the years Anke grew to be an essential part of his life and many have witnessed the delight they took in each other, describing it as a perfect partnership, joyful and fulfilling for both. When he suffered periods of rejection by the community, it was sometimes because of his impatience with what he perceived to be the conventionality and narrow-mindedness of his colleagues young and old: 'Much as I love them I find them suffocatingly old-fashioned and petit-bourgeois,' he wrote in his last letter to Dr König in March 1966. At other times it was because of his rather non-conformist nature. Then Anke was the perfect partner: strong, intelligent, warmly encouraging and able to make the necessary bridges back. And when she went through her own difficulties with colleagues, or withdrew from the invasive nature of community, he was there with his great patient, loving, faithful and generous nature.

Even as Thomas rose through the community hierarchy there was always a modesty about his tastes and needs: although he was now Superintendent, his bedroom-study was little bigger than a broom-cupboard. He continued to take his turn at the huge washing-ups and at other humble community tasks. Late one night, noises outside the windows roused his children who were astonished to see a fire engine with flashing lights standing in front of Murtle House. The following morning happened to be Thomas's birthday. When they had sung the traditional birthday song outside his door, the children opened it to wish him a 'Happy Birthday!' — but the bed was empty. A boy had set fire to the costume cupboard, a room in the basement, and although it had been put out, Thomas had spent the rest of the night wrapped in a blanket outside the door in case it should flare up again. He shopped at Woolworths where he bought all the household and electrical items he needed, including lamps — even shoes. When he smoked, and all the smokers on the estate were issued with their weekly quota of 120 Players, he smoked tiny Woodbines. He then gradually cut these down and stopped smoking altogether. His bedroom-study he kept neat, fresh and uncluttered, with the minimum of items for his personal use, including a bed barely two feet six inches wide that he had had made in the Murtle joinery. He kept nothing that he did not use and would accept no luxury, even as a gift. One Christmas in the days when Camphill was becoming quite prosperous, he unwrapped his gift from Anke — a pair of silk pyjamas. His expression of joyful anticipation as he took time unwrapping it, changed to one of dismay. Without hesitation he told her that she must take them back, that it was a quite unacceptable extravagance.

The middle years

The 1960s were both a fulfilling and a challenging time for Thomas. In March 1961 he suffered a life-threatening kidney disorder and it took some considerable time before he felt strong enough to resume his demanding workload. During 1961–62 the first purpose-designed Camphill Community Hall was built. The flexible threefold concept of a hall with a stage at one end and a chapel at the other, where the chairs in the auditorium could face either way, or even fill the stage and chapel, leaving the

Thomas around 1960

centre free for social events, was the inspiration of Dr König. The project, however, was brought to birth and completed through Thomas's initiative, with his daily visits to the site and his intimate working with the architect Gabor Talló. The form of the dove carved in wood on the stairs above the altar, and now used as the Camphill logo throughout the world, was born out of this working together. The opening of Camphill Hall at Murtle was a milestone in the life of Camphill, and was soon followed by the first Annual Camphill Movement Conference. Into this large and beautiful space members of the Camphill Movement came from all over the world to work to deepen their perception of the therapeutic tasks they had in common. Since then, many important community events have taken place in this space, which have had an impact on every aspect of Camphill life.

The Camphill Schools were now twenty-one years old and had just received a very favourable H.M. Inspector's Report from the Scottish Education Department. Now was the time to make their rather unorthodox approach to the special needs child more understandable to orthodox practitioners. Thomas was at the forefront of this move, and he began to lecture at various educational and psychiatric conferences, making valuable contacts with other special schools, training centres, sheltered workshops and psychiatric hospitals. Camphill hosted large conferences attended by child psychiatric consultants and professionals in the fields of education and child care, where they could become aware of the ideas and methods applied at Camphill, and where the Camphill staff could also learn from them. During this period Thomas became well-known and respected in social and child-care circles throughout Britain. However, it was also during these exchanges that Thomas became aware of the controlling tendency of regulation and observed how it gradually hardened into the development and practice of behaviourism. Thomas was deeply concerned about this. Graham Calderwood, who worked with Thomas during this period, describes it in this way:

Once, I sat over coffee with him, in his study at St John's, the house he shared with Anke. St John's overlooks the river Dee, and stands among ancient trees on the high shank of a rise contoured over aeons by the river itself. Thomas's study window afforded us a panoramic view of the river and its flood-plain. It was exquisite. Dusk was settling. Gathering mist smudged outlines, and peace seemed to gather with the mist.

We — or at any rate I — had been agonizing over some issue of the day, something governmental, probably, though, after some thirty years, my memory is faulty. Certainly I was bemoaning some topical craziness. But the lovely scene had reached in and made us quiet.

We sat in companionable silence. Minutes into the quiet, Thomas stirred, finished his coffee, and remarked that there was much to be said for stupidity. I waited. Presently, Thomas added that he was coming greatly to value foolishness. In those days it fell to Thomas to interview all the children on approach to Camphill. Part of this involved talking with the children's authorities, so Thomas came to know the Ways of Authority. He said more than once that, for those in authority, the Christian argument — largely summed up in the Ten Commandments — had at one time sufficiently defined the criteria of care. And then, oddly, and at first inexplicably, at some point hard to pin down, it didn't. Something had changed, very much for the worse. Thomas detected the onset of a shift that I believe can fairly be said to have largely gone to completion. He began to speak of the corrosion of Trust, and the insidious, softly-casual substitution for it of Control.

And there we have it. We can see why, for Thomas, there was much to

Thomas with J. Downie-Campbell and architect Gabor Talló (left) at the opening of Camphill Hall in September 1962

be said for stupidity, much value in foolishness: it is simply that these qualities make for poor control. Thomas went to do battle. He was by then well-known, and had earned high regard in social and child-care circles. He had every reason to believe he would be listened to, and heard. In London's eyries of power, Thomas argued passionately against Control. By his own, unhappy, post-battle admission, he failed to carry the day.

I well remember the moment Thomas stood before us all in Camphill Hall and recorded that failure. I recall his distress, which was acute, and the more poignant for being reined-in, and I recall the depression into which he was subsequently thrust, and its length. One day, months later, we passed each other. As one does, I enquired how he was. He checked, shot me a dark, inward look such as I had not seen before, and responded brusquely, 'I survive! I survive!' — then strode on.

To this major concern of his, namely the way individuals were losing their freedom to controlling influences, is added another. Thomas had been struck from the beginning by the way Steiner had attempted to apply the same rigourous integrity and intelligence that are successfully applied to the natural sciences, to questions about the values of goodness and morality. He was increasingly concerned about the relegation of morality in our society in favour of science. If, and only if morality — a prime concern for the good — is cultivated, can it grow in the world. The first step in building morality was the experience of awe and wonder in the young child. He described his concerns in this way:

I think I told you a year ago that I attended the Chinese Exhibition in London. It was beautifully set up with most magnificent works of art and skills of Old China. Long queues waited in the streets, the rooms crowded with people pressing silently and awe-struck around the lit-up exhibits.

Then a group of very young, six- to seven-year-old little children

Thomas and Anke with Hermann Gross 1976

*came flitting through with clipboards, taking notes, the only ones among
thousands who were unimpressed, not overawed; they saw no beauty
and no wonder in the exhibits but took very efficient notes on them.
When I saw this I nearly burst into tears for I knew these children had
been robbed of their most important birthright, of awe and wonder, a
wellspring of man's dignity.*

To illustrate how we all gradually become conditioned to these new and
highly damaging attitudes, he described how he went to another exhibition
a year later and, on observing again the little girls flitting through with their

*St John, carved in
wood (Thomas Weihs)*

clipboards, did not feel inclined to weep but found himself instead thinking,
'perhaps they will become more capable journalists.' He had himself succumbed to one of the most coercing factors of our society. Ultimately the
question of morality and of the good should and 'can be taken earnestly, can
become the subject of the same honest, diligent, intelligent study that has
made science so effective physically.' These things were not mere ideas or
preferences for Thomas but touched the very bedrock of his being.

Thomas had always had a real interest and enthusiasm for art and made
a point of knowing what exhibitions were on, and wherever possible, of
visiting them. He was knowledgeable about modern art and had a particular love for the works of Henry Moore, Picasso and Chagall, among others. In his leisure moments throughout this period Thomas began to
develop his own artistic abilities in the visual arts: first he took up photography, and then sculpture, which he continued to develop for the rest of
his life. In several Camphill Schools and Villages his sculptures still stand.
Thomas loved to be surrounded by art and artists and it was during this
period that he welcomed Hermann Gross, painter and sculptor, with his
wife Trude, to set up permanent home in Camphill. A studio was built for

The Lovers, carved in stone (Thomas Weihs)

Hermann, in which he painted and sculpted many of the images for which he is now known. Trude developed drama therapies, trained therapists and worked for many years with the special needs children. Was Thomas musical? Christof-Andreas Lindenberg, a musician, composer and colleague for many years, writes:

Maundy Thursday was the one time during the year Thomas would let us into the secret that he could sing: he joined in the humming of the tune 'O'er the hill and o'er the dale' that by Camphill tradition forms the acoustical backdrop to the calling of the disciples during the play.

Others, however, attest that on the long car journeys he proved that he could hold his own in a round against many a musically gifted passenger.

For the eighteen years that I lived in close contact with Thomas, I learnt that his appreciation of music was greatest for any piece composed with an emphasis on intervals, not on brilliant runs or wild chord shifts. I began to realize that Thomas pricked up his ears when I tried to make conscious use of the rising and falling intervals and their mirroring. He delighted in the songs and music composed especially for the seasonal festivals and plays, and at one conference he asked me

The Praying Man, concrete,
Murtle (Thomas Weihs)

to arrange a performance of the choir pieces of all *the seasons in*
one go.

Christof-Andreas goes on to make a most interesting observation linking the musical intervals with Thomas's sculpture:

Eventually I learned what it was with Thomas and music: he sculpted
in musical terms! I lived near the old St John's cottage (now St Bren-
dan's on Murtle Estate) where he lived and sometimes sculpted and
witnessed how he worked on an over-life-size figure that, in a second
metamorphosis, became the form with the 'raised veil,' the negative hole
as the head: a musical octave! He worked and reworked this form,
becoming the musical form master.

Another much smaller sculpture, The Lovers, *which he made for*
Anke, is one of the best expressions I know of the interval of the second.
(This stands behind his final home, now the Medical Practice at Murtle).
In the Rose Garden by Camphill House, where the urns of Karl König
and other Camphill friends are interred, he placed a Pieta made of
metal. The form suggests the interval of the fourth! When Thomas
worked on the Praying Man, *with arms outstretched into a complete*

The Praying Man, Botton (Thomas Weihs)   Pieta, copper, Camphill Rose Garden
(Thomas Weihs)

semicircle, the interval of the fifth clearly rang out. (The original, made to guard the East Slope at Murtle against children running into the River Dee, unfortunately is lost, but a similar form stands in Botton Village in Yorkshire, at an urn site.)

These forms are musical archetypes. Only later did I become aware that the wooden sculpture St John the Baptist *(also at the Medical Practice) was an image of one's own higher calling expressed by the musical prime. There it is, facing you: one of Camphill's original impulses, namely that of community building, and the path of learning, and changing oneself.*

Look again at Thomas's sculptures, of which St John *was the first, and you will find all the intervals brought into form — a musical statement. They will sound on, even when one day Camphill's music will be forgotten, singing of community forms.*

A lecture course Thomas gave on Embryology at Steiner House in London in the mid 1960s was attended by a young BBC film producer — Jonathan Stedall. Jonathan was, at that time, becoming increasingly interested in the study of Steiner's anthroposophy, and at the age of twenty-eight, had taken a year off to attend Emerson College in Sussex. He felt that he was at that time facing a choice: to remain as film maker or to go completely into some sort of anthroposophical work. Jonathan was hugely impressed by this first course and over the years by many more lectures and courses, and describes Thomas as an extraordinary and powerful speaker.

The great strength of Thomas was the artist in him. He was an artist to his fingertips. He had a poetic, imaginative faculty in him so that very profound things were expressed in poetic terms.

What art does is to raise you — you've got to move up into that level ... and that is what Thomas did. That was the power of his communication: you felt, as listeners, that you were present in the creative process. Children love made-up stories and are nourished by one's creative activity. The degree to which someone is being creative is captivating and is the exact opposite of somebody who is a know-all — which is a complete switch-off!

When Jonathan thanked him after one such lecture, Thomas's reply was '*I* must thank *you,*' and he went on to explain that he could not speak into a vacuum, that it was the audience which called his thoughts forth. He needed that interaction with other people to draw out what was living in his thoughts. For this reason, too, he had difficulties with writing; the empty page looked blankly back and called forth nothing. While writing was a real struggle, speaking was an inspiration for him. He spoke without notes. Jonathan added that good public speakers are not often good in one-to-one conversations but that Thomas was as much at ease and as creative in both.

This first course marked the beginning of a deep and lasting friendship for them both. Thomas invited Jonathan to visit Camphill. At the end of his year at Emerson, Jonathan made two documentary films for the BBC entitled *In Need of Special Care*; the first about the Camphill Rudolf Steiner Schools in Scotland, the second about Botton Village in Yorkshire, a Camphill centre for adults with disabilities. Throughout the filming Thomas allowed Jonathan completely free rein and was 'lovely to work with.' When Thomas saw the films, he was very pleased with them and showed his gratitude with great warmth. Jonathan returned in 1971 to make another film with Thomas entitled *In Defence of the Stork*; and many years later made yet a further film about the Camphill Movement, *Candle on the Hill*, to celebrate Camphill's fiftieth birthday. Thomas was sadly no longer there — neither to take part, nor to appreciate it.

Thomas worked wherever possible to develop broader participation on the part of members of the community. Being in the position of Superintendent was irksome to him, and he soon asked Henning Hansman and Friedwart Bock to take on the tasks of deputies. 'He would encourage us to form a ring,' explains Friedwart, 'and to take a strong interest in each other, to enjoy the 'otherness' of our neighbours, to go from tolerance to appreciation. Thomas himself was a living example of this attitude.' There came a moment in the early 1970s when he saw that 'the function of Superintendent as the focal-point of all the

Thomas & Anke on holiday at the Acropolis in 1964

activities was no longer an adequate expression of what we were after as a community,' so he stepped down in favour of a group of five Principals and from then on acted as Consultant to the Schools. The early phase, when Camphill had been led by Dr König — whom he described as 'a father-figure of considerable strength' — had long been left behind and the Schools were ready to continue their social endeavour in a spirit of comradeship.

Dr König had often stressed the importance of everyone's having an interest or hobby quite unrelated to his or her work. Thomas chose fishing. In a letter to Christine, who was living in West Africa in the early 1970s, Anke described the first fishing trip: how they set off for the Highlands, their little caravan carrying the new fishing tackle in tow, and how they set up camp by the chosen lake. Anke was afraid of small boats and would not set foot in the one Thomas was to use for his new hobby. This meant that, ensconced comfortably on dry land, she was in prime position to observe and describe his efforts to row himself out to a promising spot, to attach the wriggling bait and to throw his line out without it swinging round and getting caught in his clothing. Thomas was valiant in his efforts, although there was no mention of a catch that first day.

Thomas in 1979

*One of the last pictures
of Thomas and Anke,
Easter 1983*

The later years

In his later years Thomas was spending only about half of his time in Camphill, in clinics, and lecturing in the curative education Course. The rest of his time was spent in a similar way, but travelling all over the Camphill Movement, seeing children, adolescents and adults, lecturing and holding seminar courses. In addition to this he interviewed the parents of troubled children and adolescents as well as around two hundred and fifty adults a year. Between 1954 and 1983 he interviewed around twelve thousand applicants for places in Camphill Aberdeen alone. During these interviews he met doctors, psychiatrists, social workers and psychologists, and, through them, the way the world dealt with mental illness. He was growing increasingly alarmed by what he called the relentless march of scientific thinking and, speaking with the Camphill Principals in 1978 described how discussions 'have moved from openness to rigid materialistic behaviour lines and manipulation ... Modern Society is quite without ideals: politically, in art, medically and psychologically.'

In his last address for the Annual Report in February 1983, he said:

*I have had this year some really shattering experiences, particularly
with adolescents and adults. Several came with the label of psychopath,
several of whom gave me really the experience of hopelessness, of
human existences that had really gone into a realm where they could
hardly be reached any more.*

He described the unsatisfactory, even disastrous effects of
Behaviourist methods, with Operant Conditioning — a punishment and
reward approach — and of how, while there were localized, concrete
successes:

*... they were not only not lasting, but they left the person, as a person,
diminished and slackened. Behaviourism, which is followed up all over
the world with incredible enthusiasm, is hurting and harming a lot of
people. It is an expression of a force that grips the world and tells us
that improvements can only be achieved by increasing control, by
making sure that things are right and proper, that nothing goes wrong.
Behaviourism is one inevitable outcome of this attitude of control.*

He describes how control does not help anything that is living, least
of all human beings. 'What is needed, particularly in the human realm,
is tolerance, acceptance, enjoyment of the otherness of the other, and,
ultimately, love.' He went on to describe how although he had met 'quite
exquisite tolerance and love' in Camphill centres, he had also met the
anxiety that wants to exert control, to take corrective measures, to show
up consequences. He finished this, his last address, with these words:

*And my plea and hope for the future is to stress that we must not lose
this potential for tolerance and love, that we must resist this increasing
trend to feel we have to control, to manipulate, to show up the
consequences — this will have only momentary success. It will always
and inevitably undermine human values, human potentials. It is the
integrity and divinity of human existence which we must uphold,
acknowledge and further.*

Thomas was becoming increasingly aware of the growing polarization
between technology, science and economics at one pole, and moral stam-
ina and a belief in one's own purpose and destiny at the other. What was
needed to bring about a new 'enthusiastic idealism' in society, was a spiritual renewal such as that offered by anthroposophy. With growing
urgency he repeatedly addressed groups within Camphill, speaking of the
tremendous opportunity there, and of the potential danger that they
become self-absorbed and do their work 'efficiently' and forget the privilege in possessing something for which the world around was thirsting.
He reminded them of how many people, particularly young people,
passed through Camphill, and went out again as 'emissaries' into the
world:

We must be aware every day and every hour that the world around us depends on the intensity with which we learn to describe, to verbalize, to formulate, to communicate that potential of enthusiastic idealism that is the realization of that Christian way which becomes possible in our time through Rudolf Steiner.

In the last years of his life, Thomas spoke of the love he felt for those with whom he lived and worked, even the disaffected ones. When he spoke of the children with special needs he described them as 'the children whom we love but of whom we despair,' knowing that love was the essential element which helps to reach even the most withdrawn children. Thomas walked a conscious path from intolerance and impatience to a conscious enjoyment of others and their idiosyncrasies. This path took him to unconditional love.

Early in January 1983, Thomas had a swelling on the thyroid investigated. This resulted in an immediate operation and, as soon as he was able, Thomas was back at his desk, continuing the work on his second book, *Embryogenesis*. During March he set off with Anke, Peter and Kate Roth and Barbara Lipsker on a long-planned trip to Russia, a part of the world in which they were all tremendously interested, and which Steiner often described as a place of the future. It was during this journey that Thomas became aware that the operation had not been successful, and his last real challenge in this life was to find the path of acceptance.

With the help of Anke he was able to complete the work on his book, sitting up for shorter periods each day as his strength ebbed. One day he called for paper and pencils saying he wished to design their gravestone. It was to be made out of pink and grey granite and to mark their resting place in Maryculter cemetery, from which high spot can be seen the fast-flowing Dee and the lengths of both the Camphill and Murtle estates. On the last occasion that he called for pen and paper, he wrote a letter to the community which was read at his funeral service. In it he thanked all those who had sustained and supported him through the months of his last illness. 'I have believed that love endures all, is unending,' he wrote, 'Anke's love has carried and sustained me all that time.' He spoke of the strength and comfort he had received from his 'doctor-son' Nick, of the radiant strength and selflessness of his nurse, Gisela Schlegel, of how he rejoiced in the love of his children and grandchildren, and of how the flood of letters and messages he had received spoke of a love and a spirit that quite overwhelmed him. And lastly, 'I believe that if that spirit and love could be realized in Camphill, Camphill could become an invincible wellspring of spiritual love.'

Thomas gave himself up to death during the season of John the Baptist, a man whose role he had so often played in the annual pageant, a man he had carved in wood, a man after whom he had named his home and in whose footsteps he had in so many ways quite consciously trodden. Reading over his addresses and lectures, the growing urgency and passion of his words are evident. Like 'a voice crying out in the wilderness,' he repeated his call: people must wake up, think and act! John was the one he came to love, — from the time when, as a small child, he had awakened the conscience of his little sister Karin, through the many years of his searching, questioning, wrestling, provoking, inspiring, enduring and sacrificing. And John, 'Johannes,' was his middle name.

Thomas died peacefully on a beautiful Sunday morning, June 19, at home with his son Nick and his wife Anke at his bedside.

Let Barbara Lipsker, his friend and colleague of so many years, have the last word, as she reflects back to the Study Group in Vienna in 1937:

Some of us had a first meaningful Christmas experience that year when we performed the Oberufer Christmas Plays. Thomas played the part of Gallus — the mature, down-to-earth shepherd standing between the youthful, boisterous Stickl and the old, wise, slow Witok. Gallus is 'the man' giving security, having presence of mind, knowing how to deal in all situations. He is the one who leads the shepherds through the dark night, he is the first one to see the light of the stable, he is the one to put the question to Joseph: where is the child to be found? He is the first one to enter the stable and to kneel down in reverence before the new-born child.

This image of a 'man' Thomas has represented throughout all the years I have known him and been permitted to be his friend. Thomas's all important part in the whole history and development of Camphill is marked by these characteristics: Thomas the searcher, Thomas the doubter, Thomas the believer, Thomas the deeply Christian Man.

Peter Roth

(March 12, 1914 – October 14, 1997)

Deborah Ravetz

In 1955, the year in which Peter founded Botton Village, he was forty-one years old. He was to live in Botton for the next thirty-seven years. The whole of his life up till then had prepared him for this work. The years of the Nazi regime, in particular, inspired in him an existential response to the needs of the world that never lost its clarity or purpose.

If we wish to grasp the inner situation of the founders of Camphill, we need to bear in mind the horror of the demonic events in Europe at that time. We read about the early days of Camphill knowing that the Nazis were defeated. The founders — a group of largely Jewish refugees who chose to spend their lives living with a group of children with special needs — could not know what the outcome of the war would be. Bringing this fact to life in our imagination, we can feel what terrors they had to face, what courage and faith they had to find, and what a hard schooling was necessary, in order that they might rise to the occasion as they did. It is also more than moving to remember that after the war it was revealed that thousands of children and adults with special needs were the first victims of Nazi ideas of racial purification. Moreover, we now know that the euthanasia programme that murdered these children and adults served as the training ground for the people who later ran the extermination camps in Eastern Europe.

Peter's life was Botton. Everything that happened to him before its inception, his sorrows and joys, prepared him for this great attempt to create a new kind of social structure, something that was to be nothing less than a blueprint for the future.

Childhood and early years in Vienna

Peter Roth was the first of two children. His younger sister, Alix, also became one of the founder members of the Camphill Communities. His mother was the daughter of a Hungarian landowner and diplomat; his

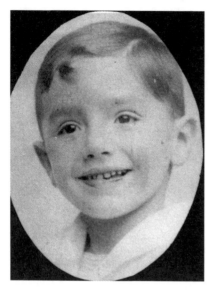

Two portraits of Peter as a child

father was a highly regarded civil engineer who had also served Austria as an officer in the First World War. Peter was a radiant and gifted child who was the privileged favourite of his family. The family was Jewish. They lived between their house in Vienna and a country estate where his father took the task of farming the land seriously. Peter suffered no hardships during his childhood despite the turbulent times in Europe as a result of the First World War. Looking back on this time in his life much later, he described himself as a turn-of-the-century Jewish Viennese snob.

When Peter was eighteen, he began his medical training. While he was at medical school he met Thomas Weihs. They were to be deeply involved with each other for the rest of their lives. Peter and Thomas both found their task in life by meeting Dr König, who had gathered a group of young people around him in a youth group. Their arrival in the youth group had a deep and positive impact. They were handsome and intelligent and exuded a radiance that meant they were compared to the hero twins of Greek mythology, Castor and Pollux, born of the union of Leda and Zeus in the guise of a swan.

The first years in Britain

Up until the Nazi invasion of Austria, when Peter fled to London, he seems to have lived a charmed life. From the moment he was uprooted from his home, his background, his training and his language he under-

The early group at Kirkton House in 1939.
Adults: Anke, Peter, Marie, Alix, Trude, Willi, Alex behind Karl König, Thomas

went a trial by endurance. His radiant and generous personality and his tireless will to release the gifts of whomever he met gave no obvious hint of the struggles that were then to be part of his life. He had a vast fund of humour. His temperament and inner resources helped him to overcome the obstacles of his life in a remarkable way. We look back on the story of the founders' escape from the Nazis and their part in the birth of what is now a worldwide movement as accomplished fact. Yet we can wonder how it felt for the beloved and privileged Peter who responded so enthusiastically to all the adornments of life — beauty, art, culture, good food and conversation — when he had to confront the many discomforts and uncertainties of being cast homeless into a world with such an uncertain and ominous future.

He left Vienna for London in June 1938 together with Anke, whom he married that same year in August. Imagine two young people, refugees in a strange city, establishing a marriage and making their living translating medical textbooks. The princely Peter also worked, improbable as it may seem, in the role of chauffeur.

Nine months later Dr König and the pioneering group finally began their life together in Kirkton House. Only a year later the tiny community had to face the upheaval of the men's internment. It was hard for both the men and the women to have to separate and not be able to support each

Peter as a student in 1932

other in a time of terrible uncertainty. Yet what we hear of that time, before and after internment, is the excitement of building that new life with its moments of hilarity, such as when Peter, gripped by artistic enthusiasm, planted seeds in a lemniscate with the result that they could not be weeded, or the incredible lessons on Greek mythology he gave to Dr König's children.

The stories of how the women moved alone to the estate that gave Camphill its name and how the men worked in an inward way whilst interned on the Isle of Man are recorded elsewhere. They are stories of overcoming and endurance. They involved choices and the struggle to stand for those often hard choices. They tell us of truly remarkable achievements. I once asked one of Dr König's children what it was like living in those early days in Kirkton House and later in Camphill. He replied that he felt that the greatest gift the adults could give to the children was that they were so engaged with life and its great purposes. He said that for him it was a joy to be a part of that time.

In 1941 Peter was released from the internment camp and in 1942, aged twenty-eight, he went to London to begin his studies for the priesthood. The medical student whose studies had been interrupted by war and who fled to the island of Britain, itself under siege, transformed his vocation.

In the obituary issue of *Camphill Correspondence, Jan/Feb 1998,* prepared to honour Peter, Christof-Andreas Lindenberg describes some of the circumstances that led to this decision. Dr König was concerned with both the medical and the religious impulse and he wanted to bring them together in what is known as the pastoral-medical impulse. Christof-Andreas says that he believed that Dr König guided Peter in his decision to become a priest. Thomas Weihs had completed his medical degree, while Peter had not. If Peter became a priest, the pastoral-medical work would be made possible in the ever-expanding endeavours in Camphill Scotland.

Peter was ordained on October 1, 1944 by Alfred Heidenreich. He then spent two years in London with Heidenreich and others before returning to Camphill with the intention of beginning the pastoral-medical work that was envisaged as part of the curative and medical work of Camphill. The sacramental life of the Christian Community was to become one of the foundation stones of Botton Village.

In 1947 Peter fell ill with polio. This illness was to change all his expectations and to demand huge resources of courage and endurance both inwardly and outwardly.

At first he was so ill that his survival was in question. When he did recover, he was so weakened by the illness that he had to learn to speak and walk again. For a long time it seemed that his physical impediments would prevent him ever working as a priest. Trial followed upon trial; it was at this time that Peter's first marriage — to Anke — came to an end. He was thirty-three years old. This was an important turning point in Peter's life. The person whom so many came to know as an unfailing source of creative strength faced and overcame the kind of challenge that can easily quench a person's idealism and crush their will for the good. In the following years Peter must have resolved to meet those challenges and to find strength and meaning entirely out of himself.

After his initial recovery Peter travelled abroad. He then lived and worked for a time in Glenilla Road, the congregation of the Christian Community in North London. At this time he became a British citizen and his divorce was granted. He returned to Camphill Scotland in 1950. Many people remember him teaching in the curative education seminar at that time. The effects of polio meant he had to struggle with his breathing and balance, and his laughter was mixed with pain.

In 1953, six years after that cataclysmic year that had changed so much, Peter remarried and moved to The Sheiling School in Ringwood. He had met Kate in London while he was working in Glenilla Road. Many people loved Peter in a quite exceptional way and there is something in the story of his meeting with Kate that may help to explain why. Karl König used to stay with Kate Elderton in London, where she ran a

Peter around 1950

small nursery class. He told Peter to seek her out during his training. He told him that despite the challenges of rationing she was a marvellous cook. Kate would later tell the story of how Peter came up the stairs to meet her. He was smoking a cigarette, the ash of which he was tapping into a matchbox. As he stood talking to her he noticed the velvet curtains, which he began to stroke with delight. This is a wonderful picture of one aspect of Peter's character, his joy in the aesthetic pleasures of the world. When Kate told this story Peter always laughed. It reveals something of his charm. Peter gave the impression that life was a serious business but that it was also immensely enjoyable. Many people found this combination of idealism and the warmth and enthusiasm for the whole of existence almost intoxicating.

Peter was completely dedicated to the ideals of Camphill. However, he also believed in what he called 'social imagination.' This meant that we must care for the whole of life and find every opportunity to make the strenuous way of life in Camphill regenerative and sustainable. He was a great fan of the cinema as well as the more serious side of cultural life. Anyone who went on journeys with him remembers the importance of meals and visits, whether it was to the Greenham Common Peace Camp on the way to a youth conference, or an art gallery or church.

Peter was interested in whatever there was to be discovered wherever he happened to be.

Not long after the move to Ringwood, Kate and Peter's son Simon was born. In the following year, 1954, The Camphill Village Trust was founded. This legally incorporated body was to be the foundation of future village developments. On September 5, 1955, Peter and Kate and a small group of other pioneers moved to Botton Hall, which was a hunting lodge set in a large estate belonging to W.F. Macmillan, the publisher, whose son, Alistair was one of the early pupils in Camphill, Scotland. The estate on the North Yorkshire Moors comprising the Hall with the walled garden, the home farm, a gate lodge and three other nearby farms had been offered in response to a great need. The work in Scotland was expanding but the parents of the children reaching school-leaving age were urgently concerned about the future of these young adults. They turned to Karl König to ask if something could be done for their children. Dr König set the parents the challenge of finding the place where community life with their growing children and the expanding numbers of co-workers joining König in his work could begin. Botton was the result.

The first Camphill Village

Botton's growth to the large thriving community of today was gradual. In the first years only the Hall had electricity and running water. The small pioneering group had to contend with many challenges including a fire burning down Botton Farm and the struggle to establish all the infrastructure of life including workshops and services as well as education and culture. The village and all its many aspects can be seen and read about in the films of Jonathan Stedall and in various publications listed in the bibliography. How did this all come about and what was the intention behind this first Camphill Village?

Many years later one of the co-workers who had been in Botton at that time described to me the first two things Peter did when he arrived. First he made sure there was a place for a library; then he ensured that there was a room suitable for the celebration of the Act of Consecration of Man. Eight years after that fateful time in which he seemed to have lost everything, Peter was finally ready to begin his life's great work. That he began his work there by establishing the inner wellsprings of the community says much about his vision for Botton. Overcoming the problems in the practical life with ingenuity and great energy was one of Botton's great achievements. However, it was ideals rather than necessity that were to inform the life. Dr König described the ideals and intentions of the first Camphill Village nine months after the new village had been received into the fold of the Camphill communities with great expectation and love. He addressed those assembled for the official opening, as his christening gift.

It is equally important, if we wish to grasp the width of intention that Botton sprang from, to read the words of the editorial written by Anke Weihs for the Michaelmas edition of *The Cresset* magazine in 1956, which welcomed this new endeavour into the world.

For many, the ideals and principles of the Village Community may seem remote and unworldly. Yet we know of no-one who has been to Botton Village who has not been gripped by the immediacy of the social attempt being made there. The moment you enter the dale, you know you have entered a new province; its newness is already inscribed into the atmosphere, it casts a spell on you — not the spell of the cloister, the retreat, but the spell of the future. The future blows like a fresh wind down the dale, and you love the feel of it in your face ...

... The resources of the earth are gigantic and mankind has taken them for granted as questionless conditions of existence to which there was no thinkable limit. But in recent months, the results of man's insatiable use of the elements have begun to loom threateningly all over the world. Earth — how many hundreds of erstwhile fertile acres slip away yearly, almost irretrievably eroded by chemical over-treatment! Water — read of the empty reservoirs, receding ground water, polluted rivers and lakes, oil-encrusted oceans! Air — good air — has become a precious thing — smog can be had anywhere, and from another aspect, our air is controlled by traffic regulations and in some parts its 'highways' are over-congested.

And who can measure those resources of moral health and creativeness which must sustain the conditions man is forging for himself, but which are equally imperilled? We are all impoverished in our joy, in our love, in our essential freedom to be whole and human.

Thus [our hopes and those of many others] are pinned upon the new Village situated in a remote Yorkshire dale ... [It] was not born out of affluence, nor are there great resources of knowledge and experience to draw on, for the venture is too new and wisdom will have to be gathered on the way ...May it carry on in strength and clarity of purpose.[1]

The first village was to be nothing less than an attempt to create new social forms out of living knowledge, social forms that were to be discovered and practised not just for Camphill but also for the world. The words of Anke and Dr König show the urgent sense of responsibility those founding members felt towards a world beset with the consequences of misguided thinking. The problems that arose out of what Dr König called the three errors were real then and are perhaps even more real now. If we think of the crises in nearly every aspect of life in modern industrial society we can feel that the intentions and ideals of the first village were never more needed than they are now. The final words quoted here, regarding the people around whom the village came into being, are also important. Dr König says: 'The villages were not intended to be institutions *for* people with special needs; on the contrary the people with special needs made possible this effort to create new social forms.'

Today, official policy for people with special needs attempts to integrate them into society and to protect their rights. Gone are the days when Camphill started where there was neither education nor a place for people with special needs in the wider community. Nevertheless, despite sincere efforts, people with special needs seldom experience a life where they are seen as a person rather than a condition. Angelika Monteux of Camphill Rudolf Steiner Schools in Aberdeen described this problem:

At a large conference on Autism in Glasgow a woman diagnosed with Asperger's Syndrome spoke of her experiences in this context. 'Why do professionals give us these names, and why do they change all the time?

'When I was in hospital with a breakdown I was told I was a patient ... OK ... I had to be a patient in my bed. Then I was moved on to a house and became a resident ... all right, I resided there. Somebody else called me a client which I did not like so much as it smells of dependence on lawyers, social workers and doctors etc. But when I was told I was a consumer I rebelled. This does not make sense; as a child I did bite a few psychologists, but I never consumed one! Why can't I just be Anna?'

This same woman went on to say at the same conference, 'Why are we always told that we have to be the same as others, and independent? What is wrong with being dependent on services, other people, help and support? We don't want to be lonely and independent, we want to share life with others — be interdependent like most people are.'

These words echo most strikingly the intentions of the pioneers of Camphill. Anna's experience of life suggests that though conditions are very different now, those original ideas are still much needed not only for people with special needs but by all of us because, as Anke pointed out, 'We are all impoverished in our joy, in our love, in our essential freedom to be whole and human.'

These words from Anke Weihs and Karl König articulate a problem and an attempt to mitigate and even heal that problem. Anna's words show us the problem has not gone away, that there is much work to be done. This work was given into Peter's care. We might ask ourselves, what did he try to do, what were his strengths and weaknesses, what did he achieve and what would his hopes have been for the future?

We know that during the thirty-seven years Peter lived in Botton, the tiny community grew into a flourishing little world that has given a home to thousands of people. Botton was intended not only to be hospitable to people, but also to impulses, which came to include a Waldorf School, a Eurythmy School, biodynamic farms, a laboratory, a church of the Christian Community, a bookshop, a post office and many craft workshops. Peter hoped that the community would build on that hospitality and become capable of supporting more and more diversity. Through initial connections with Botton many other communities began, some working out of anthroposophy, others not.

The cultivation of people

What made Botton into such a radiant success, and why was it that in Peter's time people flocked there to join in the work, or constantly returned there for regeneration? The poet Chaucer describes how when we are truly seen we become both at peace with ourselves and able to serve. The young people around Dr König were deeply inspired by the series of lectures by Rudolf Steiner called in English, *The Younger Generation,* in which a quality is described that Peter embodied: 'the ability to have confidence in the human being.' Peter had many enthusiasms. He was musical, he was widely read and very well educated; he had the inner confidence that can come from being a gifted and privileged child. However, we can only understand the glory that surrounded Botton if we understand that the major work of his life was the cultivation of people. Many have to struggle to develop interest and love for those beyond their immediate circle. This interest was Peter's greatest ability. People and their potential were his major interest; they were the starting point of anything he did in Botton. On the evening of his farewell from Botton he spoke of the need to be ever-welcoming people, of the need to keep one's doors wide open and not to be inconvenienced by the unexpected.

Peter saw the people who came towards Camphill as full of potential. His task was to meet them and release that potential as Dr König had done for him. I believe we can learn something of what insights led him to behave in this way if we look particularly at his work with young people.

A central area for Peter was his work with youth groups. Rudolf Steiner's lectures to the younger generation make clear how important is the relationship between young and old. Steiner describes how young people need to find older people who know about the spiritual origin of man in a truly modern way. The young need this knowledge, they are dependent on this knowledge, and they are drawn to the older person who wishes to give it to them as concretely as a baby who needs to be nourished by their mother's milk. He goes on to describe how the older person will need to find a way to impart this knowledge, this truth, artistically and in the garb of beauty. Peter often mentioned that Rudolf Steiner had said that the work with the young was so important that, if he had had time, he would have written a gospel especially for them.

In Karl König, Peter met just such an older person. Anyone reading Dr König's lectures and books, anyone familiar with his life and work, experienced that he gave all that he was and had learned to the upholding of the true image of the human being. His concern for the young people who became his youth group has had immense consequences. One can see how the power of striving friendship around a great ideal can create a world movement. Peter's great commitment to the young arose out of a fundamental gratitude and a sense of responsibility to what he met in the person of Karl König.

Just as he felt that his life had been invested with significance by Dr König, so he in turn attempted to do the same for every young person he met. He saw the relationship between the generations as an interdependent one. Steiner says that the youth movement must have a Janus head that looks both to the past and the future. For Peter, the young were those who 'carried a knapsack of heaven on their back' and it was the responsibility of the older ones to hear what the young had to tell. The youth movement was always present in Peter's life, and he dedicated an enormous part of his time and interest to cultivating this very important mutual relationship between the young and the old. In the lectures to the young mentioned earlier Steiner says:

Woe betide if nothing happens to enable this question of the young to be answered by the old so that the young say: I am grateful that I have learnt from the old what I can learn only from the old; what he can tell me, he alone can tell me, for it will be different if I learn it when I am old ... In the foundations of the spirit life of the world it is as though a chain were there, reaching from the past over into the future, which must be received by each generation into itself, must be carried onwards, reforged and perfected. This chain has been broken in the age of intellectualism ... Try to feel that you did experience something of the kind ... And if you sense this you will realize the true significance of the youth movement today, the youth movement which has, which must have, a Janus head, because it is directed towards the experience of the spiritual — an experience of the spiritual which carries thought so far that it becomes will, that it becomes innermost impulse.

The young co-workers who came to Camphill interested Peter deeply because they were the future. He believed that neither Camphill nor anyone in Camphill, young or old, could come into their true identity without a relationship of mutual giving and taking. That the relationship between the generations should come into healthy communion was for him as much part of helping to heal our ailing world as any of the more obvious tasks of Camphill. The chain that had been broken by intellectualism, of

In the office in Botton Village with Carl Alexander Mier in January 1956

which Steiner speaks, was an ever present and growing problem for him. His illness, he once laughingly said, had freed him from practical work, and he had transformed it into an opportunity to establish a culture where interest could be cultivated, a true culture of the heart. This was never intended to be the work of one or two people in the community. What he longed for was that it would be perceived in its true importance by everyone and would be as much part of the working life of Camphill as any of the more obvious tasks in either villages or schools.

Materialism can make one believe that life and human beings can be ordered in a mechanical and therefore efficient way. It may make people believe there is no time for anything but practical work. It may even make us value a certain kind of measurable activity more than another because it is clear and because it is actually very demanding to cultivate that infinitely more challenging quality, interest. The award-winning designer, William McDonough points out that Nature is never efficient; rather she is both abundant and effective. Peter was never in doubt as to the effectiveness of cultivating people. Abundance and effectiveness were the mark of his being and at his hand Botton grew and became the beacon known to so many. But this sense of abundance and this ability to be effective has another aspect. It is at home with diversity and it does not fear difference. In this way Peter could love and foster a huge variety of people and impulses without there being any apparent contradiction. It was Peter's abundance, his sense that there was enough room, enough time and enough space that gave Botton its width and breadth. Botton had a contemporary feel even though it was at first glance an out of the way settlement—the last place where one would normally expect to meet the breath of the future.

The new family

Peter was married to a great homemaker and yet one always felt it was a revolutionary home. Everyone in the home felt responsible and every one was welcome. In Hall South, where Peter and Kate lived for so many years, there was none of that exclusivity of the bourgeois family whose love and interest hardly extend beyond its boundaries. There was a healthy balance of family and community needs. It was clear that for both Kate and Peter marriage was a blessing, a harbour and a civilizing influence. But family and personal happiness were not their *raison d'être*. For Peter it was always a disappointment when people married and became less concerned existentially with the wider aims of Camphill.

One of the new forms made possible by the Camphill Village is the revolutionary marriage — the antithesis of the bourgeois, self-protecting marriage. Peter and Kate had such a marriage and their home became a very wide and very welcoming one. It is truly apt that Kate Roth should have given her name to the Camphill seminar on the art of homemaking. This was one of her greatest achievements. It is very important to note that although Kate's house was a byword for hospitality, Kate was involved in many other aspects of life because the villagers and young co-workers were taken seriously and given a great deal of responsibility so that life was carried by everyone.

The renewed sacraments

The new village and the renewed Christian sacraments were established at the same time. One of the early pioneers told me how, as a group of co-workers trying to support the establishment of the Christian Community,

Peter and Kate's wedding in 1953 with Tilla as their witness

they all agreed that they would all try to attend the services whether they had a connection to them or not. In doing this she had to admit that she found the service inaccessible and so she went to see Peter. He suggested she try to keep going and simply follow the words. She resolved to try again and as time went on the service became a very important part of her inner life. One can experience from this story how in the early days everything in Botton was seen as part of the whole. This had much to do with Peter whose great strength it was to include rather than to differentiate. However, we also know from conversations with Peter that the experience of the War helped strengthen this attitude. He described how, in those uncertain times, the anthroposophists in Britain hardly knew whether anything of anthroposophy had survived on the continent. They felt that not only anthroposophy but the whole of Christian Middle European culture was under threat. There could be no hesitation to help each other as movements. Peter's gaze remained fixed on the far distant future in which a true Christian culture would have emerged and the divisions between the world and the church would have disappeared. With this as an ideal, he established the services in Botton. The unity of church and community could be experienced in the fact that the service took place in what was also the village hall.

Botton was not only host to the sacraments but also for many years host

König's visit to Botton in the late fifties

to the British Priests' Synod. Many priests spent their time as a practicant there, and many priests owe their vocation to the Christian Community having a home in Camphill. As time went on there came a point when the congregation and the community needed to find a separate identity. This was hard for Peter to accept. He tried to find a way of coming to terms with this need for differentiation. He spoke at this time of how he had discovered in his reading that, from the level of the archangels and upwards, the movements may be united but that on the earth they must be separate. Within Botton both co-workers and villagers became members of the Christian Community. In this way the congregation and the community established separate but interdependent identities. Eventually a free standing church was built to embody that separate identity. Peter had left Botton by the time the new church was completed, but he attended the opening in one of his last public appearances. He radiated support and good will.

Education and the arts

It is possible to experience in the bearing of a person who has seen education as a never-ending process, a certain youthful energy and plenitude. The role of education as an essential nutrient throughout one's life

Peter with Päivi Lappalainen in Fohrenbühl in the 1980s

was an absolute reality for Peter. He knew that the health of the individuals in the community and that of the community itself depended on the quality of the adult education he and others tried to bring about there. He knew that the strenuous daily life in a Camphill community could only be maintained if we constantly returned to and worked on the ideals out of which the life had arisen. They needed to be enlivened and renewed to throw light on the ever-changing landscape of a developing community.

In Botton, the Introduction Course had the role of introducing the new co-workers to the community and explaining what it was about. It was also a place where the new person could find an orientation for the next step in his or her life, whether this was in Camphill or not. To the people responsible for this course, Peter said: If a person in the Introduction Course does not understand you then you must learn to say, not there is something wrong with these people, but there is something wrong with the way I am speaking with them.

He encouraged the course facilitators to search for the language that each group needed. In this way the course, though it had a basic intention

Home sweet home

and structure, needed to be flexible. Its task was to solve the riddle that the participants brought with them and to hear what they were bringing to the community.

Peter's words to the course leaders illustrate that part of his thinking which informed all the different aspects of education in the community. Peter was a reader of signs. The confidence he inherited from his broad education and background and his bright and naturally enthusiastic nature meant that flexibility was not a threat to him. The forms of adult education in Botton were often allowed to fall away in order that a new and more appropriate form might be found for a particular constellation of people and abilities. The festivals, the summer schools for all the visitors, the courses with villagers and co-workers separately and together, the courses with older or younger co-workers, the courses with special groups like the farmers or eurythmists, were opportunities for each individual to grow wider — to become a world citizen. Culture was not an accessory or a luxury; rather it was the source out of which we would gain the insights that would enable us to meet the challenges of daily life. Peter's aim in adult education was *Bildung*, which an older member of the community described as 'forming and developing one's soul and intelligence.' Adult education activities often meant that practical life, though important, had to give way. Peter knew that if the practical work was not informed by ever-widening understanding of oneself and the world it would become drudgery. It was his longing to light a fire of enthusiasm in the soul of everyone in Botton, an enthusiasm that would lend buoyancy and energy to the building of a new world. Education in its widest sense was the kindling he used to light this fire.

One of Peter's most enduring contributions was his inspirational fostering of the arts in the community. He was a radical composer who wanted everyone to feel equally interested in the village music and to feel called upon to compose too. Through him, the Eurythmy School came to Botton, enriching the life of the village greatly. He felt all the community plays should be periodically revised and rewritten and he continually encouraged people to do this. He once even told someone to rewrite Steiner's *The Philosophy of Freedom!* He was as interested in the visual and written arts; he wanted people to paint murals, to write poetry and novels and to develop all of their gifts for the enrichment of the cultural life out of which our ideals spring.

Peter never stopped reading and discovering new things that would throw light on how to live more creatively. He talked often about how we can only understand life and each other by noticing and observing how we struggle between two poles, one that makes us feel better than we are and one that makes us feel worse than we are. In life he asked that we search for the third possibility: modest self-confidence. Out of this the arts were to be developed. Many people rose to the occasion, giving lectures and taking on tasks in the life of the village, which they did well, though they would never have known they could but for Peter's urging.

The citizen of the world

Peter lived in Botton and Botton was his work but he also always lived there as a Camphiller, a priest of the Christian Community, an anthroposophist and a world citizen. He knew countless people through his travels and involvement and was a prodigious letter writer. He was as encouraging and helpful to every person he met as he was to his colleagues in Botton. Through him Botton was known and valued worldwide. His interest stretched to every corner of the globe and brought the whole world into Botton. In this way it never felt like an isolated or limited place. He did not believe in self-sufficiency and he was never parochial. He once said that it would be more in line with our ideals if we took the biodynamic produce grown in Botton to give it to the poor in Middlesbrough, buying our groceries in the cheapest supermarket there.

Many roads led in and out of Botton. The production of food and Camphill craft products connected the community to the world. Visitors of many nationalities, of varied faith or none, came to Botton to learn how to create something similar in their own situation. Peter was always ready to respond, to share experiences and resources, to facilitate and help other community-building endeavours. Botton was partly helpful or responsible for the development of many other communities, anthroposophical and otherwise, both in Britain and abroad, in rural and urban settings. His work for the wider Anthroposophical Movement was likewise generous. He was prepared to travel nationally and internationally to meetings and conferences on both inner and outer themes if there was anything he felt he could do to strengthen the work of Camphill, the Christian Community or the Anthroposophical Society. He was renowned in meetings for his far-sightedness, for his humour, which could dispel tension, and for his ability to listen to everyone as if they were right, trying, by his example, to foster similar attitudes in those around him.

Peter knew a lot, and had a lot to give but he often gave it indirectly. For example, every week an article would appear in the *Village News*. This article was often a response to some situation that needed to be addressed in the life of the village. By writing about the situation in this rather indirect way, Peter tried to avoid the role of leader. His dream was always that everyone in Botton would feel responsible. He placed his wise thoughts into the public arena in this way hoping to create a space in which the rest of the community might become active. One of his greatest acts of confidence towards his fellow human beings was the way he tried to be there for the community, but as one among many. In this way he placed the sacred trust of this emerging world firmly in the hands of everyone who lived in Botton. What it was to become lay in each individual's power to help or hinder. Peter's attempts to befriend people, even those whose ideas were alien to him, had at their root the hope that out of friendship an interest would grow that which would make it possible to have a positive influence on those alien ideas. This indirect approach was a form of social artistry.

There is a little story that describes Peter well. The sun and the wind both agreed to try to persuade a man to take his coat off. The wind blew and battered at the man, who drew himself together and buttoned his coat even tighter until the wind had to admit defeat. The sun on the other hand shone mildly on the man who relaxed, opened himself and took off his coat. This was Peter's approach to everyone. It had one aim only, to open that person to the possibilities of his or her true self and to release that person's gifts for the world.

This image of the sun describes an attitude that can create openness, which is the right atmosphere for a meeting, and in this Peter was a master. However, in a one-to-one meeting in which there was danger of disagreement, he rarely allowed it to become apparent who he really was, or where he really stood. Rather, he would remain as it were in disguise, talking instead about who the other person was, even expressing approval of ideas quite alien or harmful to what he was trying to foster. He always tried to be tolerant and to keep an open mind, and that was one aspect of his flexibility.

But Peter had an Achilles' heel. He had a physical fear of falling and he could not bear heights. As soul qualities, these translated into a fear of struggle. He could not bear to be at loggerheads with anyone. The consequences of disagreement in the soul realm can have something of the quality of falling or of losing ground. In the realm of human relationships, not to disclose, to remain an unknown quantity, is a way of remaining in disguise so as to avoid the danger of being fixed to one point of view. This may prevent one falling into extremes but it can also be problematic. We know that every complex organism needs an immune system, a way of distinguishing between itself and the world. The immune system is the biological identity that says: 'This is I inside and that is the world outside.' In the realm of the soul, this identity counterbalances the virtues of tolerance and acceptance. Peter had a very strong sense of identity, but if letting that identity be known meant struggle, he simply left the field. With his sun-like quality, Peter could be interested, could listen to and could befriend a person, but he could not assert himself nor his often selfless and farsighted point of view.

This irresolute side of Peter could create confusion and lack of clarity. In these situations Kate was a good counterbalance, but often not even she could persuade him to come out of disguise. It was clear therefore that those around Peter needed to guard against becoming dependent on him. While remaining respectful, one needed to have a strongly developed sense of who one was so that Peter experienced dialogue and not acquiescence. He never turned against anyone, least of all someone who disagreed with him. His role in Botton was one of mild and non-coercive leadership. When he was surrounded by people with sympathy and understanding for his vision all was well, but when he was surrounded by less open people or those with rigid or inflexible opinions, problems arose.

In the same way as Peter remained in disguise and set boundaries he would also not set the boundary of what Botton was. For this reason, Botton never had problems with a strong and dominant older generation who found it hard to share responsibility. Instead, it had problems with keeping its identity and not becoming 'all things to all men.'

The Camphill Community has an outer and an inner form. The inner form of the community was the wellspring out of which the daily life was informed. Although it is beyond the remit of this chapter to describe the inner form it is necessary when describing Peter to refer to certain aspects of its content. Peter always had a leading role in the inner community. He was responsible during his life for what was called the 'Upper Room' and there he put into practice one of his greatest ideals, finding connections with other spiritual streams. He was the first to invite someone who was not a member of the inner Camphill Community to an Upper Room meet-

ing, something eventually taken up by others. He was also responsible for finding and translating *The Royal Art*, one of Steiner's lectures that was to become important for a particular aspect of the inner community connected with research. There is one paragraph in this lecture that has much to do with Peter's aims. There Steiner says:

Although our age is not so advanced as to be able to control living Nature, although that cultural epoch has not yet come in which living and life giving forces come to be mastered, nevertheless there is already the preparatory school for this ... The time will come ... when humanity, deviating from its present tendency, will see that deep inward soul forces

*cannot be decided by majority resolutions; that no vote can settle
questions involving the limitless realism of love, involving what one feels
and senses. That force which is common to all mankind, which expresses
itself in the intellectual as an all-embracing unity about which there can
be no conflict, is called Manas. And when men have progressed so far that
they are not only at one in their intellect, but also in their perceptions and
feelings, and are in harmony in their inmost souls, so that they find
themselves in what is noble and good, so far that they lovingly join
together in the objective, in what they have in common, in the same way
that they agree two times two makes four ... then the time will have arrived
when men will be able to control the living as well. Unanimity — objective
unanimity in perception and feeling — with all humanity really embracing
in love: such is the pre-condition for gaining control over the living.*[3]

This paragraph was seen as the star over a particular aspect of the inner
community, but is also the star over Peter's life. He tried to build a social
form directly out of work with the threefold social order as described by
Rudolf Steiner, and he tried to fill that form with life-giving content that
would help every individual in the community to find the strength to give
their particular contribution.

Peter had no personal ambition and shared everything he knew as a
brother. Through this, together with his unquenchable love and interest, he
tried to release the forces of his fellow community members that they too
could share in the building of this new world, that they too could feel responsible for realizing its potential and living up to its radiant early vision. By
sharing his task in this way he made both himself and his work vulnerable.

What response does this call up in those who had the privilege to see
his vision and to experience his love, in those who never met him but
glimpse the need we have for a new world such as the one he tried to
foster? Clara Westoff wrote, on hearing of the death of her friend the
painter Paula Modersohn-Becker:

*But as to the effect of the death of someone near on those left behind,
it has long seemed to me that it can be none other than a higher
responsibility; doesn't the one who has passed away leave behind a
hundred undertakings to be carried on by the survivors, if they were
sincerely involved with each other to any extent. It is clear that the deep
intensity of a noble and seriously searching person radiates an energy
which increases abundantly. Her task was not art alone as she once
said, but the process of life, for which we gave up everything in order to
share its wealth.*

Peter inspired just such a sense of higher responsibility towards the
many undertakings still to be carried on. Our only response must surely be
to continue to foster the village impulse with an ever-warm interest in our
fellow human beings.

Alix Roth

(June 24, 1916 – May 25, 1987)

Claudia Pietzner

Alix was the quiet one in the group. Initially this quietness and shyness was her natural disposition. Later in life, as her relationship to people and the world gained in meaning, her inner silence and capacity for restraint became conscious, deliberate qualities. She knew the value and importance of these qualities and lived them whole-heartedly. Her inner silence allowed for a higher life to shine through, be it in the form of ideas, ideals, the reality of spiritual beings or the inspiration of a friend. Her capacity to hold back allowed others to shine and recognize themselves. Alix's interest in others was genuinely more developed than her interest in herself, yet at the same time she knew who she was: a pupil of Michael, the guiding spirit of our time.

There are few records of her life, really. Alix herself liked to say that her life was Camphill's life and then she would add how mighty a life it was, how she wouldn't have wanted to miss any part of it and how grateful she was for it. In her presence, what was not said was at least as important as what was said. Similarly in regard to her entire life, the overarching characteristic was the importance of the invisible: what can be gleaned from what is not apparent. Her whole striving was to inspire trust in the ever-present spirit world.

Alix first met Dr König as a patient. He was the first person in her life by whom she felt known and understood. She joined the Youth Group who studied anthroposophy with him and met for the last time on March 11, 1938. They had resolved to flee, each one separately, to meet again in a new country and begin to live anthroposophy. Alix made her way to Scotland via Zagreb (then in Austro-Hungary), where she spent a few months waiting for papers. Alix spent twenty-five years in Camphill Scotland (a school for special-needs children aged five to eighteen with a three-year seminar in curative education), five years in Brachenreuthe, Germany (a school for special-needs children with a farm offering courses in curative education and biodynamic agriculture), and came to Village

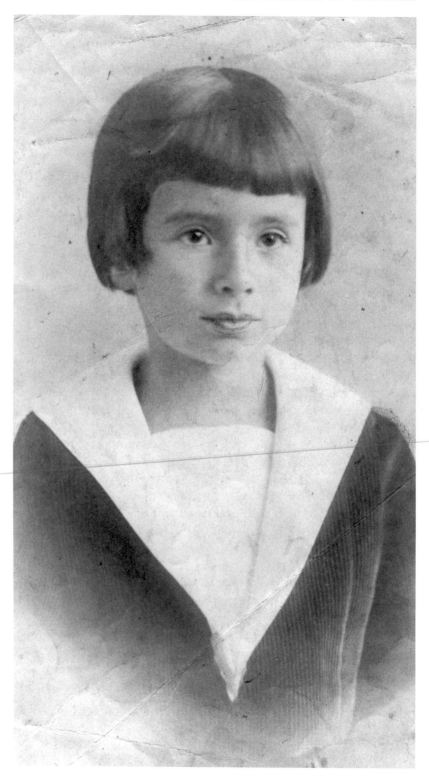

Aigues-Vertes on Lake Geneva in 1969. Aigues-Vertes is a village for adults with developmental disabilities. It includes a farm and many craft studios. Alix was instrumental in bringing about the construction of the church and cemetery at the time. During the years of her activity, Aigues-Vertes was a lively village with a strong community. Today, the village has a more institutional character. Many Camphill friends, including myself, left after Alix's death; the remaining group had to find other solutions for the management of Aigues-Vertes.

Anke Weihs tells us:

Alix's father was a civil engineer of a high order who did a great deal for the State of Austria. He finally bought himself a large estate with a castle in Upper Austria which he farmed, as he was a farmer at heart.

He was an extraordinarily good-looking man, who had been an officer in the First World War and still had his military carriage as well as a beautiful baritone voice and a very kindly character. He was not at all Jewish in his appearance although he was Jewish by blood. Alix's mother was Hungarian; she was the daughter of a large landowner in Hungary who also worked in the diplomatic service. Alix was born on June 24, 1916, in the middle of the First World War as the second of two children, Peter having been born in March 1914. Although there was famine in Austria, even among the well-to-do, it seemed that the Roths were not affected by this.[1]

They lived in a big house in Vienna. According to Taco Bay, to whom Alix recounted the story during the last stages of her illness, Alix was:

... cared for by a Nanny, and the world into which she was born did not really interest her. She did not play, not even with the one doll that was given her. She did not like to eat; she did not speak, but rather sat on a chair which she remembers being placed on and not moving away for hours on end. She could read the thoughts of the adults and realized that these did not really tally with what they said. It all made her feel that she did not belong to life, while her brother Peter, a radiant boy with curly black hair, was always the centre of attention. Her apathy caused great concern and in the course of the years she was taken from one doctor to another. They were all equally puzzled and the reports from them including well-renowned specialists only added pages to a steadily increasing file.

Just a few weeks at school, however, and she was back to how she had been before. Her desk was full of scraps, bread not eaten or only nibbled at. The teachers complained and at last offered to give her a somewhat decent report if only her parents would be willing to take her out of school. Somebody had the idea of sending her off to a boarding school in England, but she did not learn anything there either. Her only

*interest lay in what the other girls told of far-away countries where their
parents (all well-to-do people in colonial service or the like) had sent
them for their education.*

*A year there was enough to have her sent back to Vienna. No
change was noticeable and the next attempt at furthering her
education, which remained practically a blank sheet, was to send her
to another girl's school for the wealthy located on the lakeside near
Lausanne, Switzerland. Here she remembers hearing of Napoleon, but
basically her interests lay anywhere but in the subjects being taught.
She smoked. One day the head of the school told of a girl with a
hunchback who was to come. To make her not feel awkward, the girls
were asked if anyone was prepared to share a room with her. Alix
volunteered and befriended this very sad and often tormented person.
It so happened one day that the girl, in one of her recurrent
depressions, threw herself into the lake, and Alix pulled her out and
saved her life. This act filled her with deep satisfaction and with a
sense that there was purpose in life after all.*

*She did not know what she should do in her life, however. Later a
constant dream of hers was to one day have a large house with many
children.*

*Back in Vienna, her health or lack of it and her apathy continued to
be a frustration to her parents. She feared and disliked her mother,
though she did find comfort with her granny, who had a soft spot for this
very unusual girl and also an interest in spiritual matters. She was a
theosophist and had heard of a doctor who had a similar outlook. It was
thanks to this grandmother that Alix met Karl König, the man who
'saved her life,' as she put it. He made her feel that she could be herself
and eventually opened the way to what in Camphill became 'her life.'*

*The first interview stands out clearly in her memory. She was used to
being presented to yet another doctor, but this one was different. He had
the big file of her previous physicians and specialists lying before him,
but looked at her for a while and smiled:*

*'This cannot be as difficult as all that,' he said, putting her
immediately at ease. When he gave her permission to smoke and drink
coffee, her worst fears abated. Within a few weeks of his treatment she
had regained sufficient strength and weight to commence what gradually
became a life of devoted care and hard work. Before she made the
decision to step into curative education in Scotland, however, she
learned to be a photographer. She chose it as an occupation she could
perform without too much contact with a still largely threatening and
hostile world while focusing on select parts of it and processing the
negatives in an atelier of her own.*

Trude Fleischmann's photo studio, where Alix was an apprentice, was

Alix as a teenager

the number one atelier in Vienna, all the artists had their pictures taken there and it remains a successful photo studio to this day. Lotte Pietzner, Carlo's sister, worked there all her life and was later responsible for their archives. I came to know Lotte during the years in Aigues-Vertes and surprisingly or not surprisingly she knew many of my family members from having photographed them at the Opera or the Burgtheater. Alix had a keen interest in artists, and especially in the artists alive and active at the beginning of the twentieth century, so she rejoiced in the unexpected closeness to the spirit of that era which lived in my family. She 'adopted' my family, saying: 'You don't know how much it means to have a family again, when one is all alone.' Alix loved my family and the various occasions we spent together.

I came to Aigues-Vertes in 1977, twenty years old, on the recommendation of Hans Spalinger. He had told Alix that I was a rather worrisome young woman and maybe she could help me. After explaining the needs of the community in Aigues-Vertes to me, Hans asked me how long I could imagine staying, and apparently I answered 'as long as I am needed.'

When I first met Alix, I was astonished how she greeted me. She did it in a very conscious yet unspoken way, half asking 'who are you?' and half saying 'we know each other.' She held my hand and looked into my eyes

In Kirkton House in 1939 with Andreas König

a little longer than customary. It was formal and warm. Over the following ten years of our friendship, I watched her greet many people. It was always this very conscious moment with a touch of formality. Even when she was rolled out of the recovery room sore and exhausted following surgery, when she saw that her friend the Camphill nurse Turid Engel had come to visit her, she pulled all her forces together, stuck out her hand and joyfully greeted her in the same conscious manner. There was never a reason to let go of any acquired attitude. Each greeting was a meeting from I to I.

Her appearance was dignified and graceful, no unnecessary movements, never hasty, never too slow. She had an unusual face, which could be totally uninviting if she didn't want to be inviting. Once coming home from a trip, she said to me: 'You know, people never talk to me on the plane because they don't know what to do with me, a strange old lady with a long nose in a wrinkled face.' She could easily pass by unnoticed in public when she chose to be nothing more than a face in the crowd. And yet, what a presence she had in the context of the Camphill Community and the School for Spiritual Science! She had acquired true knowledge of herself and carried her being. She decided when it was appropriate for her to reveal herself.

She often did so in the context of the Bible Evening. As she folded her hands to speak or listen to the opening verse, she appeared to be showered in gold. Then, as she proceeded to interpret the gospel, her fiery gaze seemed to pierce and lift the veil between the here and now and the reality of Christ's presence in the surrounding ether realm. She spoke warmly and thoughtfully, mindful of the participants around the table as well as other spiritual beings that were being nourished through her word. I could experience her groundedness in both worlds and her nobility, which lay in a deep sense of gratitude and blessing for having been granted some understanding of the mysteries of our time. Alix's extreme sensitivity to the power of the word was certainly related to the fact that she did not speak until the age of four. Even later in life she doubtless suffered a great deal from being halting in speech and slow to formulate. With a certain amusement she recalled how at the end of meetings Dr König would often prompt her, saying: 'Well, perhaps Alix has something to say about this too?'

As a remedy for her silence he gave her the following story, which she later passed on to me.

THE SLUGGISH TONGUE (A HASSIDIC TALE)

Once in eastern Galicia, perhaps in the town of Tarnopol, there lived a man learned in the Torah, a tzaddik by the name of Hisla. He was a good man, hardworking and God-fearing, and never forgot his fasting or prayers.

*He was well-loved, and he could speak in such a way that many
people found his words a source of help and comfort.*

*And so it came to pass that one day he was asked to join the council
of the congregation of the Temple to be a voice for right judgment and
true piety.*

*When Hisla began to come to the gatherings of the elders, however,
he kept his silence. His first thought was that he ought to listen to what
others said; so he listened with strained ears as the affairs of the Temple
were discussed. He had thoughts of his own, but he felt it surely could
not be his business to speak.*

*'The others know it anyway, so to what purpose would my speaking
be?' he thought. Thus it often happened that the gathering had dispersed
without Hisla's counsel having been heard.*

*The tzaddik of the community, however, found his mind returning to
Hisla, wondering: 'Why is he so slow to speak? Often he knows which
way to go and what to do better than we, yet he does not open his mouth
and say it.'*

*One day, the tzaddik sat rocking his head back and forth, pondering
the sluggishness of Hisla's tongue, when there was a knock on his door
and a child entered and said:*

'The snake has bitten him.'

*The tzaddik took the words into his two hands and contemplated
them. 'The snake has bitten him.' It was a round phrase, round as an
apple, and it weighed like a fruit upon his hands.*

*'You must bite into it,' said the child. And the tzaddik took the word-
fruit, lifted it to his mouth and bit into it. The moment he swallowed the
first bite, his heart began to beat faster and he felt sick. The blood left
his face and his hands began to tremble.*

As he sat there sick and suffering, the door opened and in came Hisla.

'What is ailing you, tzaddik?' he asked in amazement.

*'The snake has bitten him.' said the tzaddik. At first Hisla did not
know what the teacher meant, but suddenly his heart filled with
compassion and he fell on his face, saying:*

'The snake has bitten me.'

*At those words the eyes of the tzaddik shone and he said only: 'Hisla,
Hisla.'*

*From that time on Hisla became eloquent. The word of God could
now avail itself of his tongue, and often in the council of the Temple he
was a giver of good counsel and true help.*

A few months after I arrived at Alix's house in Aigues-Vertes, it was Dr
König's death day. Ignorant of that fact, I entered her room to ask her
something. She looked up from her desk and I saw that she had tears in

her eyes. She told me then that it was twelve years since Dr König had died and that he had promised to come and fetch her 'soon.' Alix was definitely not sentimental, yet occasionally she opened her soul and revealed what lived deep in her heart. It left me feeling honored because I realized the magnitude and importance of their relationship.

Alix loved to prepare festivals! Whether it was Easter, Christmas or Ascension it had to be Easter, Christmas or Ascension everywhere in the house, and in our souls. After the clearing and cleaning were done, all the boxes belonging to one festival were brought up from the cellar to the living room. She opened them all, and first we gazed at what was in them and rejoiced in the beauty and artistry of the various decorations. Then together, with a tremendous amount of joy and love, we took one piece after the other and hung it up or put it somewhere. This had nothing to do with decorating! It was bringing Easter or Christmas into every corner of the house, and at the same time awakening anticipation and preparing a space for the festival in our souls. Making everything beautiful included hanging appropriate pictures and paintings, and all this took quite a while. Then it was enough, and it was time to let the preparation continue inwardly. Alix would always think of something helpful for me to read, often lectures and sometimes poems or stories. Later, when we were resting or rehearsing music or drama, she quietly added a little something here or there, maybe to surprise the child in each of us. It definitely heightened the experience. Not only were we all drawn in by her enthusiasm, but the festivals were real. There was nothing artificial about them, no meaningless tradition, only conviction and dedication to connect with the mysteries of life through the gateway of each festival. It was a great opportunity for each individual soul and for the community. How could one ever imagine missing any of the festivals, including birthdays? It was a sin, and so was carelessness. I remember one Christmas when the gardener brought a tree that was unsuitable and ugly. Alix was very upset, because it was really important for the signs and symbols hanging on the tree to be properly visible. Not to have given foresight and attention to that in choosing the tree was neglecting the importance of celebrating Christmas in a new way.

The following words were spoken by Peter Roth, her brother, describing his experience before her open coffin:

Alix was someone individually carrying the glory and width and
burden of Camphill from the past into the future. Dr König once said that
the beginnings of Camphill were in ancient Egypt. Devotion to the
smallest thing is so much one of the primary impulses of Camphill. It is a
transformation of the ancient Egyptian drive towards death and matter.
But out of the human deeds of conscience will be built the physical body
of Christ as out of compassion the etheric and out of awe the astral body.
Our faithfulness towards order, physical necessities, physical

Alix with her camera in Heathcot in the 1940s

*perseverance, our insistence that our spiritual life can only shine when
we have done justice to karma ... transformed into the stars of Camphill.*[2]

As a young person, Alix related to Mrs König and Dr König as new-
found parents. She expresses this in a long letter to her friend Erika
Kellner* dated November 11, 1940, Milltimber, Aberdeen.

*And now I have parents all of a sudden, new parents — Dr König and
his wife. Often I am living like children do in their childhood, blissfully
happy in the warmth and love of true parents. That is more than just lovely,
it is unfathomable. Though I had known for a long time that Dr König
could only be father, since we felt so close, so familiar from the beginning, I
really hadn't known that I would someday have the experience of having a
mother. But it happened, and it has grown stronger and clearer all the time
and now it is more wonderful than ever. It seems like a great mercy that it
is so, and often I can't comprehend how, in a time of such awful pain and
misery in the world, I should be able to experience something so beautifully
quiet. That is how it is with our whole life here. The wheel of the world
turns exactly the opposite direction from the wheel of Camphill. But not
because we do not want to know anything of the world and want to*

* Erika Kellner was a very close friend of Alix during the years in Vienna pre-
  ceding her departure from Austria. Hans Lassner, at the time a medical student
  now a retired physician living in the Dordogne, France—introduced them to
  each other. Erika Kellner later became involved with the work of Albert
  Schweitzer. Dr Lassner told me that Erika later in her life changed her name,
  married and moved to America.

withdraw, but in great part for the children's sake, since they need to grow up in peace and quiet, because that is the only way we are able to help people and give them strength. Many come to us, many begin really to breathe for the first time when they experience our world, when they walk through the garden and see the children's eyes shining, see them working with spades and shovels, living their lives with independence, walking around on their own, and the teacher is never one to be feared, but just one they can quietly look up to, one they can ask anything, who just keeps watch over their lives from a distance, tending and protecting ...

Alix never lost sight of the need to foster peace, harmony, rhythm and morality through Camphill life. Yet another side of Camphill life from its beginning is charmingly described by Anke Weihs in the opening address she gave at the memorial evening for Alix on June 1, 1987:

... and again tonight I mention the scrubbing, the furniture moving and would like to say that Camphill was born out of the work of our hands. It was not born out of meetings, it was not born out of planning but actually born out of the will, out of the work of our hands and it was reverent work ...[3]

Alix used to say 'big hands can carry a lot.' Her hands were unusually strong compared to her delicate frame, yet they were agile and never looked as if they had done any scrubbing. In fact they looked somewhat similar to Albrecht Duerer's 'Hands of an Apostle.' With them she tirelessly transformed, ennobled and blessed matter. On her right ring finger she wore a ring that Dr König had designed for her: a square, green tourmaline below a triangular red tourmaline set in gold. The following poem accompanied the ring:

Grün ist Hoffnung
Und
Rot ist die Liebe.
Grün ist Leben
Und
Rot ist Not.
Grün ist Werden
Und
Rot ist Tod.
So schließen sich Hoffnung
und Werden und Leben
Mit Liebe
Und Not und Tod
Um deine Hand.
Sie aber liegt in der meinen
Umschießend
Uns beide.

Green is Hope
And
Red is Love.
Green is Life
And
Red is Distress
Green is Becoming
And
Red is Death.
And so Hope
And Becoming and Life
Join with Love
And Distress and Death
Around your hand.
Yet your hand lies in mine
Enclosing
Us both.

Christmas 1959

Alix had a wide variety of human relationships, and she helped many to sort out their life questions. One didn't necessarily notice how observant and sensitive she was and how she took a person in with his or her circumstances and peculiarities. In addition she had an extraordinary memory and never forgot what she had been told. It allowed her to see together the fabric she was placed into. It informed her initiatives as well as her recommendations to those seeking advice. Alix distinguished very clearly how she wanted to relate to a person. As a result her friendships as well as many other relationships were fine-tuned and highly personal. When Alix had to face the fact that her cancer had spread and that her days were numbered, she told me how good it was that all her relationships were 'in order' and that there was nothing more for her 'to do' in this life. Her unique spiritual authority and power in the realm of human relationships were experienced and accepted by everyone. Other friends' experiences, descriptions and memories illustrate this.

Anke Weihs writes:

The community began to grow and I might have to speak a little personally because Alix and I seemed right from the beginning a team, to move furniture, but also to move transcendent furniture, to move other things in other realms of the Community.

We were somehow always part of each other although we were very different. When the Community developed we were often placed at each side of Dr König in the various structures and formations that we had.

Later on when the six Regions of the Camphill Movement were formed Alix and I were the two so-called secretaries of the six chairmen and together held this chairmen's group, so to speak, in our embrace and we had a long and deep dialogue with each other. Sometimes we seemed distant from each other as things in the Community changed but never really, and right up to the last moment even through the telephone, we both sensed this sistership that had been given to us, that had been, in a sense, invested in us. Alix was a very strong figure in Camphill; she was central also in the lives of many. She was very upright and forthright, forthright sometimes to a degree which seemed hard and yet there was a tremendous integrity in her. She was, I would say, a member of a true knighthood to many who came to meet her. Very often our functions were interchangeable; we deputized for each other in many overt and in many subtle ways and therefore I miss her, though not in a mournful way.[5]

John Byrde adds:

Alix was one of the finest people one could turn to if one had a real question. She listened on the level one really wanted to exchange on and was so frank that failure to agree was of little import as the conversation continued inwardly long after one had gone home.

Alix created that space for the other in which he could meet himself both in his aspirations in life and in what he still had to achieve. I experienced this gift of hers as the fruit of a life imbued by spiritual striving and service to other human beings in their becoming. In all she did she loved to serve the spirit but had no pretensions about her ability to do so. After an event in which her participation had been crucial she asked 'Was it all right ...?' with such humility that whatever had not been, became all right.[6]

Margit Engel contributes:

When I arrived in Camphill thirty-six or thirty-seven years ago, I experienced Alix as a rather silent presence. I remember a College Meeting we had with Dr König. At the end of the meeting she read the reversed, the Cosmic Our Father. She spoke it in such a modest way, in such incredible modesty. Then she shook hands with each one of us, looking into our eyes with such strength of direction that it could touch, could even move one's destiny.[7]

Her brother Peter's words give a flavour of Alix and Dr König's relationship:

... Alix stood next to and in front of Dr König. In her being she helped him to transform the destiny of anthroposophical medicine into the social realm, so Camphill could grow. We know that Ita Wegmann was a friend of Rudolf Steiner. With him she created anthroposphical medicine ...Alix was in her being a nurse. She helped to achieve the transformation of medicine into social art, into the deepest striving and impulse of Camphill ...[8]

Conversation with Joan Hinchcliffe-Rudel in 1948

In a letter of 1948 from London Dr König acknowledges Alix's crucial support:

... Last Tuesday when we held the festive concluding session of our gathering, each person spoke what was especially on his heart. I said more or less the following:

Out of despair over the collapse of the Anthroposophical Society I tried to build Camphill; I did not want Rudolf Steiner's impulses for humanity to become social reality to fail because of human failings.

You, Alix, helped me so in this building, that any thanks in words are completely insufficient. For out of trust and love you sought to pour all your strength and your life into it.

Let us continue down this path together. Through it your life has found a fulfillment and mine has become more beautiful. Let us keep striving towards the goal until the end of this century.

Portrait around 1954

Souls that burn for the spirit,
Hearts that beat for Michael,
Spirits that work for the Good,
Find their dwelling
Here on earth.
Thus I give my hand to you—
I am your friend,
And will remain so.
Ever yours
Dr König[9]

Two years later, in 1950, Alix reconfirms to Dr König their common path:

... That was the twelfth Easter festival that we have spent together.

On the first Good Friday walk, when I was still a little girl walking next to you, my only wish was that this path would never end. We walked toward the evening sun and you spoke to me of so many things. And in recent days it keeps coming to me how through all its stages of transformation, this wish has actually been fulfilled ...[10]

With Karl König in 1954

In deepest gratitude, Dr König wrote from Thornbury on Christmas Day, 1952:

These last days, as I've been wondering and wondering what I should really give you, the answer kept coming to me: 'Nothing.' What should I give you, after all?

At Christmas we give gifts wherever we have failed to keep faith with someone, to purchase a kind of indulgence for the wrongs that we have committed over the year. But there is no question of that in relation to you. You have my complete faithfulness because you are the only human being who has never asked for it or expected it. You have never forced me to do things I have not done out of inner freedom, or out of necessity. For that I will never be able to thank you enough. But most of all for being the only one who has kept pace with me, because you trust in my angel even more than I ...[11]

Barbara Lipsker wrote:

The healing impulse was strong with Alix ... in her concern for nurses' training and in her relationship to Kaspar Hauser. In the early years we had very ill children in Heathcot, many very young children. Alix helped to care for them. Some of these children died. That was when Dr König wrote the Christmas Story: He described his vision of the Land of Life and Truth where the souls of these children were whole, where these children who had been so ill could walk, climb, talk and jump around. These souls gathered around Kaspar Hauser

At Camphill's 21st birthday party

were preparing a Ring for the future. In these last years many, many souls have gone into the Land of Life and Truth, not young souls now, but old souls who gave the best of their lives to create an earthly Ring, to create places of healing around Kaspar Hauser here on Earth ...[12]

These words are complemented by Gisela Schlegel's description of Alix's connection to the stream of nursing or nurses which was so very much at Dr König's heart.

He felt strongly that a new way or attitude of nursing should come out of Camphill and when I had left and gone back to Germany as a nurse, a few months later Alix wrote and said: 'It is about time you came back to take up your nursing impulse in Camphill.' So I did come back. All this time Alix was a link between Dr König and the nurses, and a great deal has been born out of her impulse or wish that this could live in Camphill. She has been a link between us and Dr König and then a link between Hans Heinrich [Engel] and us. And in the last years it was with Carlo, where everything that had to do with nursing was inspired by Carlo's artistic impulse.[13]

Alix and Carlo guided three retreats for the Camphill nurses in those last years. Together with others, I helped host, cook and surround these retreats. It was clear that this work further uncovered the very essence of the Camphill impulse, which can be expressed in Rudolf Steiner's verse 'In Michaelic Times':

*Alix and Thomas in
1968*

*Victorious Spirit
Flame through the weakness
Of faint hearted Souls.
Consume their self-seeking,
Ignite their compassion,
That selflessness
The life stream of humanity
May live as wellspring
Of Spirit reborn.*

How did Alix help transform anthroposophical medicine into the social realm, as Peter said?

Alix referred to herself as a child in need of special care. She experienced the beneficial effects of inspired medicine in her own body. She developed strength, security, and trust by slowly overcoming her state of apathy. Through meeting Dr König her interest in the world, in people and in the workings of the spirit was sparked. She was able to find again and connect to this 'warm light' where she knew her true home was and without which earth existence was unbearable. Once she had found it again, she remained faithful to it all her life. She cared for it, she radiated it and she was a servant of it. Many children found their home in this soul-spiritual atmosphere, found their way to themselves again.

Alix's extremely slow incarnation into speaking was hard for her, but at the same time she became highly sensitized to what lived and expressed itself in the silences. She also had control over her speaking. Alix used the word as a sword of truth at times. She consoled and encour-

In later years

aged many desperate souls, she remedied and saved situations. In short, she had aquired a command of the word sufficient to build community.

Alix's capacity to read people's thoughts remained, but the disappointment she experienced as a child metamorphosed into an earnest, warmth-filled seeing of human frailties and imperfections. She encountered people in a pure way, without agenda or any kind of discrimination.

She had taken up her cross, and in her presence many found it possible to do so for themselves again. Alix wanted the roses that unfold as steps of soul-development are taken, to be celebrated, or at least to be noticed. They serve as windows into a light filled social realm, where the forces of destiny live. She trusted these forces of destiny fully and collaborated to the best of her ability, serving the Spirit of Humanity.

Through the help of Dr König, she found community in working with what her incarnation presented her with. On her path as a nurse she also learned to include the wisdom of the stars. Under Dr König's guidance, a Camphill nurse had to be aware of the astrological picture of each day, to be prepared for what the day would bring.

*Alix, having opened the new
foyer of Camphill Hall in 1986*

In the years that I knew Alix she continued to be a leader of inner affairs, but she had also stepped into an official leadership position in Village Aigues-Vertes. This task, as well as the responsibilities she carried for the Camphill Movement and the School for Spiritual Science, made up her areas of activity. In addition she fostered and maintained precious relations with the Christian Community. Needless to say, her correspondence was extensive and the phone rang constantly. There were numerous days when she literally had no more than fifteen minutes to herself. She was able to accommodate all the demands because of her discipline, foresight and heart wisdom. Her capacity to see the spiritual and evolutionary importance in anything she did allowed her to bear an enormous amount of stress without ever losing perspective or humour. She maintained peace and harmony for herself and those around her because 'there is a time for everything.' And so she lived, doing the right thing at the right time.

In contrast to this extremely firm, disciplined and conscious side of her stood her contagious and expansive laughter and her joy in sensory experience. Everything from dining to travelling was part of life, always to be kept in measure and lifted into the spiritual, yet also to be lived fully.

These qualities made her a welcoming, generous host and added spice and expectation to any performance, excursion or travel.

Born on St John's Day, Alix's being was imbued with some of the radiant, golden, cosmic light experienced at that time of year. To the best of her abilities she lived in harmony with the cosmos and helped others to attune themselves to it as well.

Selfless self-consciousness, which is Michael's signature, became the fruit of her lifetime, emerging through gratitude, modesty and knowledge of higher worlds. When I asked her once how she did it, she responded with a story: Once a meditant asked his teacher 'How did you learn to meditate?' The teacher's response was: 'Don't ask me to stir up the ashes.'

Alix died three days before Ascension Day. Her unbending and earnest efforts were lifted into the space of the ten days before the Whitsun event. Alix loved community building. Her detachment from personal karma freed her to fully support Dr König's task, and together with the other founders she laid the foundation for the community.

Peter's formulation of how Alix carried herself, and thereby the community, can stand as an inspiration for any community builder. This is a birthday letter Peter wrote to Alix from London in 1945:

... I tried to spend some time in thought about you, about the Community, how it was and will be, and one of the things that occurred to me is that you are the only one who has never burdened the Community with her personal well-being or non-well-being; that people always take it for granted that you can handle your problems yourself

and that you, so to speak, always carry something unchanging with you through the vacillations of the various and changing soul landscapes of the others. For all of us this is a great and magnificent blessing, and it is actually a mystery to me how you manage to do it; but I believe this makes it possible for something objective of the Community always to be attached to and supported by you, and then for the others as well; it was so beautiful to be thinking of these things ...[14]

Drawings by Peter Roth.
Top: From Wilhem Meisters Wanderjahre
(left: dedicated to Thomas and Henny,
right: dedicated to Hans Schauder).
Below: Irish Sea from Internment Camp, Isle of
Man, dedicated to Anke.

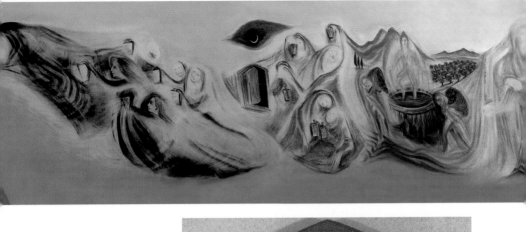

The Prodigal Son *and the* Workers in the Vineyard, *paintings by Carlo Pietzner in Botton Hall, Yorkshire.*
Top: West wall
Left: South
Bottom left: South-east
Bottom right: South-west

Overleaf:
Stained glass windows by Carlo Pietzner
Top: Silvester and Heinrich von Ofterdingen. Brachenreuthe, Germany.
Below: St Andrew, Aigues-Vertes, Switzerland.

Carlo Pietzner

(January 26, 1915 – April 17, 1986)

Hartmut von Jeetze

Among the founder members of Camphill, Carlo Pietzner stands out in creativity and charisma. Tall, fair, well-spoken, his personality radiated a distinctive air of certainty and decisiveness, as someone able to encompass both worldly as well as spiritual or personal matters. Carlo was a cosmopolitan. Close friends descibed him as a master of life, a conductor, 'a foreseeing, forethinking, fore-willing human being, as if wrestling with impulses coming from a future stream of time ... Promethean.'

Carlo's presence could be felt in whatever role, passive or active. His voice could at one moment have an imperious quality, and then lend fire and buoyancy that would confirm important moments in Camphill's development. And there were moments when he appeared to be struggling to harness the unique strength of idealism. He was instrumental in the founding and developing of Camphill, starting at Aberdeen in 1941, then moving westwards to the Belfast area in Northern Ireland, and subsequently to Pennsylvania and New York State for the last twenty-six years of his life.

To write about Carlo is important for two reasons. Firstly, a deep love for a person who has given so much to so many, without whom the work of Camphill is unthinkable, which is particlarly true of the work in America. Secondly, a still deeper and shared concern of Carlo's: his concern for the future of humanity. This prompted him to focus all his strength on assisting the younger generations to prepare them for the needs of the future and their tasks as thinking and serving human beings.

With this in mind, let us look at Carlo's childhood and youth. Ursel Pietzner, his wife shares the following:

There is evidence, that already from his youth, Carlo was very much a

Carlo's parents in Austria

loner. Already in his youth he moved around a lot. Little is known,
however, about the details.
    Carlo grew up in a middle-class family. His father was a
'Rittmeister.' He loved to socialize. His mother was a housewife. He had
two older sisters, one of whom still lives in an old people's home in
Vienna. Grandfather Pietzner was court photographer to the Austrian
Emperor and established a photographic studio that was famous for
many decades in Vienna. The family went bankrupt and Carlo's father
did not help the situation: the parents still lived in their minds in the
afterglow of the Austrian Kaiser Reich. But not Carlo, who was born in
1915.

I do not know much more about his background, he hardly ever talked
about it, did not feel 'at home' in his family.

Carlo was a good student, went on from school to the Art Academy in
Vienna, graduated *Summa cum Laude.* He was in the master class, obvi-
ously very gifted artistically. There he met, and became friends with
George and Vera Kalmar, who joined the Camphill Village in Copake in
the early sixties on Carlo's invitation, having 'found' them again in New
York.

With Christof Andreas
Lindenberg and Christl Bender
at Heathcot in 1953

During Carlo's student years and the early Karl König Youth Group years, he was friends with Peter and Alix Roth. He often spent time at their parents' place, Kattau. He received food packages from them as he was poor, starving and thin.

He was an important element in König's Youth Group; studying, conversing and arguing as well as participating in the Oberufer Christmas plays. Among those attending the Youth Group he was one of the few non-Jewish members.

In 1938 he went to Switzerland; then to England, where he stayed in the Lake District; and to Canada, where he was interned.

He came to Camphill in Scotland in 1941, thereby reconnecting with his friends of the König Youth group. There he became principal of one of the four estates of Camphill, Heathcot House, where together with Janet McGavin and Barbara Lipsker, they took on the care of severely disabled children, among them many who were afflicted by autism, or paralysis.

Carlo went on to found new Camphill centres; he lectured widely, held conferences and workshops and through his special gift in art he led retreats on the seven arts as well as teaching in seminars.

He designed many stained-glass windows; he also designed buildings in cooperation with the architect Joan Allen who designed Rainbow Hall in Beaver Run, Fountain Hall in Camphill Village Copake, NY; as well as many other buildings. The stained glass windows which Carlo designed can be found in chapels as far apart as Norway, Switzerland, England and

A relaxed moment with Hans van der Stok in 1953

Germany. The first of these is found in a church in Belfast, in Northern Ireland.

Carlo edited books, wrote articles, plays, and many poems; as well as a novel, *Wiegand's Freunde.*

Carlo was often away from his home in Glencraig for meetings in Scotland, England or in the U.S.A. He had two residences, commuting between Copake in New York, and Downingtown — later Beaver Run — in Pennsylvania. In the early years he spent more time in Beaver Run with his family, also was more involved in the life of the school (children's admissions, meeting with parents, at festivals, and so on.). Later, after his children had grown up and left, Camphill Village in Copake became his residence for the last years of his life.

In conferences, meetings, and the processes of community building, he was always somehow central, charismatic, interested in and helpful to young people. He initiated new methods in how to approach workshops, retreats, conferences, festivals, taking his approach directly out of the wellspring of the Arts themselves.

Reginald Bould sheds light on what occupied Carlo in his youth:

Once, when we were travelling in Italy, Carlo told me, that as a young man he hitch-hiked through some parts of Italy and was provided with board and food, paid for by re-painting wayside shrines.

Ursel mentioned Glencraig, as the Pietzner family's home in Ireland.

Carlo with his three children, Christiana, Cornelius, Clemens (front) around 1967/68

Before we look in more detail at his time in the U.S.A., we should consider Carlo's work in Ireland.

When Carlo and Ursel moved to Ireland in 1954, it constituted a major expansion of Camphill. In the words of Reg Bould:

Carlo's move to Glencraig (1954), was a major event in the history of Camphill.

It certainly was a step towards America. He made quite an impression when he gave a talk to the Union members of Harland and Wolff shipyard in Belfast. Usually they allow a person ten minutes to speak. But they asked Carlo to continue for more than half an hour. They then decided to give sixpence per week out of their pay packets for the Glencraig Community.

This led to working parties that came at weekends to work in Glencraig. They repaired all the glasshouses in the walled garden and later helped to build the first house. They wanted no payment — but asked Carlo to talk to them!

To understand Carlo and his relation to the Camphill movement, we must remember that in addition to establishing Glencraig in Northern Ireland, he was also active in other areas of Camphill life, for instance, in the arts.

At the beginning of each year, during the early 1950s, Karl König, as the founder of Camphill and chairman of the Camphill Rudolf Steiner Schools, presented an Annual report. These reports were a kind of 'State of the Union Address' for Camphill. They were important in more than

*At the
Camphill Hall
opening 1962*

one sense. They signified a step in the development of Camphill in the
world. In these annual reports, accomplishments, goals, decisions and
future steps and goals for Camphill were vividly presented. Decisions
were reached about who would go where to help establish a new place,
such as the Sheiling Community at Ringwood. Options for future tasks of
Camphill were considered.

At the end of one of these reports, Karl König, suddenly said: 'But
there is one thing dear friends, we must do in the coming years: We must
build a House for the Arts. But I can't do it dear friends! One of you, or
some of you should consider doing this.'

I am convinced that this was the beginning, the seed point for one of
the main impulses Carlo brought to realization: to give the arts a place in
Camphill.

Insignificant as this remark may appear, it throws a light on how Karl
König related to his founder co-workers. It gains in importance, especially
in the light of one of his earlier statements about the youth group that he
had gathered around him in Vienna, when he said about Carlo:

*Carlo Pietzner also belonged to this group. He had studied at the Art
Academy in Vienna where he proved to be a gifted graphic artist and
painter, highly appreciated by his teachers. He was an artist through and
through and has always remained so. He was a poet, wrote novels and
with astonishing speed and accomplishment he learned to express
himself artistically in the English language. In Vienna he had become a
friend of [the novelist] Robert Musil and in Prague, where he fled in the
summer of 1938, he had long conversations with Oskar Kokoschka. I
mention this because with him a stream of modern art entered our circle.*

In 1960, the call sounded for Camphill to take up work in America.

Even before the move to America, Carlo, inwardly and outwardly carried the impulse of Camphill in a way that allowed its essentials to motivate other human beings. At the same time, he was known for his ability to assist in the coming about of new ventures. Among other things, Carlo was a Class Reader in the Anthroposophical School of Spiritual Science, was treasurer of the Camphill Village Trust in Great Britain, Seminar teacher in the newly established curative education training course in Scotland, and gave lectures to parents, and to members of the Anthroposophical Society. In addition, he became known for his ability to assist human beings who asked him for advice, either about outer tasks they had to carry, or questions for guidance on the path of self-development. With the move to Copake, New York and Downingtown, Pennsylvania, a new phase of Carlo's life and work began.

One of Carlo's unique contributions to the field of curative education is the 'Colour Shadow Display with Music,' a potent therapy for restless or emotionally disturbed children. Carlo established this colour light therapy first in Heathcot, Scotland as early as 1949. It is practiced very succesfully in many other Camphill centres.

Among the plays Carlo wrote, '... and from the night, Kaspar' may be the most remarkable. To this day it has continued to be a powerful endorsement of the ideals of Camphill.

The contributions that follow are from some of his many friends who shared the work of Camphill.

A disciplined life by Margrit Metreaux

When I think of Carlo now, and my experiences of him, I think mainly of his abilities and above all, in big letters, the word: DISCIPLINE. This penetrated everything Carlo did. He approached any activity, big or small, mundane or artistic, in a disciplined manner. It was part of his daily life, flowing into his surroundings. One became part of it; simply by having a household next door to him. Of course, there was something exacting about this. One had to be on the alert in all that one did, simply by the order one had to uphold in oneself in the daily conduct of one's life. There was also a magical quality to it.

I remember one of the big events in the early years of the village in Copake: the occasion of the dedication of the 'Black Elk' memorial. It was a powerful event: the inauguration of a place where our human endeavour could reach out to spiritual beings. After the ceremony had taken place, Carlo disappeared. He never lingered!

Carlo could be inspired by tasks, festivals, but above all, by people. Then his artistic abilities could flow and he could create in an extraordinary way. In his paintings, especially, this came to expression. Painting was not for the sake of creating a beautiful artwork, but to give expression to a spiritual or community event. The execution was quick and therefore the paintings at times appeared unfinished. Again, no lingering!

He had an enormous wealth of vocabulary and could write wonderful verse. He had a great need to express himself in writing. There remains a wealth of his plays, poetry and articles. Only toward the end of his life did he ask for more time to be able to write! His creative abilities were entirely put at the disposal of the Community. It was his conscious endeavour to be socially creative which had nothing to do with 'socializing,' but everything to do with living artistically, to put art into life; to let it become part of life. He called into life the 'social art.'

One could experience that there was a teaching in all this that flowed as much as the arts themselves. It required discipline of us as human beings for it to be able to flow through us. All this led to the coming about of the art retreats.

In the nine months between November 1972 and July 1973, Carlo, together with Joanna van Vliet and Renate Sachs, conducted art retreats six times with the same group of people. Here we experienced Carlo the teacher. We were led through six of the seven arts, each event lasting one to three days. As with all retreats, these occasions had to be well held in our consciousness. They were high moments and were the beginning of similar occasions elsewhere: moments where elements of our human artistic creativity could become interwoven with elements that might aid the enlivening of our social life. In the wake of these first art retreats, Carlo was called upon by the whole Camphill Movement to guide more of them.

The social art also flowed into the work with the School of Spiritual Science. We learned how to conduct members' meetings. The whole Village became aware of the importance of the arts, especially in the celebration of festivals. The Village life could begin to support and accompany inwardly moments of celebration; be they seasonal festivals, work by the School of Spiritual Science, conferences, concerts by visiting artists, plays, and so forth.

There were times in the village when 'the stars were just right' and Carlo noticed it. Sometimes, they were not! Either way, Carlo was able to activate spiritually forces that are still blossoming.

Carlo needed people around him. He needed to be inspired to do the work that had to be done. That was very obvious when I was not there in the fifties and early sixties, when Renate was also absent during her illness. Her totally selfless presence, care for the village and assistance to Carlo were absolutely essential, often deflecting what could have been hindering to development. Carlo had personal friendships, but these were also in relation to the development of the work and life here.

With Hans Müller-Wiedemann and Georg von Arnim July 1966

It was always special when he returned from vacationing with the family, usually to Copake. Sitting at dinner with him, one was transported into a different sphere. Perhaps it was a little like the conversation and mood around Goethe's table must have been! It has to be said that the preparation for these vacations was quite exciting and a strain on some people — and their sense of humour — since everything had to be 'just so.' Even the nearest and dearest could not escape the tension of these preparations to get everything ready — and on time!

I believe it is true to say, that he gave his life to the development of anthroposophy and the Camphill Community.

A memory of Carlo by Erika von Arnim

On April 17, 1986, at the noon hour, in the seventy-second year of his life, he took leave of the earth and crossed the threshold to the spiritual world. Many friends came to the U.S.A. from far and wide to accompany him on his way into the spiritual world. From the wealth of the contributions given at the festivities by younger and older people, it was apparent how strongly the destiny of Carlo was involved in determining the destiny of many people in their relation to Camphill.

Carlo died during the forty days between Easter and Ascension. At that time after Easter, the light of the Risen One ever and again appeared to His disciples and apostles. He taught them, spoke to them; and His 'Peace be with you' accompanied them during these forty days.

Carlo with his camera

The time, in which we live today, can remind us of this event after Easter; for the Christ is close to the earth. Actually He is with us. When we are together in His name, we can perceive His message of peace.

As long as I knew him, since 1951, Carlo was deeply connected to the light of the forty days. Several of his creations, specifically in the art of painting, seem to have been inspired by the air and light of this festive time. He was an artist in manifold creativity and in many places in the Camphill Movement we find pictures painted by him, specially cut coloured glass windows in festive halls and chapels, sculptures, and many other creations. His poems breathe a special mood, and his plays have helped in determining new approaches to many a festival in many a place in the Camphill Movement. Carlo's untiring endeavour to bring new approaches and dynamics to the conduct of conferences and retreats also bears witness to his immense creativity.

Carlo's overriding task was to offer his artistry to the service of social endeavour: to use the arts to place our striving as human beings on to a new level of relevance to mankind and the spiritual worlds. The great stained glass windows in the festive hall of Föhrenbuhl, and in the Johannes Erigena building in Brachenreuthe, were created by him, as was the Kaspar Hauser Play, first performed many years earlier.

Then, there was Carlo's ability to elicit from us our hidden artistic capacities, talents and enthusiasm. The effect of this has been to accomplish a very noticeable degree of enhancement in the cultural-spiritual ambience of many Camphill institutions, and elsewhere. We can look back on this legacy with gratitude.

Carlo's deep connection to anthroposophy was such, that it was of great importance to draw from this wellspring, in such a way that its living strength could flow into the curative, educational and social-therapeutic work, and into the social forms of our establishments.

He was a citizen of the world, but one who was especially strongly connected to the Middle European impulse. With regard to this, Carlo saw his task as a 'bridge-builder' wherever he was active in different countries. Since the beginning of Camphill's work in Germany in 1958, he showed a deep interest, giving advice, and visiting us every year.

Carlo's special concern was the many young human beings in the Camphill Movement; their questions, inner development and schooling for their future tasks; be this within Camphill, or for other manifold goals in the service of humanity.

In 1954, together with a group of young friends, Carlo built up the work in Northern Ireland. Here he received the great new task from Dr König to begin the Camphill work in the United States of America. Wherever he worked, his relationship to everyone, the parents of the children in need of special care, the young people and the adults, was a special and warm one.

He died in Copake, in one of the villages for adults with special needs, after a long and severe illness, accompanied in the last weeks by his relatives and friends.

One of the founders of Camphill by Andrew Hoy

While I was in America I had once again the opportunity to watch the movie *Casablanca*. It had been filmed in 1942, or thereabouts — when I must have been six years old — and is considered to be a cult movie, on account of its ability to endure. It seemed to have many of the right ingredients, including the special chemistry that existed between the two main stars of the film — Humphrey Bogart and Ingrid Bergman — and it can still entertain us. In fact, I had to be alert to recognize in it much that is no longer current in terms of human values.

Casablanca was made soon after the Camphill 'movie' had begun to roll. The latter also had a fabulous cast, incredible chemistry, and with a similar background of disjointed lives. I do not mean to appear flippant in placing *Casablanca* and the birth of Camphill alongside one another, but to evoke a sense of the time in which they took place. A certain amount of 'lacquer' with something of the quality of film celluloid has begun to cover these early years of the Camphill Movement, that leaves us feeling ever more remote from what took place then. Perhaps a kind of embalming has occurred. Even my childhood, in which I experienced air raids and rockets, has something of this dreamlike quality of a movie. Sometimes, it is hard to believe that it all really happened.

I once interviewed Peter Roth on the subject of the youth groups that were active around Dr König in Vienna. One of these groups concerned itself with those artists and painters who died during the First World War and whom Dr König had felt were an expression of a new age of 'Michaelites.' This activity preceded the decision of some members to move to Scotland and begin the work that has come to be known as Camphill. I even visited the König house on Anastasius Gruen Gasse in Vienna — and still the gap remains. How could such a group of young people be torn from their environment and create a new social order — and form it with a group of people who were also outcasts?

I know that *Casablanca* has left its imprint on the American language with, 'play it again, Sam' and 'Here's looking at you, kid.' I like to think that Camphill has left its imprint on any number of languages. However, apart from this, and the period in which they arose, the two 'movies' could not be further apart — but again, with each of them, you would have to be alert to notice what is essentially different today.

It was with Carlo that I had the closest relationship — for twenty-five years — though we only lived on the same estate during relatively short visits. Nevertheless it proved to be a continuous and very fruitful relationship. A noticeable transition occurred with the death of Karl König in 1966. Carlo had felt deeply indebted to him and it was with this event that his artistic spirit went through a renaissance. I can recall the first pastels that he created directly following Dr König's death at the Lake of Constance. It was this awakening that led up to the series of seven art retreats that Carlo led during the fall of 1972 through the spring of 1973. He was able to do so with the musical support of Renate Sachs and with Joanna van Vliet as the eurythmist.

This was to become one of the turning points of my own life. Carlo had given many seasonal lectures that were a constant invigoration to our life in the American region, and yet this series of seven artistic retreats inscribed the selves more deeply into our existence. The retreats were based on the address by Rudolf Steiner known as *The Nature and Origin of the Arts*. Carlo had felt that anthroposophy, despite its growth and many achievements, had failed when seen against the achievements of the world. He felt that we ought to begin 'to know differently — and through the medium of Art.'

Perhaps outwardly, we could recognize that this attempt failed. It has not been one of our greatest successes. And yet, this impulse remains within the realm of intention and potential. As a seed it will be available

*Visiting a children's sanatorium at Karlovy Vary (Karlsbad) in
1964 with Karl König and Alix*

for fresh growth through any number of spring seasons. We tackled each
of the seven arts with such an intensity for a period of two and a half
days — and with no time for loose chatter — and with considerable
preparation for each retreat, that the memory of them still leaves me
breathless. These were days that had been taken from the fullness of
everyday life. Kimberton Hills was founded during the course of the
series, and almost inevitably outer disturbances occurred to challenge
our wish to continue.

Perhaps one of the enduring features of *Casablanca* — if you will
forgive me for returning to it — was the unwillingness of the two main
protagonists 'to ride off into the sunset.' The last minute twist of the plot
persuades us that the story is not over. I have this feeling, as I have
stated, about Carlo's work. The inner impulse of the art retreats was to

At Aigues Vertes

try to persuade us to transform our outer existence; our social forms; even ourselves.

There is a tendency to feel like orphans in the absence of Dr König and that close circle of people that accompanied him when I was six years old, and yet we have to recall that their teachers — those who were called disadvantaged, or handicapped — are still our teachers today. They are able to mirror our own inadequacies. And yet human values have changed. These people no longer appear to be disadvantaged in quite the same way. There are many more with far greater needs whom these friends of ours may be able to help. In looking back I feel the need to look ahead as well.

How can our life companions help us to move on? How can they help us to widen our vision? Another thought arises; will Camphill have to disappear in order to make such a step possible? Will a re-founding of Camphill still be within our reach?

Camphill Village, the art retreats and the summer pageant

Meanwhile they were getting near to the place where they were going, and He made as if to go on. But they urged Him and said, 'Stay with us, for it is near evening and the day is now drawing to an end.' And He went and stayed with them. And when He had sat down at table with them, He took the bread, blessed it, and broke it and gave it to them. Then their eyes were opened and they recognized Him. (Luke 24:28–31.)

The very first retreats were held with the same small group, Class members and Community members, focusing on the arts from an anthroposophical aspect. There were six retreats held between Fall 1972 and Easter 1973, sponsored and nurtured by the Camphill Community. One retreat was in Beaver Run, the others were in Copake, Camphill Village. What was the purpose of these art retreats? That through the living practice of art together we may find new social forms, new ways to meet each other.

I clearly recall the challenge to learn to see differently; to look at things growing: a leaf, a flower, or anything, in such a way that its inherent nature-being may be released.

Walking now through the beautiful world of nature in Copake Camphill Village, twenty-eight years later, I try to look *into* the depths of the shade in the thickets; *into* the stillness surrounding the Black Elk Memorial Ground; *into* the stillness before and after the Offering service; *into* the lie of the land of the Herb Garden, of the Farm. I find my looking becomes listening as my gaze becomes less focused, and I become aware of a Presence that would embrace me from behind, by the Being of a tree, a pond, a water lily, a dragon fly.

And this Being speaks to me thus: 'It is not enough to come with the idea, you must *perceive.*'

I try to understand perception, the true childlike perception that is the prerequisite preparation for the process of developing empathy, in order that I may truly see what is called for.

In the stillness, in the silence, lives a Being that can spring out of the past, inspiring the flow of history in its search to serve the Good.

The *Summer Pageant*, by Carlo Pietzner, was performed for three years running at the height of summer in Camphill Village, Copake. The last of the art retreats mentioned, coincided with the third performance of the *Summer Pageant*. To mark this occasion Carlo added two parts to the Pageant. As I reread the Pageant, carrying in my heart this need to hear the 'call,' a message speaks to me out of the scenes of the pageant:

Scene 1: the sharing of bread; the 'telling' of music; the judging of souls.

Scene 2: the silencing, the death of the music of Pan.

Scene 3: the birth of song: Non Nobis Domine ...

Scene 4: the inspiration of Mozart; the message of redemption, love and friendship; of a new brotherhood.

Scene 5: again the silence, no voice, no song, awaiting the song that Kaspar carries, of the bond of new hearts ...'Come, let us gather, watch and see.'

Scene 6: The Girl says: 'Be still, death, no more, no you kill, every word kill, you trying-to-be-friend kill, your Jim kill, your house kill, your thoughts kill, you murder death.'

*And later:' but I will die my own and come, seed in the earth and rain
and sun and come, and come again ...'*

*Ever and again the theme of silence, of stillness, is waiting there, to
be* perceived, *and out of this perception to feel, the new life, to hear, the*
other.

A memoir by Paula Lindenberg

Carlo's standing in the group that gathered about Dr König, as I understood from descriptions of those who were together in Vienna, was different, as he was not from a Jewish background, as most of the others were.
But his being was committed to that work that had established itself in the
study with Dr König of that Youth Group. He was an artist *par excellence.*

I can't tell much about his life because what I have to bring is more personal in character. For one thing he was certainly instrumental in my staying in Camphill. When my father brought me here I was not at all sure that
this would be my place. Carlo became a second father to me, and then a
teacher and guide. His artistry was not only in colour and form, but in
many different ways. In the use of language, poetry, stories and particularly strongly in the light of the elements, he was very creative, for
instance in making up celebrations, such as the Little Folks Winter's Tale,
where the four elements are beautifully enlivened and made present in the
life of the children's community.

I was present when for the first time, we were allowed to hear that story
as it built itself up throughout Advent. I was also privileged to be part of
the group that started Glencraig; pioneering Camphill in Northern Ireland
at Easter 1954, where Carlo was very much the guiding spirit. And I'm
sure many people will support me when I say he was remarkable; what I
would call in German: a 'Weltmensch'; a human being of the world. He
took the world in his wide embrace, and could communicate his message
wherever he went. He reached many hearts and souls of parents and
friends in Northern Ireland.

It seemed most remarkable, bearing in mind his close connection to
Glencraig and Northern Ireland, that the decision should be made that he
go to America.

On the last Open Day he addressed almost a thousand people outside
Glencraig House on the big lawn (where there was still a huge, beautiful
tree, no longer there) saying 'You all say we do such good work, we are
so patient, we are such wonderful people but you must learn to understand
and accept that we would not be here and would not be what we are without Rudolf Steiner.'

This big public speech had arisen from the fact that there had been a

At Carlo's 70th birthday

serious question at the time whether one should perhaps remove the name Rudolf Steiner from our work in Northern Ireland. But in this spirit he would confront people, and it reached many people very deeply.

In the realm of the community I still very often met him. He wrote something for the community in Copake, for a celebration on Palm Sunday at the Black Elk Memorial. He had a very strong connection to Palm Sunday, the threshold into that week of weeks. I think this was one of the most important things he ever wrote.

A Song of Praise to the Elemental Beings
We come to praise the Earth,
The waters clear thereon,
The multi-moving airs,
And all trans-pulsed by fire.
We come to praise the earth,
Of soil and rocks their beings.
We come to praise the waters,
Of brooks and waves their beings.
We come to praise the air,
Of wings and gales their stirrings.
We come to praise the fire

That gives as it consumes.
We come to praise the earth,
Fair city of the Lord,
His New Jerusalem.
He enters as a child
He dwells there as a God
He rules it as a spirit
This New Jerusalem.
Each man as child must enter,
Then God as word indwells
The soul moved by the spirit:
A New Jerusalem.
That to the city comes.
We came to praise the city,
The city of the Lord.
We came to praise the stones
That bear a crystal new.
We came to greet the waters,
Which run with precious blood.
We came to watch the breath,
Twixt ox and ass its beat.
We came to fuse the fire
Our coming with His praise.
We came to praise the earth
We came to praise the sheath
Each child must wear for entry into Jerusalem.

He had a strong connection to Jerusalem. In the most difficult circumstances he succeeded — as was his wont — in crossing the border, into a part of Jerusalem where, at that time, in 1958, it was forbidden to go. He could see the city from above, and there, in perceiving the city he had a mighty experience. He only shared this with us two and a half weeks before his death. He gave his last talk at Easter 1986, and was by this time unable to stand for the full length of the talk. There was an interlude with eurythmy, after which, finally, he could speak about what he had experienced in Jerusalem. From where he stood he perceived Jerusalem as the great altar of the earth, with two figures, one in red and one in blue standing on either side. Although he did not fully understand this vision at the time, out of his commitment to anthroposophia there arose in him the certainty that he had to be a pupil, to earn and receive his white garment, to celebrate together with the red and the blue figures on either side. I bring this because it moved me deeply at the time, but also when I remembered it later, when he crossed the threshold into the spiritual world. Exactly a week later, my father, Hans van der Stok, who was a close friend of his, followed him into death.

In the *Golden Blade* 1986 there was part of a lecture describing how the dead perceive the earth, a lecture by Rudolf Steiner from April 1, 1918. Rudolf Steiner describes there that we have to learn to build up our powers of imagination in such a way that we can work together with those who have crossed the threshold. In doing so, we could perhaps learn to perceive that the whole vast eastern part of the earth would shine in a deep blue with a touch of purple, and the whole west in a fiery flaming red. Between East and West, the earth is perceived in a greenish hue. This imagination is indelibly inscribed for me when I turn in thought to the being of Carlo. His ever-active spirit reached and enthused many young people in America and in other countries of the world with the living message of anthroposophia, thus kindling the striving for renewal into the future.

Conclusion

It was well known that Carlo's enthusiasm as an artist was such, that out of his heart he could embrace you with genuine love. This could however, suddenly change.

This trait was well known. Many of us met it and pondered about it a good deal, wondering what could have been the cause of it.

It was only recently, in the course of writing these contributions, that, while reading a lecture Rudolf Steiner gave on June 12, 1919, I suddenly understood something of the enigma that Carlo presented to many human beings who met him. In this lecture, (lecture 5, from the cycle *The Inner Aspects of the Social Question*, GA 193), Rudolf Steiner, in considering the characteristics of that time, speaks about the melancholy that one meets on the faces of those human beings who have just entered their earth life, which he says, is the result of what these souls experienced just before they entered their earth incarnation in meeting the souls of those who had just come back up from their earthly incarnation.

This is not the place to discuss this lecture, except for quoting the cause Rudolf Steiner outlines for this:

Something lies at the root of this, which especially for the materialistically permeated outlook of our time is extraordinarily difficult to grasp: That just since this world-historical point in time, in which the wave of the materialistic world conception has reached its peak, is in truth the one, in which the strongest spiritual power that ever wanted to enter human life from the spiritual world, now wills to enter human life.[1]

With this situation in the background, we may be able to begin to better understand Carlo, his strong uncompromising commitment to his work and his equally uncompromising wish to help light the candle of the spirit in the human beings whom he met. It also sheds a light on his enthusiasm and the immense confidence and expectation he had of those around him: to draw attention to the fact that the light of the Risen One is at all time with us, even today.

In the light of this, his occasional disappointment in people becomes equally understandable. It could be quite powerful when he found no response from those who, he had hoped, could help the cause of Camphill.

It was my intention to open a small window, so that something of Carlo and what he stood for might convey itself. This may best be accomplished by words he once formulated about our relationship to the Spirit of our time:

Offer your pride and
Receive your poverty!

Offer your challenge and
Increase your charity!

Offer your ounce and
Bear your obedience!

At the door of the gate
Where Michael stands.

Marie Korach

(August 4, 1915 – October 28, 2002)

Nick Blitz

In the crisp autumn dawn of the day on which Marie died, a delicate moon still hung in the pale sky, and the geese were flying northward. She was the last of the Camphill founder members to cross the threshold and with her death an era of Camphill ended.

Camphill and anthroposophy were what had sustained her during her life, through more or less constant social difficulty and ensuing loneliness. She was probably unique amongst the Camphill founder members in being asked to leave Camphill by Karl König, and then later being invited by him to rejoin the Community and its work. As in so many aspects of her life, Marie was totally committed to Camphill and to Spiritual Science, but with this commitment went a lack of openness and flexibility to other situations and viewpoints, and this isolated her from truly developing communion and community with others. Yet, through her demands and challenges she stimulated community building in those around her. In those who were able to maintain a relationship with her she enabled a greater sense of self. Her biography, perhaps in a unique way, illustrates the struggle of community life, the intense engagement with others and with oneself, without which the fruits and joys of community living cannot be attained. These struggles are alluded to in diaries she left behind, one covering a few months in 1942, and others from more recent times. In 1942 she writes:

July 21, 1942. Conversation with Trude about my path: until the fall 'we' was my only possibility of existence — I knew nothing of myself — that broke down and I had some experience of myself cruelly lit up — pain death — the world had died, my pain was the only thing that lived — the wounds are healing now. I step for the first time bearing my own weight forward.

That diary closes with these words:

November 24, 1942. I am alone in a chaotic flow, from nowhere comes help from nowhere stillness, no clear thoughts, no real joy, everything swims and from everywhere comes fear.

Many years later she writes:

December 21, 1989. I suddenly see the past in absolute and almost painless clarity! I had driven myself onto the rocks 45 years ago and there I was foundering and slithering from one stark rock to the next — life passing me by — and I in rigid pain observing the lesser guardian in everybody — nobody would or could help.

Marie's social difficulties were also the result of her superior attitudes. She was well aware of this and recognized that in this way she was very similar to her mother. In Park Attwood Clinic Marie was known as 'The Queen.' This attitude would have been difficult for many of those working with her who would not have felt comfortable in the role of 'servant.' However, through her intelligence and application, she was able to develop a high degree of professional competence in a variety of pedagogical fields; initially curative education, and then Waldorf Education. Later, she worked more in the fields of speech and form-drawing, and taught in the Training Course for Curative Education. She was also active in promoting the Community's cultural and spiritual life.

A further significant element in her life was the field of health and medicine. As a young adult she had enrolled in the medical faculty of Vienna University and studied for four years, but was unable to complete her medical degree once Austria had become annexed by the Nazis. She was forced to flee the country. Much earlier in her childhood she had been a near neighbour of the Roth family and had played in the local park with the two children, Alix and Peter, who were also to be two of the founder members of Camphill. At university, Peter, and his close friend, Thomas Weihs, also a Camphill founder member and who was to become the father of her son, were students of medicine in the medical faculty at the same time as Marie, although further advanced in their studies. It was through Dr Karl König, first as his patient and later as a co-worker, that Marie came to Camphill, and it was there in the early days that she met Dr Thomas Weihs. Her son Nick, in later years, also went on to study medicine. Later, this early link with medicine was sustained, but in a changed form through her failing health and the deep connections she made to a small number of doctors who cared for her. At different times she referred to two of them, along with Nick, as her doctor 'sons,' and in the case of one of them she fostered and held on to an even more significant relationship.

What she expressed as a possibly karmic relationship to this one doctor was of immense importance and comfort to her over the last fifteen years of her life. In him she found the trust, acceptance and possibly even the love that she so needed and craved as described in the following entries in her diary:

November 24, 1989. I was broken so many times that I don't know

*how I will be able to stand another breakage. I ask you to put the arm of
your soul around me and hold me still for a while and let me heal — this
is all — is it too much?*

And a few days later she adds:

*December 8, 1989. I plunged into deepest night of despair and then
you were with me and held me and gave me back to life. You came, did
you know? You were with me the first time ... the threshold looms almost
physically and tears me in and out — I am nothing but a prayer ... but
gradually a love greater than mine is with me.*

Later, other diaries from 1996, 1998 and 2002 speak of the ongoing significance of the relationship to her in the context of her continuing struggle to come to peace. This peace she was able to find in the community of
Park Attwood Clinic, where she was a regular patient and guest over the
latter part of her life. Here was a therapeutic environment where she felt
very much at home, and from which she received much, but to which she
was also able to contribute, both socially and culturally.

Marie's early life

Marie has described her early years up to the time she was forced to flee
Austria in some autobiographical notes that follow.

*A friend once looked at me, shook his head and said, 'Who are you?'
I will try to give an answer — to myself.*

Far back and beyond in the landscape of life there is a Dreamwalker.

*I think that the town you are born in is as important as the parents
you were born to. The town in my case was Vienna, a town still in my
blood, a town most suited to dream walk.*

*A Roman fortress two thousand years ago at the Donau, a mighty
stream flowing from west to east:* die *Donau, a great and somewhat
mysterious female, in contrast to her masculine counterpart* der *Rhein
flowing from south to north. In the old days there was a steady traffic of
trade of salt and spices along these rivers, which eventually led to the
rise of the town Vindobona which grew organically like the rings of a
tree. An enterprising multi-lingual settlement merging Germanic and
Slav tribes. Vindobona became the seat of the Habsburg dynasty in the
thirteenth century and eventually became Vienna, the centre of the
Austrian Monarchy which grew through shrewd statesmanship rather
than land grabbing battles and war: marrying the right princess at the
right time as in* Tu felix Austria nube.

*Sixteen different nations and languages eventually lived together in
peace fructifying and enriching each other wonderfully in a multinational
brotherhood not known anywhere else. In the sixteenth century the*

daunting attack of Islam against Europe by the Turks was halted at the walls of Vienna. Chased back by the much feted Prince Eugene, they left in such a hurry that all their sacks of coffee stayed behind! Thus Vienna brought coffee culture to the rest of the world: innumerable shades and tastes of coffee to be ordered these days in the veritable Kaffeehäuser. You can sit for hours with one cup of coffee, being served a fresh glass of water and reading the newspapers of the world and meeting your friends, not to speak of enjoying the sumptuous cream cakes.

But more important than this was the music of Gluck, Haydn, Mozart, Beethoven, Schubert, Mahler, Brahms and Strauss, all sons of Vienna, played by the most perfect orchestras and woe to a wrong tone or tempo heard by Viennese ears — they whistled mercilessly!

All the different nationalities merged into a cosmopolitan people. A peaceful and liberal time between the two world wars allowed thousands of Jews from Eastern Europe to come and settle down, and hidden gifts and talents came to flower, offered gladly to their hosts. Writers, poets, musicians, politicians played their much appreciated part in Austrian life.

The parents I came to

My mother was the youngest of ten children. Her father, like thousands of Jewish people from all over the old Austrian empire, had come to Vienna and settled down peacefully during an amazingly liberal time. They were either hard-working craftsmen or shopkeepers. My grandfather, Herr Raschovsky, was a diligent, quiet shoemaker who managed to start a shop which soon became one of the best in town. He probably worked too hard and had too many children — he died in his thirties, leaving my beautiful, strong-minded, grandmother in charge of the shop and children. She was the polar opposite of her late husband and took over family and business like a field marshal. As the older siblings married one by one and the shop was sold, there was not much left to rule over, so my grandmother became increasingly difficult. It fell to the youngest daughter — my mother — to stay with her and look after her.

At twenty-five she was introduced to a witty young lawyer who had recently moved to Vienna from Moravia. Dr Otto Blitz fell head over heels in love with her and asked for her hand. Strong-willed, gifted and hard working, he was by then a bank lawyer in one of Austria's oldest banks.

Photographs of him show a man always with a cigarette in his mouth, not too good looking but tall, masculine and with a noble high forehead. Not interested in the Arts, he passionately pursued his hobbies. The biggest one was to play chess. One of the old Cafes was

Marie's father (1930)

Marie's mother, Stephanie

the Kaffee Central where men of this calibre played this noble game to
the early morning hours when the head waiter wanted to go to bed: at
that point he took away their chess figures and switched off the lights.
Thus my father would happily buy an expensive opera ticket for my
mother, take her there and leave her to the 'boring music,' before
making a bee-line for the Kaffee Central. My beautiful mother, always
exquisitely dressed, was often plagued by people staring at her. The
Viennese are very good at this and like to turn round and go on staring,
whereupon my dear father would pull the most frightening grimaces
and when he was in the right mood, put out his tongue. He was by then
'Herr Director' of the Credit Anstalt Bank. In 1937, just before the
Nazis came into Austria, father's chain smoking caught up with him. He

succumbed in a very short time, dying as upright and unorthodox as he had lived. I remember seeing him the last time, already semiconscious, holding his little chessboard and playing with two figures challenging each other and murmuring stoically 'Sie verstehen mich nicht, sie verstehen mich nicht' *[they don't understand me, they don't understand me].*

My queenly mother was in no way outgoing, but was always surrounded by admirers and was a very good cook and hostess, holding court wherever we were. Her outstanding gift was to care for others and nobly support many friends. She was a true 'lioness' which did not make life easy for the two of us, for I too was born in Leo arriving as the First World War loomed. I was in a hurry to come to the earth. Photos of me show a beamingly happy toddler. I see myself riding cheerfully on my china potty before I made my first steps. Grown-ups trying to be helpful were discouraged by loud protests of 'Mali alleine *(Marie alone)!' Loved and spoiled by all, I had no problems.*

My first two memories go back to when I was two and a half. I was told that I was to have a little brother and awoke one night to see my mother sitting in the dim light lacing up her high boots.

Standing up in my cot I hear myself saying: 'Ist der kleine Bruder schon im Sanitorium?' *[Is the little brother at the clinic yet?]*

Well he was, the next morning, and I was taken to see him with a bunch of primulas — not quite knowing what to make of him.

Rudi, Marie's brother, emigrated to the United States in 1939, fought in Korea, and became professor of economics at Nashville University in Tennessee. Marie, with her particular world view, often wondered how she could have a brother who was so different from herself.

Becoming myself

It seemed to have started with myself jubilantly riding on my china potty through our flat. Life was being on the move. When I could eventually walk I soon found out what else my legs could do. I see myself with a skipping rope in the streets of Vienna, or a wooden hoop and stick that would propel me along the pavements.

Alix and Peter Roth lived around the corner and we would spend many afternoons playing hide and seek in one of the beautiful old parks, the Belvedere, racing and hollering at the top of our voices.

Carlo Pietzner and his family also lived nearby and were close friends of the Roth's. They went on holidays with them to the country. Although Thomas Weihs is not mentioned and probably was not known to her then, his family were also living in the same part of Vienna at that time. Peter

Two childhood pictures of Marie

and Thomas both went on to study medicine at the same university where they became close friends. Marie followed them to the same university a few years later. Thus, some of the earlier connections of Camphill were formed.

After the First World War I became the pupil of a Russian dancer, one of many Russian Aristocrats who settled in Vienna after the Bolshevik Revolution, some of whom came to our house and brought a new world to us. I also learned to ride horses bare back. I loved swimming and once swam across the Danube, and I loved ice-skating too on the big open air skating rink to live music. I got myself pieces of silk and improvised whole dance dramas, variations of a theme, finally learning ballroom dancing and spending many nights waltzing. It was movement, movement, movement, never serious sport and certainly no competitive ones. Life was all sunshine without care, grief or sorrow, and I Marie ... danced, skated, skipped through it with no cloud so far.

My well-meaning parents did something rather terrible when out of pure opportunism they baptized us in the Protestant Church 'to make life easier for you.' So we grew up in a total spiritual vacuum, not fathoming that the Protestants were to become the most ardent Nazis.

Half consciously I revolted against this situation; I never had myself confirmed but swindled my way through the boring Protestant girl's school not ever doing my homework. I almost succeeded but failed in maths. It was all a tragic swindle.

But next to these inborn gifts and forms of self-expression a totally new world opened up and filled my soul; the world of nature. Withdrawn and expelled from city life I met it, when after the war, people could again spend their holidays in the countryside. My parents decided to go to the Austrian Lake District, the mountainous lakes of Steiermark, not the big flat lakes of Carinthia. They rented a big wonderful peasant house where we from then on spent many weeks every summer. The big subterranean caves and passages where salt had been mined since prehistoric times and the deep mountain lakes gave this piece of earth a very special almost mythological character. Its warm-hearted humorous people spoke a lovely musical dialect. Their agriculture was still an old culture, all the work being done entirely by hand according to the yearly seasons and the Christian festivals. I remember the peasants climbing up the mountains with bundles of wood on their backs at St John's time. On this evening the entire mountain chain was crowned by log fires burning through the night. This land was Christianized. Life on the lake too, had its own style. There were long flat-bottomed boats called Platten *rowed by one person standing with a long oar at the back of the boat and manoeuvring it in a joyful way across the water. Life had style. So had the costumes; men wore embroidered leather trousers, green jackets with horn buttons and black hats with big game trophies attached.*

We became true friends with the peasant family who owned the house that we rented and my soul drank in the ancient rites and customs of Austrian peasantry. The village priest went around all the fields sprinkling holy water on the earth and blessing every field. Every few minutes along the footpaths a small crucifix would stand under its roof. The whole village was in church on Sunday.

All this was without any bigotry, was utterly self-understood and in good faith. I was deeply part of it all and became one with this piece of earth, taking long walks on my own and since then having my strong connection to plants.

Sitting on the train taking me back to Vienna I silently wept, life in town was a prison. This was the pre-Camphill child.

Things begin to happen

One day my mother told me to see a certain Dr König. I went and sat for three hours in a full waiting room and eventually was told by this strange man with a big head who looked right through me, what a superficial lass I was. However, when I heard him speak at his big public lectures of a new way to look at life and the world, I was sure I knew all this, it did not sound strange at all.

The Nazis came in March 1938 and found many good Austrians who hailed them, and Austria fell like a rotten fruit in twenty-four hours, without a shot being fired, into Hitler's arms. Life began to be very ugly. I was once stopped in town and made to sweep the pavement of a street — I was so furious that I went and bought myself a new hat! We were really saved from worse things. My brother, who had just ended his military service, was able to emigrate to the United States, and my mother to Scotland.

I was somehow guided towards England where there were two openings for women, either as auxiliary nurses in a hospital or doing domestic work. Dr König advised that I should become a nurse. Leaving Austria meant that one was stripped of all financial assets, referred to as the Reichsfluchtsteuer *[tax on fleeing the state], an absolutely perfidious term.*

Dr König himself, and the Youth Group around him, to which I had not really belonged beyond having known Peter and Alix Roth since early childhood, wanted to emigrate together. They had reached the point when they did not only want to study anthroposophy but wanted to live it. They therefore wanted to emigrate together but no country would have them. Dr König, who had, as the only Jew in Pilgramshain, to leave Silesia came back to Vienna with his family where he built up a huge private practice. At the time of the Nazis annexation of Austria he declared that he had had to leave once and that this time Hitler should leave ... this of course was only wishful thinking.

Marie's life was changing dramatically at this time. From being part of a secure, comfortable, upper middle class family, and being well established in her medical studies, she lost her much beloved father, her family, her home and almost all her belongings, her country and her future — inasmuch as it was mapped out at the time.

Arriving alone in London she began work as an auxiliary nurse at King Edward VIII Hospital in Ealing. She described the work there as being hard and regimented. However, she was not completely alone in London. It is clear from Karl König's diaries that they met on five occasions between January and March 1939. Marie recalled meeting him at

*Marie and her brother Rudi
in 1931*

Piccadilly Station where he told her about Kirkton House and invited her to join the founding group. This she did, arriving at Kirkton House in time for the official opening on Whit Sunday 1939. A year later, with the men interned, Marie was one of the six women who managed the move from Kirkton House to Camphill itself on June 1, 1940. Those early days in Camphill are remembered for the remarkable and unique intensity with which they were lived. There were long hours of very hard work, powerful human interactions, and a driving commitment to inner work and outer study often going on late into the night, and beginning again early the next morning. Some of this is touched on from Marie's perspective in her diary covering four months in 1942. In it she makes the following entries around the time of her birthday:

August 4 — my twenty-seventh birthday. Dr König was in bed and I visited him. It was the step of healing of my 'imaginary suffering.' I must say 'yes' to my situation. He is good and positive — when I accept self-knowledge from him. What pains and shocks me is my sick pride and egoism. I must try harder and remain still!!

August 7 — the Lord has taken my spirit — he will return it to me when my heart gives up this pride and selfishness. Serve with joy!

Aug 13 — early this morning I suddenly had an experience of deepest distress. A new strong experience of pride — It is certainly still elusive and must transform to courage but a strongly devoted courage not a destroying annihilation.

August 16 — in the afternoon with Dr König. 'I have climbed out of

the bath of egoism but just look into it which is also a form of egoism.
Through that I am cut off from everything.' He gives me 14 days!

During that short period reference is also made to the brief, but very close relationship she had with Thomas Weihs. She comments on the possibility of their engagement but then writes despairingly of the ultimate breakdown of the relationship.

Then, on October 16, following a conversation with Dr König, she writes, 'I'm expecting a child! It's already four months.'

At that time although Thomas was still married to his first wife Henny and had a two-year-old daughter, Chailean, Thomas and Henny had separated and Henny had moved out of Camphill. The prospect of being a single mother with an illegitimate child during those times must have been very daunting for Marie. In January 1943, Dr König wrote a letter to Marie's mother Stephanie, describing in some detail the circumstances around Marie's pregnancy and the arrangements made for the birth of her child. Also, he wrote that her situation in the community would not change because of it, and that although he did not know what would become of the relationship, he hoped Thomas and Marie would become reunited. Why things had turned out that way he was unable to say but he believed that in spite of everything it was positive. In reassuring her he concluded: 'and I request you truly to believe that my wife and I will try our best during this time to be substitute mother and father for Marie.'

However, in later years, Marie related to her son that Dr König had told her she had ruined her life by becoming pregnant. During the first eighteen months of his life, Marie intimately describes, in a book given to her by Alix for the purpose, her tender love for her son Nicolas. But it was never possible for her to make a home for them both, and for considerable periods Marie and her son did not even live together — such were the conditions in Camphill in those early days for some in the Community.

Later, two of her former Camphill colleagues shared their own reflections from those early years. In 1989, Irmgard Lazarus described how in response to Dr König telling her she should seek a friend, responded:

Then I would want Marie to be my friend. Firstly, when we stood in a circle or at other times when I looked at her, I wondered how can one be at the same time so ugly and so beautiful — for the features of the face are really not so beautiful — even when she was young. But something radiated out from her, which I noticed at once. Therefore I could say 'I would like her to be my friend.' And this friendship has lasted until now. We do not live together now but when I visit Camphill I always stay with her. This is not always so easy because she is so dreadfully critical. Not quite so much any more, nor with myself, but always to hear the

Marie at the time of her studies

*Marie with
Thomas playing
with the König
children at
Kirkton House*

*criticism! She never forgave Thomas and Anke, right till the end when
they came together. She wrote to me after Anke's death, that they had
really made peace, Anke and Marie.*

More recently Diane Basil reflected from the time in the mid 1940s
when she lived with Marie in Murtle House:

*In those days Marie was a most sincere and devoted seeker and
follower of a meditative path. She was very serious, and completely new
to the harsh realities of practical life; with her pronounced melancholy
temperament I think she must have suffered more than any of the others
in the group who escaped from Vienna. But in fostering all the
inspirational thoughts and plans for the future, which Dr König spoke to
us about on most evenings, Marie must have played a major spiritual
part in the development and expansion of the Camphill movement.*

It was Marie who responded to Karl König's vision of a shared meal
and Bible reading every Saturday evening to conclude the week and pre-

pare for the Sunday and the week ahead. She did this in the face of considerable opposition from her colleagues, but only through her positive affirmation was Karl König able to proceed with introducing the Bible Evening to Camphill. This act was of immense significance to the development of the Camphill Community.

A time of wandering

Early in 1951, at the age of thirty-six, after twelve years of pioneering the work of Camphill in Aberdeen, Marie and her son Nicolas sailed for the United States. The following fifteen years could be described as 'wandering in the wilderness.' There was an element of exile from Camphill, but it continued to be her spiritual, if not her actual physical, home during those years. A life-line was maintained by Karl König and to a lesser extent by Peter Roth over the years so that, in spite of serious difficulties, they were somehow able to maintain a positive human connection. In her diary of January 15, 1998, she wrote:

But then I really read Peter's letters from 1956 to '57 when I was on the run and he pleading and wrestling with me to take on sense — I must have been totally maladjusted *— fighting and leaving nothing but burned bridges behind me ... it suddenly comes home to me in a shattering way ... and you, Peter, are like my guardian showing the truth from beyond the threshold. Have you become my guardian? I feel in good hands.*

Marie's base in America was with her mother and brother who lived in Berkeley, California, but she soon teamed up with a somewhat eccentric older anthroposophist, Minerva Brookes, who lived in a logging community called Hyampom in the wilderness of northern California. There Marie, with her son Nicolas in tow, attempted to begin curative education work and for a time had two young people with disabilities under her care. Unsurprisingly however, the project foundered and Marie returned to the San Francisco Bay area. By now the immigration authorities were looking for her because her visitor's permit had expired. In an attempt to forestall her deportation she married Werner Korach, a fellow anthroposophist, but to no avail: she and Nicolas were forced to leave the country at the end of 1952. During her spell in America she still seemed to have the total confidence of Dr König, who had written a glowing reference in support of her attempt to start curative education work in California. On a personal level however, he referred to her loneliness as being an opportunity for her to work at some of her social difficulties.

On Marie's return to Britain at the end of 1952 she joined the Camphill

Sheiling schools at Ringwood in Hampshire where she continued her curative work as a eurythmist. She also looked after children and worked as a class teacher, something she had done for many years previously in Aberdeen. Within months of her arriving at Ringwood, however, difficulties emerged and Dr König wrote from Aberdeen:

If you believe that in this manner the issues of life and work can be resolved, then only disappointment can follow. It is very painful for me to experience your continuing lack of insight and how instead of seeing the difficulties in yourself you continue to see others as being at fault. If you have no other possibility but to feel constantly offended and unjustly dealt with then your heart will freeze.

By summer 1955 difficulties had reached such a pitch that Dr König wrote Marie a very outspoken three-page letter asking that she leave Camphill. He suggested that she seek work in Germany as a teacher or in any other position that she could find, and spend two years working at her difficulties after which she should consider whether she could look him in the eye again.

Marie moved to Germany in the summer of 1955 and her son Nicolas went to boarding school at Wynstones, spending most holidays with his father Thomas and his family. Alone in Germany, Marie had a number of jobs including that of doctors' assistant before starting as a special needs teacher at the Krefeld Waldorf School on April 1, 1957. There she taught different groups of children with mild learning difficulties, and others, a variety of subjects including German, Mathematics, History, English and Eurythmy. Between January 1957 and July 1958 she and König re-established a good rapport and nine letters from him attest to that. She invited him to visit the Krefeld school to give lectures and see children with special needs, which he was able to do. However, by the end of the year difficulties were developing and Marie was ready to

Marie and Nicolas

Marie and her class in Pforzheim Waldorf School

move on. But König was emphatic in responding to her request to come back to Camphill, that there was no point in attempting a flight into the past, reminding her why she had separated from the community and that it was right that she went her own way. He also wrote:

I can under no circumstance *recommend you to any school and must also ask you not to use my name as reference point in this connection. It is necessary that you at last forge your own destiny alone; I will gladly stand by your side* personally *but not as Dr König. You must learn to differentiate between them.*

This advice was obviously not well received, but König denied that he had written harshly to her and referred back to her long-standing difficulties. In a letter he wrote shortly before Christmas, after Marie had written to Alix requesting that she spend Christmas in Aberdeen with her son Nicolas, he made it quite clear to her that she would not be welcome, and that she should instead meet Nicolas in London.

Marie left the Krefeld School at the end of 1958 with an appreciative reference and enrolled at the Pedagogische Institute in Darmstadt in April 1959, in order to obtain a State teaching qualification. Having gained a year's exemption, based on her past experience, she graduated with a 'Good' teaching Diploma a year later. From there she moved to Pforzheim taking over the first class at the Waldorf School. She took that group of children through to the sixth class, and then started once more with Class 1. She also taught English to all the classes in the school. This was a positive time for Marie, as well as her pupils, their parents and the school, as her reference attests. She was also able to re-establish her connection with Dr König who, at her invitation, visited the school and lectured in Pforzheim. Between 1961 and 1964 his interest and concern for her well-being was expressed in eight letters, and in the last two of them he invited her to visit him in Brachenreuthe.

Karl König died on March 27, 1966 and Marie moved to Föhrenbuhl, one of the Camphill Community Schools on Lake Constance, in the summer of that year. Her time of 'exile' had ended but she only returned to her original 'home' in Camphill in Aberdeen eight years later.

For very many years until her death Marie had a large photograph of Karl König on her desk. On the back she had written:

Why did you never uphold me?
Why did you discard me?
Why did you not light the candle in me?
I am not one of you —
I had to go it alone to become myself.

And at some other time she had added: 'I was not ready.'

These words poignantly describe her experience of those years, as well as one of the challenging aspects of community living, that of commitment.

Back to Camphill

Marie spent six years in Föhrenbuhl from 1966–72 as a class teacher. She also taught on the Training Course for Curative Education. She was now in her late fifties, and was suffering from increasing health problems, and so the possibility of continuing as a class teacher was in question. The time was ripe for change and Marie moved to Camphill's Karl König Schule in Nuremberg to train and get further experience in therapeutic speech work. This came to a difficult end in the summer of 1974 culminating in a period of hospitalization. From this low point, she was invited by her former colleagues in Camphill, Aberdeen to rejoin the Community there, and she arrived back in Murtle that same year. Soon after, she took on Rose Cottage with its three young boys and a young co-worker, until the time came for the boys to move on when it was realized that the house was not really suitable as a children's unit. There, Marie was at last able to put down roots. She began to make a garden, planting roses and other flowers that she cared for with great love, faithfully supported for many years by Mr Allen, her gardener, who worked diligently under her watchful eye.

Marie finally also had her family around her. Her son Nick, with his wife Karin and their three daughters had joined the Camphill schools in

*Marie's 70th
birthday*

Aberdeen in 1973 when he took up medical studies at Aberdeen University. In 1979 Marie's mother Stephanie was brought over to Murtle from hospital in Vienna where she had been diagnosed with a terminal illness. Although these two did not manage to share Rose Cottage for long, the invigorating north-east climate suited Stephanie well and she lived to be almost one hundred years old, dying in 1988.

Marie continued to be very active in the life of the schools and in the Community, doing speech and remedial work with both individual and small groups of children, contributing to the Training Course in Curative Education and to the cultural and spiritual life of the Community. She also spent periods of time in the late 1970s at Coleg Elidyr supporting their work and later during the 1980s she was a regular visitor and contributor to the work of the Pennine Camphill Community. Jane Luxford, one of the founder members of that community, describes Marie's visits thus:

The relationship between Marie, Pennine and ourselves as co-workers can only be described as golden!

She would regularly come and spend time with us, teaching students in the class, and young co-workers in the Introductory Course. I would

*'look after' her, so we would go out for lunch and shop like a mother
and daughter, yet without the complications of a blood-tie.*

*In her eyes, everything we did in the Pennine was wonderful. She
seemed to overlook sometimes half-cooked lunches or untidy rooms. It
did not matter.*

*She would often say we were all great people. I think she felt the wind
of pioneering in Pennine, and felt refreshed herself by that wind.*

*Marie was instrumental in finding an adaptation of the Waldorf
Curriculum for youngsters of sixteen and over who had not attended a
Waldorf School earlier. She had found a German curriculum for this
purpose and had translated it. We still use it to this day.*

*Marie came to the Pennine Community for many years for a week's
visit. Gradually, as her age progressed, she would teach less and the
visits would be more social. For us, as 'relatively' younger co-workers,
it was marvellous to have Marie coming, seeing what we did and being
so positive about everything. Through that, our confidence in what we
did was also strengthened.*

In 1996, Marie's dream for her 'own' home was realized when, with sav-
ings from her pensions, she was able to finance the building of St Bride's, a
small bungalow on Murtle estate. This home, with its guest room housing
occasional visitors, was one of the greatest joys of her final years. From it
she could continue to enjoy caring for her garden with the help of Mr Allen.
Retaining her independent nature, and with the support of her faithful and
forbearing home-help, Aileen, she was able to enjoy outings to good restau-
rants, buying nice clothes, and perusing the *Independent* newspaper with her
critical eye. Having this small personal income also meant that Marie was
able to give regular financial support to a number of individuals and chari-
ties over many years, including Oxfam, the Aberdeen Waldorf School, the
Christian Community, and Park Attwood Clinic.

She also engaged very actively with Community processes, writing two
papers for internal circulation within Camphill and keeping herself well
informed of Community developments. Nora Bock adds:

*Her zeal for the mission of Camphill as vehicle for Anthroposophy
was like a burning flame that often allowed far too little rest and
patience for her to realize that her intense idealism swept her well
beyond the limitations of others.*

*Often, we sensed the tragedy of a destiny that did not permit such a
fiery will for the Good to be channelled more harmoniously into
Community striving. Equally, how infinitely worthwhile were the rare
moments when her creative mind and wakeful conscience found the right
moment to blend with others! However, it was particularly in personal
relationships, that she could give freely of her positive strength, which is
remembered by very many to whom she gave lasting guidance.*

Her thirst for greater knowledge and understanding of Spiritual Science was also unquenched to the end, with heavily underscored lecture cycles constant reading companions on her coffee and bedside tables.

Peter Howe, who lived on Murtle Estate for many years while Marie was there recalls:

It was not easy being a friend to Marie. She was never a comfortable person and friendship for her was not about reassuring each other but about questioning and challenging, particularly in relation to the principles of the spiritual Camphill Community. Many were the times one was met by what seemed quite aggressive cross-examination and, less forgivably, many were the times the phone was put down in mid-conversation. However, one discovered over time that however many times the friendship foundered, Marie was always able to meet you on the next occasion openly and honestly, and to begin again. There were no apologies but there were also no grudges.

Another thing that I personally appreciated was that when I moved out of Camphill to live independently, Marie was one of very few people who would regularly contact me to find out how I was, and who took a real interest in my new life. For her, there was no question that one's commitment to Camphill and its inner community was unaffected by such a change, and that living in a Camphill centre is just one aspect of a diverse and spiritually great community-building endeavour.

There was also another side to Marie, a part of her soul that loved humour, could laugh freely and enjoyed nothing more than being teased by young men, especially if they spoke German with an Austrian dialect.

For the last twelve years of her life she also enjoyed the support of Jennie Tanser, who writes:

For eleven of the twelve years I have worked as art therapist with the Camphill Medical Practice, Marie and I travelled an artistic path together. She shied away from the flowing elements of watercolour and much preferred the medium of pastels. We worked with many motifs, but particularly with images of Rudolf Steiner's Soul Calendar, and the world of the elemental beings for which Marie had a particular feeling.

One day, I was a bit exasperated with her because she was being 'impossible' and wouldn't agree to anything I suggested as subject matter; and I said 'Oh Marie, you are just too old for therapy!' She replied 'You're right Jennie, you'll just have to do it instead!' We laughed a lot. She had an intrinsic artistic talent which reflected a real beauty of soul, which sadly she somehow didn't quite allow to blossom. The last series of images we worked with were those of the transformation process from the egg to the butterfly.

Another theme Marie worked on was that of Mother and Child (or the Madonna and Child) of which she left a number of beautiful small pastels.

Marie at 81

Yet in spite of moments of joy, and the outer comforts of St Bride's, she continued to be lonely and unhappy, at times increasingly so, in these later years. This expressed itself in her declining health and a growing need for medical, nursing and therapeutic support. The provision of this at Park Attwood Clinic was of immense importance to her. Her relationship to the clinic and to many of those working in it went well beyond that of a patient, and she enjoyed a number of Christmas and Holy Nights there. In this way she was able to bring her own experience of community building to a similar active process going on in Park Attwood.

Marie's highs and lows during these last years are described in her diaries from 1996, 1998 and 2002 in which she wrote brief but revealing comments on her situation. What is evident, and was also evident on meeting her, is the continuing and singular lack of balance and harmony of her experience; events and people are either wonderful or terrible. In this, one cannot but think back to Karl König's warnings from the 1950s. But what is different is an element of self-knowledge that was perhaps lacking then.

On her eighty-first birthday, Marie wrote the following notes in her diary:

August 4, 1996: morning in peace at home but *find diaries of 1989, 1990, 1991, 1992. Oh, on what shattering path have I been led; what wounds in body, soul and spirit.*

In the afternoon there was a birthday celebration and a housewarming, and she continues:

I am surrounded and taken in by loving *hearts — people are* good *— there is peace and warmth on the greening lawn.*

And on the next day she continues:

August 5, 1996: I am so full of gratitude *for everything. My* heart sings *in my house — the house opens its heart to tired house-mothers and young co-workers on free days — it feels good.*

Sadly this dream was never fulfilled; tired house-mothers and young co-workers would not have felt free to relax there, and she would have struggled with the reality of others sharing or using her space. Some days later she continues:

August 8, 1996: my astral body has hit and hurt so many children and people — it now hits and hurts me

I can see it.

Am I allowed to pay it off?

Ghastly pains.

And later she writes:

September 17, 1996: I am in excruciating pains and then N. rings to tell me full of glee about the regional community meeting and H.'s wonderful talk on the rhythms and the group's decision to take up the rhythms and meet on Friday. I recoil inwardly and she tells me if I don't believe in it I should not come. *That sends me reeling in black despair, the small cupola again out of sight — 'if the others don't go that way you must follow* them *and not* yourself!?' *I crack up and spend half the night praying —*

February 9, 1998: have sorted out all *letters! Dr König — what a monster I was — but what faithful good friends stood around me and I did not recognize* them *sufficiently, battled with them as well — poor Marie.*

Then, with reference to her doctor she adds:

You were the only one who broke through the barriers and lit a little flame — which broke into a huge conflagration and almost burnt me — and you.

You stood it, you saved me.

June 27, 1998 I am exhausted — don't go to the play

lie on bed and feel what is going on in me

my thorns fall off, the wounds heal — it is good and easy to be 'nice' — I start to like myself and to like to live and people flock to me —

It is truly midsummer. I love my garden and talk to every flower — the roses come; life is good.

Two years later, in the summer of 2002, having failed either to find a place for herself in Park Attwood for long-term care, or to secure the services of a nurse from Park Attwood to live with her in St Bride's, and having resisted over a number of years offers to move to Simeon Care for the Elderly, it was apparent even to Marie that she could no longer manage alone. Periods of respite were therefore arranged for her in two local nursing homes, initially for the time of the School's holidays. Marie was very happy in Culter House Nursing Home, and was making arrangements to live there when she had a severe stroke that rendered her speechless but left her fully conscious. It seemed as though her critical tongue had been stilled whilst she took the final steps to the threshold. She died on October 28, the day she was to have been discharged from respite care, and returned to rest in St Bride's, as ever in control of her destiny. Perhaps now, on the other side, she will be able to join her colleagues in harmonious intent as the geese fly north together.

Marie wrote her last will on May 28, 2002. In it she said:

My life forces leave, I think I am going, I am ready.

This life has been a battle between darkness and light, towards the end the light increased.

Camphill called me — I always gave my best. It was hard to see that the best was not good enough.

There are no achievements but many seeds for the future — my love for the earth and her children sustained me.

I thank all those who were my faithful friends in hard times. I will try to be of help.

Marie

WILD GEESE

You do not have to be good
You do not have to walk on your knees
for a hundred miles through the desert, repenting.
You only have to let the soft animal of your body love what it loves.
Tell me about despair, yours, and I will tell you mine.
Meanwhile the world goes on.
Meanwhile the sun and the clear pebbles of rain
Are moving across the landscapes,
Over the prairies and the deep trees,
The mountains and the rivers.
Meanwhile the geese, high in the blue clear air,
Are heading home again.
Whoever you are, no matter how lonely,
the world offers itself to your imagination,
calls to you like the wild geese, harsh and exciting—
over and over announcing your place
in the family of things.

From Mary Oliver, Dream Work.

Alex Baum

(August 31, 1910 – November 4, 1975)

John Baum

*His faithful and constant devotion to the common work was an
immense help. In later years his wide range of knowledge was
able to be transformed into wisdom.*[1]

Karl König

Alex Baum was the oldest of the Viennese Youth Group that developed
under the leadership of Karl König and later went on to found
Camphill. He was part of the 'old' Youth Group that had formed by
1929, the members of which helped each other to grow beyond their
Jewish background and find their way to anthroposophy and
Christianity.

Dr Lotte Sahlmann, who worked with Alex and his wife Thesi in
Scotland, Bristol and the Sheiling, described him:

*Alex was interested in human beings. He was very reliable spiritually.
He was the spiritual guide of the Sheiling. He was the quiet point
around which much moved. He stood back a little, so that he could see
life. Alex had spiritual experience; he could help young people, and
formulate the questions that came to him. Alex was incarnated in the
head, not so much in the feet and hands. He had a fantastic memory, it
probably came from childhood.*

Looking back over Alex's life, Anke Weihs wrote these words:

*... he revealed (little) of his own activities. One feels that his was not
merely a self-imposed reserve; it was a cloak he wore in obedience to
some higher factor in his destiny.*[2]

Anke had worked with him and followed his life for many decades
and when he died wrote an obituary where she brought together the
major themes of Alex's life.[3] Her words introduce each part of this
chapter.

Alex Baum in Finland, Whitsun 1975

*Arthur and Rosa
Baum, at home,
around 1938*

Childhood

*Alex never lifted the veil that hung over his childhood and
boyhood to those of us who 'knew' him for over thirty-six years.*

Anke Weihs

Alexander (Alex) Baum was born at home on August 31, 1910, the only child of Arthur and Rosa Baum in Alsergrund, the district of Vienna famed for its poets and thinkers. His parents had emigrated a few years earlier from Hungary; his mother from near Lake Balaton, his father from the west, near the border with what is now Croatia.

Arthur and Rosa had married a year before in the Jewish Temple and had moved into the bride's home. By this time Rosa was established as a *Kleidermacherin,* a seamstress, working from home. Arthur worked as a clerk.

Whilst his parents worked, Alex's beloved grandmother, Katharina (Katti) Paski, had all the time in the world for him. She was widowed by the time Alex was born. Her son, Sandor, Rosa's brother, died of tuberculosis at the age of twenty-six in 1908. Did the family move to Vienna to help Sandor receive medical treatment? Was Alexander named after his uncle, Sandor, who had died so young? Sandor would often have been spoken about as Alex grew up and we can imagine that the family memory of his life and death were important in Alex's childhood.

Opposite Alex's childhood home in Hahngasse was the Tandel Market, a form of bazaar: a large hall with two hundred stalls. Stella Maria Hellström, who grew up in Vienna, fled in 1938 to Sweden and started Camphill's work there, remembers the Tandel Market from her childhood:

*Hahngasse with the Tandel Market on the right and the Telephone
Exchange behind. The man is walking past Hahngasse 2 and 3.
The picture was taken when Alex lived there*

*Clear in my memory is the smell of the Tandel Market. I have met it
again in oriental markets. A mixture of smells of old carpets and
material, cooking utensils and tools. The small stalls stood next to each
other in a row and were, with their windowless interiors, like small caves.
Because the stalls were small, most of the things lay on the road in front
of the stall. The seller sat on a chair nearby. The people were poor, that
was easy to see, and they spoke different languages and dialects.*

*The Tandel Market was a paradise for small children's eyes and,
through the friendly warmth of the people, it was specially attractive.*

Alex's good friend, Heinz Frankfurt, who grew up in the neighbouring
street, describes the Tandel Market, which played such an important role
in Alex's childhood:

*The area was Catholic, not at all Protestant. There was a synthesis of
religion, art and social life with trade — and the Tandel Market. At that
time everything was allowed on the Tandel Market. Plays with biblical
themes were put on in the churches, outside there was music and
dancing, and shouting, loud cries. There, all Viennese were real Jews.
All was a Viennese-waltz, until March 12, 1938. Then friends became
foreigners and enemies.*

At home the family spoke Hungarian, so that Alex knew two languages by the time he began at his local school where, a hundred years earlier the composer Franz Schubert had been teacher. It now bore his name: Schubert Schule. When Alex started school, on Saturday, September 16, 1916, his father was called up for military service, and that same autumn the old Emperor died.

At the end of the First World War the new young Emperor abdicated and the Austro-Hungarian Empire was divided into two countries with language being the criteria for division. Alex's parents had to choose between Hungary, where his parents had their roots, or Austria, where Alex had been born and where they lived. They chose Austria, becoming Austrian citizens when Alex was eleven years old. His grandmother, then seventy-two years old, remained Hungarian. She lived until Alex was fifteen years old, dying on Christmas Eve 1925.

Youth — and the Youth Group

Alex studied Chemistry in Vienna. Very early on, he encountered the Christian Community that made a deep impression on him, and he was one of the very first to join Dr König's Youth Group.
Anke Weihs

In 1920, at the age of ten, Alex began at the secondary school (Realschule) of the 9th district in the Glasergasse. The eighteen-year-old Karl König had left the same school just weeks earlier. Shortly before his fourteenth birthday, after only four years at secondary school Alex left and began working in a shirt factory. Nearby, in Wasagasse, was the Wasa Gymnasium, where Hans Schauder, Rudi Lissau, Bronja Hüttner and Edi Weissberg had started secondary school. The four were in the same class and their friendship would last throughout their lives. From an early age, Rudi had worked to convince the others about anthroposophy.

By the time Alex was eighteen he had made contact with the Youth Group that had formed at the Wasa Gymnasium. In 1929 Alex, at nineteen, was one of the oldest. Hans and Rudi and the others at the Wasa Gymnasium were eighteen. By 1931 Lisl Schwalb (later Schauder) and her good friend, Sali Gerstler, (later Barbara Lipsker) were part of the group, then both nineteen. Trude Blau (later Amann), still younger, joined around this time.

Hans Schauder remembers that his friendship with Alex developed especially through their love of the opera and of long walks. Looking back, describing the friend of his youth, he wrote:

Alex was a mysterious figure. He was always very cheerful. I think I

Alex at the beginning of his university studies in 1933, at 23 years of age

was closest to him. He was in the best sense a free spirit. He was not bound to anything — not to school, not to a group.

Memories of the time in Vienna are alive, of Alex, of his enjoyment of life. There was an interlude when he went to Paris. When he came back he ran up to my flat on the fifth floor to tell me about Paris. For me he came out of nothing, he had no past. He had an impulse to get into something new.

Alex was an opera-goer. At the opera one queued and the queue moved like a snake. One picked up one's ticket and rushed to the fourth floor gallery. There was a special feature of the opera. Once a singer had established himself he had a Gloria. Richard Schubert was an established singer whose voice was hoarse. He was loved and we all copied his hoarse voice.

Alex loved certain words, especially words that produced certain sounds. I remember a key word, for all young people, particularly Alex. There was a leading tenor called Leo Slezak. He was called the *'göttliche Leo'* — the divine Leo. He was Czech, and all called him the *'gättliche Leo,'* pronouncing it in the Czech way.

Alex was a very important part of my life, a very quiet part of my life.

In 1933, nine years after leaving school, and after studying at evening classes, Alex took the school leaving examination, the Matura, and passed with distinction. In autumn 1933 he began to study chemistry at the First Chemistry Laboratory of the University of Vienna.

After completing his basic studies, Alex began research for a doctoral degree. He worked in the laboratory of Prof. Hermann Mark, in collaboration with Dr Engelbert Broda, who, as an outspoken communist, was imprisoned several times in the 1930s.

Following the annexation of Austria in March 1938 Dr Broda escaped to England taking with him part of Alex's doctoral degree research. This became incorporated into an article published by the Faraday Society in London: 'The Absorbability of Chain Molecules, by A. Baum and E. Broda.'[4] Later, following internment in 1940, Dr Broda went to work for the 'Directorate of Tube Alloys,' the code name for the Atom Energy Project.

Whilst Alex's one and only scientific paper was being published in London in July 1938, he was fleeing from Vienna, not knowing, and seemingly never knowing, of its publication. Years later Alex said that he had been content working in the field of chemistry and believed he would have continued, had events not taken such a dramatic turn. The research he was doing on polymers and plastics was exact and intellectually refined. At the same time he found an inner home in the Youth Group, which first opened the door for the world of nature and culture, then opened it for anthroposophy and Christianity.

Annexation of Austria — and flight

> Alex experienced the abrupt termination of his studies as a result of the Nazi annexation of Austria in 1938, and he fled the country, leaving his family behind, never to see them again.
>
> Anke Weihs

On Friday, March 11, 1938, the German troops crossed the Austrian border. In the Königs' house that evening, the Youth Group met together. They made a collective resolution to meet in another country and work towards building a community focused around those in need of special care. On the following Wednesday Alex went to the Chemistry Institute and Prof. Mark wrote a reference for him. Now began the search for escape options. He obtained a visa for Italy, ostensibly to study the language. He had to queue with thousands of others waiting for passports and

Alex in 1938, from his passport

permission to leave the country. On the evening of July 3, his mother helped him to pack. What should he take with him? The few official papers were placed in a little leather wallet together with pictures of his parents in their flat, showing their big radio in pride of place, and his beloved grandmother sitting outside watching life go by. Next day, at the time the plane took off, his mother stood at the window of their flat. *'Jetzt fliegt er weg* [Now he flies away],' she said. He was flying into the future. They were left behind.

Hans Schauder travelled to Italy the same day as Alex. On arriving he cried out to Alex that his hearing was damaged by the flight. He could hardly hear! Alex calmly said to him that if he would take the cotton wool out of his ears, it would certainly help.

From Milan, Alex managed to travel to Switzerland. In Geneva, in August, he received a visa for the U.K., but did not use it. Decades later, on a visit to Switzerland, he stood by the lake in Geneva together with his wife and youngest son, Tom. He told them how he had entered France illegally by taking a pleasure steamer from Geneva to Evian on a Sunday, when French border guards were not on duty. He travelled to France because it was where Dr König was trying to find a haven. König had written from Paris to the Youth Group telling them of the great possibilities in France and asking them to learn French.

By October 1938 Alex was back in Paris, the only other city he had lived in for any stretch of time. A few weeks later he was baptized there in a Lutheran church. This monumental step for a young man born into the Jewish faith must have been quietly prepared for in the years with the Youth Group in Vienna and through his contact with the Christian Community there. His flight from Vienna had broken all outward bonds to the religion of his ancestors.

Towards the end of 1938 the situation in France had worsened and it was clear that there was no prospect of either staying or carrying out any work. In December Karl König travelled to England and some days later wrote to the Youth Group members about Kirkton House, an old rundown Manse near Insch in Aberdeenshire. By then, Alex's permission to enter Britain had lapsed. To avoid being returned to Austria a physician friend gave him refuge in a hospital in Paris, where he stayed for over a year, faking tuberculosis, living a life of uncertainty and fear, whilst others around him were sent back to Austria.

Meanwhile, in Vienna, his parents had had to give up their apartment, and his mother her workshop. They moved to a house where Jews were packed many to each room, just a couple of hundred yards from Gestapo headquarters. Their fate was sealed. They had to carry a *kleinen Abstammungsnachweis*, 'a small proof of descent' where it stated that they were Jewish. From April 1939 onwards they had to take the compulsory middle names for Jews, Israel and Sara. Each day regulations tightened around them and escape routes closed. His mother gave Alex's Kirkton House address in 1940 to her friend, Elisa Rubik, the mother of her one-time apprentice Edith, with the request to write to Alex if anything happened to them. Although Elisa Rubik was Jewish, she was married to an Aryan, and thus she managed to survive the War.

On August 26, 1939 Alex was finally given a visa to visit Britain for twelve months. He travelled the very next day, arriving in Folkstone just a week before war was declared. He took the train immediately to Insch, and the community's old car collected him, breaking down on the way to Kirkton House. There he had to sleep in a box room that not only served as a place for ironing, but also as telephone booth, office, and linen cupboard. Discovering that certain odours made him light in the head he realized that the room was also used for medical purposes. Alex moved to nearby Williamston, until a more suitable room in Kirkton House could be found for him. Anke described Ales at that time:

He looked like a broken man as a result of having to simulate illness for so long a time. He was in a precarious state of health, besides being very melancholic and withdrawn. All during his months at Kirkton

House, he seemed not quite able to fit in, to find his place among us or the right kind of work. One remembers his heavy form and incredibly sad face — always a little on the fringe of our activities.[5]

Collar the lot — internment

> *When the men were interned in May 1940, Alex went too ... The unmarried men were sent overseas to Australia or Canada..*
>
> Anke Weihs

Winston Churchill's infamous expression 'Collar the lot' shows the panic that the Battle of Britain brought with it. On Sunday May 12, 1940, all the men were interned. Alex was listed to sail on the *Arandora Star* from Liverpool to Canada. The captain protested most strongly about the dangers of overcrowding, demanding the number of passengers be halved. The authorities refused to listen. On July 2, 1940. the *Arandora Star* was torpedoed by a U-boat seventy-five miles off Ireland, and sunk with a loss of 743 lives. And Alex? 'At the last moment his name was removed from the list of those sailing, and he was kept back to wait for another boat.'[6]

Why Alex's name was taken off the list at the last moment, is a mystery. By fleeing from Vienna, Alex had by his own action saved his life. Now it slowly dawned on him that by missing the *Arandora Star,* his life had been saved, but this time by an agent other than himself.

Alex was by then well versed in anthroposophy and probably knew of a lecture Rudolf Steiner gave on the mission of Christian Rosenkreutz, in which he spoke of the significance of becoming aware that one's life has been saved:

You were saved by something akin to chance and since then a second life has as it were been planted on the first; this second life is to be regarded as a gift bestowed upon you and you must act accordingly ... A man who can recall such an occurrence — and everyone sitting here can discover something of the kind in their lives if they observe closely enough — has the right to say to himself: Christian Rosenkreutz has given me a sign from the spiritual world that I belong to his stream.[7]

As a silent witness of this realization, in later years Alex had in his study Rembrandt's picture of *A Man in Armour.* Steiner allegedly identified this as being a portrait of Christian Rosenkreutz.[8]

Alex sailed for Canada on another ship some days later. Once ashore he chose work that allowed him to read whilst he attended to his duties; for instance, while working as a painter he would sit on a ladder and read until a supervisor came to make him work. Later, working as a medical orderly he was able to read, as there was not much work to do.

Peter Howe relates hearing, he thinks from Alex himself, that on arriving in Canada, Alex had the experience of knowing the place and of having been there before.

Camphill in the War

In the course of 1941, Alex was released and returned to Britain and Camphill. He was greatly restored in health and began to take his place among us and in the work we were building up together. Not being a practical man, it was quite a while before he found a task most suited to his abilities and temperament. For a while he took over the kitchen in Camphill House where, stirring in the pots, he looked for all the world like a medieval alchemist mixing his substances! ...

Alex had acquired a formidable knowledge of Rudolf Steiner's work, and possessing an enyclopaedic memory, he became for us an infallible source of information as to when and where a particular lecture was held.

Anke Weihs

Barbara Lipsker recalled: 'In the very first years in Camphill, until Thesi appeared, Alex is in my memory a warm-hearted friend, a "quiet water" who carried in his depths knowledge, wisdom and a kind of superiority.'

Therese von Gierke (Thesi), who was to become Alex's wife, had come to England at the beginning of 1937 to help William Mann, one of the pioneer Waldorf school teachers in Britain, with his children, Christopher and Roswitha, whilst his wife, Liselotte, was convalescing. The Nuremberg Laws of 1935 'For the Protection of German Blood and German Honour,' affected Thesi because her paternal grandmother, Lilli Loening, was Jewish, and had married Otto von Gierke, a lawyer, later Professor of Law at Berlin University. In 1939 her father asked Thesi if she would return to Britain, adding, 'If you leave Germany, we may never see each other again.' Her father could not imagine leaving Germany, even though he had various offers abroad. She was determined to leave. Her father's premonition was fulfilled — he died just after the War. Thesi had left Germany because she was determined to marry a person of her own choosing, and not be restricted to those of Jewish descent.

Thesi came to Camphill in the autumn of 1941. During that summer the Viennese group had discussed whether they should take in others, as the growing work called for more hands. When Thesi arrived Dr König led her up to his library to show her that he had her father's, Edgar von Gierke's, book on pathological anatomy.

Thesi had come to Camphill to look after the child Tilla König was expecting. When the child was stillborn, she took on other tasks; yet children, especially small children, were her lifelong interest. Thesi came from a family of academics and had been educated at a Gymnasium (Grammar School) in her hometown of Karlsruhe in southwest Germany. She loved small children and had a talent for practical work. In Camphill she met Alex, who, despite having grown up with his mother's sewing workshop at home and having left school before he was fourteen to work in a factory, was not practical by nature.

At St John's 1942 Thesi and Alex went to Karl König to tell him that they wished to marry. They could not know that in November 1941 Rosa and Arthur Baum had been amongst nine hundred and ninety nine people transported from Vienna to the Minsk ghetto which had just been 'cleansed' by killing thousands of Russian Jews.

The Baums had been met with dreadful conditions. No records tell of the exact fate of the many thousands who lived and died in the Minsk ghetto. Three survived from the Twelfth Transport, the group which had included Alex's parents.[9] On Tuesday, July 28, 1942 an 'Aktion' was planned. Some twenty-five thousand Jews were assembled in the Yubileynaya Square in Minsk. The leader of the Jewish council in the Ghetto, Moshe Yaffe, was ordered to speak to them and calm them down, but instead he shouted that they should run for their lives. He was killed, as were most of those assembled. If Alex's parents had managed to survive the harsh conditions for the seven months since the Twelfth Transport from Vienna had arrived in the ghetto, it is probable that they died then, with those brave words of freedom ringing in their ears.

Thesi and Alex married on Monday, February 22, 1943, with Willi Sucher and Karl König as witnesses. It was the middle of the War and in his speech König spoke about a Jewish boy marrying a German girl. That day was also Dr Ita Wegman's last birthday. She died ten days later. Her picture always hung in Alex's study. He felt a deep affiliation to this close co-worker of Rudolf Steiner, who had founded the medical work inspired by anthroposophy.

After Alex and Thesi were married, Alex spoke to Dr König telling him that he would like to take over the garden in Camphill. König thought it a splendid idea. Alex said he wished to have three boys as garden apprentices and teach them gardening. Later, light-heartedly, Alex said that the reason for his wishing to take over the garden was that his predecessor, Peter Roth, talked far too much to get any work done.

Thesi and Alex's first child, Christopher Karl, was born on March 25, 1944. Another staff child, John Christopher Rohde, who was born a month later, also in Camphill, was nursed by Thesi at the same time, because his mother was too ill to feed him herself. Thesi continued nursing him for seven weeks while his mother hovered between life and death.

After the War

> *Alex emerged more and more as one of the teachers ... It was as a*
> *leading member of the Teachers' College when St John's School*
> *was founded in 1948, that Alex spent the remainder of his years in*
> *the North.'*
>
>   Anke Weihs

Alex and Thesi's second child, John Lewis, was born on August 24, 1945, on the same day and in the same place as Susan Bould, the third child of Reg and Mollie Bould, one of the first English couples to have settled in Camphill. Mollie needed immediate surgery after the birth and was unable to feed her baby. Consequently, during Susan's first month Thesi found herself once again nursing two babies. Susan and John, together with another staff child, Barbara Cooke (formerly Koch), were christened by Peter Roth in January 1946; his first christenings after being ordained in London fifteen months earlier.

In September that year, a letter was posted in Vienna. It was addressed to Alex Baum, of Kirkton House, Culsalmond, near Insch in Aberdeenshire. The writer had found the address in the rubble of her bombed out house in Vienna. In 1940 Alex's mother had given the address to her friend, Elisa Rubik, in case anything should happen to her and to Alex's father. The letter, bearing the Austrian Censor stamps, arrived at Insch, and was readdressed to Camphill. Alex opened the letter and must have read it many times. He put it in the small leather wallet, in which had been placed the few papers he had needed when he fled from Vienna, together with the photographs of his parents and his grandmother. Nothing else was ever added to the wallet throughout his life. He spoke to no one about the letter. The writer had written that if he contacted her, she would be able to tell him a little about his parent's fate before they were deported. He never replied. The wallet lay untouched in his writing desk — a silent witness to the world of his childhood and youth.

In 1947 Peter Roth was one of three in Camphill struck down by polio. Throughout the middle of that February Peter was critically ill. Then, on February 17, while preparations were being made for a children's carnival in Newton Dee, a tragic accident resulted in the death of eighteen-month-old Susan Bould. It was at this time that Peter began to recover. Karl König experienced an inner relation between the death of the child and the recovery of the man.

Whilst still living in Camphill Lodge, a third child, Angela Katherine, was born to Alex and Thesi on March 30, 1947. The birth took place in Camphill House, with Janet McGavin as midwife and Lotte Sahlmann as doctor. Angela was the first child to be born in Camphill House since the estate had been bought seven years before. Years later her mother told Angela that Lotte had read a Steiner lecture to her during her labour.

Karl Schubert, the first curative teacher at the first Waldorf School in Stuttgart, visited Camphill in October 1948 to open St John's School. Alex spoke to Karl Schubert asking for pedagogical advice and some weeks later wrote a letter thanking him and asking further questions concerning the children in his care. On Christmas Day Karl Schubert replied, giving advice and concluded:

It was a very great joy and a beautiful experience of humanity to see and to speak to you. What you have experienced as a coming to life of thoughts and intuitions does not have its origin in me but has revealed itself in the harmonious sounding together of souls. You yourself have called it forth from the realm of human spiritual depth! Therefore, I would like to thank you ... that such a conversation can become fruitful. The spirit of Camphill may also have co-operated; it lends wings to the human endeavour.[10]

Karl Schubert died some weeks later. His portrait was always in Alex's study.

Soon afterwards the family moved to Newton Dee. Irmgard Lazarus described the struggles Alex had to find his place in Camphill:

The really deep friendship with Alex came about through misfortune, because Newton Dee was too big for him and also for Thesi. And he re-acted to this in such a way that he could not move (inwardly) at all any-more. He was, as it were, inwardly paralysed. Despite fundamentally being a good teacher he could not cope anymore with the lads in school. They were far too often sent out to stand in the corridor. I spoke to him on many occasions. I had the experience of kneeling in front of him begging him to find his will again, to become active, but he was quite unable to do so.[11]

At the beginning of 1950 Camphill was asked if someone could help in St Christopher's School in Bristol. Thesi and Alex offered to take up the challenge, and they, as well as Lotte Sahlmann moved to Bristol.

On October 18, 1950, Karl König, in answering a letter from Alex, wrote: 'I am very amazed how your handwriting has changed; it is a very great advance. Hopefully it will hold.'

Anke Weihs, in her obituary of Alex, took up the significance of changing one's handwriting:

Alex neither had it easy with himself, nor was he an easy person to live with. He had a strong streak of pessimism, even negativity, often to the point of considerable brusqueness. But he had another quality, which I can only call 'chasteness,' childlike and fresh, which enabled him to wrestle through difficult moments to great kindliness and goodness. Rudolf Steiner said that a person can do much to change his character if

Alex with his six week old daughter, Angela, on his arm. The children (from left): Chris, John, Helen Cooke (formerly Koch), and Nick Blitz, in the Camphill walled garden in May 1947

he makes an effort to change his handwriting. Very early on, Alex made this effort, which was indicative of his self-imposed discipline in struggling through from the negative to the positive, something which was astonishingly discernible in his later years.

Anke was referring to these words by Rudolf Steiner:

When a man consciously changes his handwriting, he is obliged to pay attention to, and to bring the innermost core of his being into connection with what he is doing. The etheric body is strengthened in this way and the person is made healthier.[12]

Thesi was thankful in later years for the experience of running her own household in Bristol, and continued helping with community accounts for decades. After a year in Bristol the family returned to Camphill, moving into Murtle Cottage, now called St Andrew's.

On December 20, 1952 their fourth child, Thomas George, was born. A few weeks later, in January 1953, there was a great storm over the whole of north-east Scotland. The enormous trees on Murtle estate swayed in the winds. Many were uprooted and fell. Friedwart Bock saw that a tall spruce next to St Andrew's was cracked and listing dangerously towards the house. The family, and all the others living there, were quickly evacuated, and baby Tom was carried over to the library in Murtle House. After the

Sunday morning outside Newton Dee Chapel ca. 1952. From left: Nina Oyens, Kate Roth, Hans Jürgen Trier, Alex, Gerda Babendererde (von Jeetze) Leonie Wronker-Flatow (van der Stok), Peter Roth

storm the tree was felled. In all, a total of a hundred and fifty-nine trees on the estate fell in the gales.

Shortly afterwards the family moved to rooms in the basement of Murtle House, commonly known as the 'dungeon.' So many children lived in the house that seventy people regularly sat down to eat in the dining room. There was more than enough work to do. Morwenna Bucknall recalls Sundays as a time when Alex and Thesi tried to make room for their family: 'I can remember in Scotland that the Baum family used to go for a Sunday walk together — not a usual sight in Camphill in those days.'

During the years in Scotland Alex studied all of Shakespeare's plays, and together with Richard Poole, produced a memorable production of Macbeth with the Newton Dee boys and Cairnlee girls in the leading roles. They also worked together producing *Twelfth Night*, as Julian Sleigh has related when he wrote about Anke Weihs, after her death in 1987:

There was that marvellous production of Twelfth Night *in the Hut at Newton Dee. We had two producers, both very different: Richard Poole (who played Malvolio, unforgettably) and Alex Baum. Both had direct insight into what Shakespeare had in mind, but Shakespeare apparently enjoyed causing confusion by inspiring them differently. It was*

St John's School (Camphill) teachers outing to Cairn O' Mount in 1953. From left: Phyllis White, Hans Heinrich Engel, Elisabeth van der Stok, Richard Poole, Gloria Vincent, Morwenna Bucknall, Friedwart Bock, Rosemarie Kilwinsky, Ella Snoek (van der Stok), Wolfgang Beverley, Hans van der Stok, Alex Baum

wonderful to watch Anke bring about reconciliation when differences of approach threatened to shatter the whole enterprise. Anke was Viola/Cesario, and I had the privilege of being her twin Sebastian. In that performance the drama transcended that written by Shakespeare. Alex Baum was the Sea-Captain, and unforgettable too was the way he interrupted the delightful sword-fight between Anke (Cesario) and Reg Bould (Sir Andrew); with his booming voice he called out 'Put up your swords' and waved his own sword in the air. In the process he shattered the stage lights, plunging our little stage into sudden darkness. Feste (Günther Schubert) won lots of applause from the Newton Dee boys when he appeared with a broom to sweep up the broken bits.[13]

Eighteen and a half years, just one moon node after fleeing Vienna, Alex moved with his family to the Sheiling, Ringwood. He was to live there just another eighteen and a half years. Waiting for their luggage to follow from Scotland, the family stopped off for a few days in London where they visited the Natural History Museum. It was rather frightening for the four-year-old Tom, but his father reassured him that the animals were 'only stuffed.' In Westminster Abbey it was Tom's turn to reassure other visitors that the dead monarchs, glorified in their tombs, were 'only stuffed.' Tom became a professor in later life, with international tourism as his area of research.

The Sheiling — a childrens' village

For someone with so little practical ability and whose heavy body
was always a hindrance, Alex's life's deeds are truly manifold.
                                                                    Anke Weihs

When Alex and Thesi travelled south, in early spring 1957, the Sheiling needed people committed to staying. The Sheiling had begun as a Camphill Community in September 1951, but few of the co-workers had stayed for any length of time.

In 1957 Sheiling House and Watchmoor, then a small cottage, together with a rented house, Westmount, made up the community. Heathland, sand and heather dominated the landscape, with signs of a forest fire on the charred fence posts towards the forest. There was still a wartime bomb crater, in the corner of the field that would become Alex's garden when Linden House was later built.

Lotte Sahlmann had been working with severely ill children in the Sheiling Schools, Thornbury. At the end of the 1950s she moved to the Sheiling, Ringwood. She recalled: 'In the Sheiling, Ringwood, where the soil was dusty, like ash, with little life forces, we helped maladjusted children to work with the earth. In the Sheiling School, Thornbury, where the soil is good, the task was primarily to work with children, many of whom were very ill.'

In his first years at the Sheiling Alex explored many of the stone circles, barrows and ancient monuments in the south of England. On a visit to South Kennet, a large barrow near Silbury Hill in Wiltshire, Alex had a similar experience of recognition to that which he had had in Canada in 1940. Dorette Schwabe, who has lived in the Sheiling for many years, describes how he 'raced up' the hill, fired by enthusiasm, telling her that he felt he recognized the place.

Over the years Alex had become interested in photography, finding it a useful and practical tool to further his explorations. He devised and had a frame made for his camera that could convert it into a half-frame camera, thus giving twice the number of pictures on one film. At home Alex converted the kitchen into a darkroom and developed and printed his own pictures.

Alex identified himself strongly with the Sheiling. On a visit to Gloucester with his family he met a man who had lived in Camphill some years before. Seeing his children waiting patiently, the man asked, 'How many children have you got?' Alex thought a moment before replying, 'Sixty-four, I think!'

Among those who worked closely with Alex at the Sheiling were Eva Sachs and Hanne Drexel. Eva Sachs recalls:

In daily life Alex was experienced by others as being a very modest and human person. He was interested in people and loved to help on all levels, being very brotherly and warm-hearted. He was a man of vision and great knowledge, happy to share his 'riches.' He encouraged others, who felt secure in his presence. In conferences and meetings he was forward thinking and had visions. He pursued his ideas with tact and brotherliness.

Alex did not practice art but was enthusiastic and acutely aware of its value. He had a very good judgement in this realm.

He gave many lectures on the most varied subjects. One could always go to Alex, because he was a friend. One could share a real conversation with him.

Hanne Drexel adds: 'Alex loved his garden and he loved the earth. One often met him kneeling on the ground, weeding his vegetables.'

Alex was especially concerned with young people. Sandra Stoddard, who worked at the Sheiling between January 1974 and July 1975, relates:

Meeting Alex was a turning point in my life and has always stayed with me. I returned to the UK when I was twenty-eight from California where I had worked as a secretary for years, and knew very firmly that this was the time to explore what possibilities there were in the work I really wanted to do. I had time to think about this quite deeply and three points came into my mind — firstly, that working with children should be residential and not a nine to five job; then, that it was important to me to learn and study whilst working and not just wash faces and send them off to school; and thirdly, the word 'community' came very clearly to me. So I set off exploring the usual routes to children's homes and residential social work etc. then heard about the 'Steiner place at Ringwood.'

So I wrote asking to visit, and received a reply from Alex. As soon as I entered the gates of the Sheiling I knew instinctively that was it! I met Alex who seemed at first quite a strange person but also friendly and comfortable to be with. When he introduced me to Dr Lotte she immediately said: 'Well, we don't need any one at present,' but he must have had some inkling through his connections with the younger co-workers and indicated to me that I might be offered a place soon.

Alex was always someone to whom a young person could go to talk and find a listening ear, he was interesting to talk to and he always showed personal interest in the young co-workers. Later, I learned that he was thought to be more connected with the younger people than his own peers. His seminars and obvious connection to the Northern Mysteries reached into one's soul, and I can still hear his deep, melancholic voice reading the Elder Edda. 'Nine days I hung on a windswept tree' is such a strong image relative to Christianity and Easter that it always reminds me of Alex.

In 1964/65, fifty years after the First World War began and twenty-five

Stonehenge 1958. Alex
guiding a group.
Foreground: Magda
Lissau, behind: Michael
Hopkins

years after the Second World War began, Alex was working at understanding the burning question of nation and race, which had affected his
life so decisively. As part of his endeavours in this difficult field, he spoke
on different occasions on the theme:

The problems of nation and race play a big part in the events of our
time. Together with hardened ideologies they are the main agency dividing
humanity in a way that was unimaginable in former centuries. How can
humanity overcome these hindrances? War is obviously not the answer.

The generation of 1914 to 1947 saw two great world wars fought in
the name of Nationalism. The Treaty of Versailles contained the idea of
national independence, defining as nation, people speaking the same
language ... we have seen how this peace, the peace of the treaty of
Versailles, resulted in a Second World War. This time however the
concept of race came in ...

We must come back to our original question. How can we solve
within ourselves the problems of nation and race? Rudolf Steiner makes
some suggestions regarding this matter. He asks, 'Where do we look to

Carnival 1959 in the Sheiling. Alex with a pupil. Eva Sachs on the right

find the different nations?' We find them in looking into our soul. There we find the Italian, the French, the Greek, the German and the Englishman. Our soul is as wide as the nations of Europe.

There is a great difference between race and nationality. It is possible to change one's nation. In the realm of nationality we are flexible. The question of race is very different however. It needs to be grasped on a much deeper level. Perhaps it can only be understood through the biography of the individual.

The human being does not only consist of Body, Soul and Spirit, he also has a biography. We all carry within us the biography where past, present and future are interwoven. We all can look back to our childhood or look forward to old age. We carry our biography with us from birth to death. If we consider that seriously, then we might grasp what destiny is, and that to be born into a certain race is part and parcel of our biography. In the soul we can find the nations of Europe, in looking at our biography the races of the world.

We need to widen ourselves immensely in order to fully grasp and appreciate the gift of each race. At the same time it would be ever more important in understanding our fellow human beings to really try to understand the meaning of each individual biography. (August 1965)[14]

Our Nativity Play has shown us history, where the possibility of peace among nations was founded. There exists another play from Oberufer, the

The Baum Family in the New Forest 1960:
Alex, Tom, John, Thesi, Chris and Angela

Three Kings play, which tells the Christmas story according to St Matthew.
The three kings follow the star and a counter image is displayed in a
fascinating, cruel and shattering way: Herod, plotting against Mary and
the Child and murdering the innocent babes. He is shown between two
figures, the captain and the devil, the latter advising him, the captain
executing his orders. To experience this evil Trinity, was to experience
Hitler between Goering and Goebbels. This evil Trinity has survived the
actual death of their human carriers. It is still active, sowing the hatred of
races, sowing the evil that has sprung up meanwhile. Is there an answer to
the problem of race in the play? Yes, there is. According to an old
tradition, one of the kings is shown as a coloured man. Just as we have to
turn to the host of angels in the Christmas night to find the shrine of peace
for the nations, just as much have we got to look to the Star of the wise
men to find the solution for the problem of race.

So let us look to the Glory of the angels and to the Star of the wise
men. May the humbleness of the shepherds fill our hearts and the
wisdom of the kings our heads that Christ may work on earth.
(December 1964) [15]

In a dream, Dorette Schwabe had visualized a new chapel in the
Sheiling and had made a cardboard model of it. She has described how
concerned Alex was to find the best time and form for laying the foundation stone. Joan de Ris Allen, the architect of the chapel, wrote about
this:

The foundation stone was laid by Alex Baum at twelve noon on
September 5, 1972, the twenty-first anniversary of the day when the
first children came to the Sheiling Schools, Ringwood. The foundation
stone was made of copper tubing with a copper triangle at the top.
Within were placed three small boxes made of olivewood from
Bethlehem, the first containing gold, the second frankincense and the
third myrrh, for the Chapel was to be dedicated to the Three Kings.
The Stone was placed in the floor beneath the front of the future Altar.
At the time the walls were already about one-and-a-half metres high
and the workmen sat on top of them, watching the ceremony.[16]

Alex knew the Christian Community from Vienna before the War and
was involved in its work. The Christian Community was active in
Camphill during the War and he was one of the early servers, together
with Irmgard Lazarus. He worked with the intention that the services of
the Christian Community would be held in the Sheiling. Later, he was
asked to lecture at the priest seminary in Shalesbrook in England.

Alex loved to travel. In his imagination he travelled far and wide, though
in everyday life his cumbersome body did not make moving over the earth
easy for him. He had never learnt to drive, so he walked or used public
transport. The path to the letterbox in the Sheiling was well worn. Every
time he had written a letter he would walk there and post it with a real sense
of deliberation. The postal service enabled his initiatives to travel far and
wide. The path to the Sheiling library was equally well trodden by Alex. If
he wished to get hold of a certain book, he would spare no trouble. If the
British Museum was the only library with a copy, he would travel there. He
found it a great joy to open an old library book and have to cut the pages
because nobody had read it since it was published some hundred years earlier. Books took him travelling through centuries of history and culture.

He left his mark locally. With his characteristic swaying walk he could
regularly be seen on his way to Ringwood, a shopping bag in his hand,
and if anyone was close enough he might be heard reciting a favourite
poem.

In the Sheiling Thesi taught the children weaving, worked with the
finances and in the house, as well as supporting Alex's concerns and
increasing travel. In his last letter to Thesi, Karl König encouraged her:
'You should know that Alex is dependent on you, far more than you are
on him ... You must not only hold your head above water, but also help
him to swim forcefully on.'[17]

Eva Maria Rascher wrote about the formation of the Eurythmy School
in Camphill, and Alex's artistic inspirations:

Alex was full of new ideas as to how one could bring about new
centres for painting, music and eurythmy. He was deeply concerned that
we should integrate the arts into our communities in the right way, and

it was through his initiative and help that eurythmy training was able to come about within Camphill ...

During the last years of his life, it seemed as though Alex's artistic inspiration was very much concerned with the image of the Swan. He worked with us on the Schwanengesänge *by Schubert. When he returned from his journeys to Finland and Norway, he gave beautiful courses about the* Kalevala, *and in connection with this could not rest until I had found the music for the* Swan of Tuonela, *by Sibelius. In this music, the journey of the soul after death is described.*

Alex gave several lectures about Edvard Munch, in which both the artist and his pictures were very much brought to life for us. There was one lecture that was particularly vivid. He showed us the picture of a drowning man; only his head could be seen rising above the waters, and behind him were two swans. He then described carefully how Zuckmayer went to Bruegge at night. The boat went out onto the water, on which the silver light of the moon was shining. He lost consciousness and saw the swans rising out of the water. Alex explained to us that this is what we experience after death. The images he evoked during this evening linger unforgettably.[18]

At the beginning of 1974 Alex wrote to Christine Polyblank, daughter of Thomas Weihs, about the possibility of founding a Waldorf school for the children of the Sheiling families, as well as children from the wider community. She quoted the letter in an article in an issue of the Ringwood Waldorf School magazine:

'The Sheiling has gone through a number of transformations. We had for a long time hardly any staff children. That has changed and families have started to come. With this the question of the schooling of the children has arisen. I think the only constructive idea is to start a little school for them. There would be enough children to start a combined class 1–3. Heide Hoffmann has a little play group where more and more children from the surroundings join. That could in due course feed the school. There would be accommodation available and a classroom possibility. The only question would be to find the right person. Could you imagine that you could undertake such a thing?'

Christine soon visited the Sheiling, and noted:

Alex led me through the almost jungle-like undergrowth of Sticklebirch in search of a little cottage reputedly hidden away at the bottom somewhere. He believed it to be called Folly Farm ... Alex thought at the time that a preservation order had been served on it by 'a group of elderly ladies in Ringwood' mainly because it was thought to have once given refuge to Lord Nelson as he passed through the area. As the cottage could not be pulled down it remained standing empty.

It was rather small but peering through the windows we could see

Thesi and Alex at the Sheiling

*Alex at his writing
desk in Linden House*

that it was in good condition, merely covered with dust. We had the
distinct feeling that it might be waiting, keeping itself in readiness for
some good purpose ...

On September 16, 1974, a group of about twenty-one people gathered
in the largest room of Folly Farm Cottage for a ceremony to mark the
founding of our Folly Farm School (now Ringwood Waldorf School).[19]

Christine remembers Alex speaking about the word 'folly' describing
how Shakespeare often uses it to mean fantasy or imagination. 'Imagination,' he suggested, could be a leit-motif for us as the school developed.

Christine reflected on Alex's role in her life: 'When I look back over
my life I have to recognize the strong influence of Alex. The result of his
letter to me, was that it imparted purpose and direction to my life. He
pointed out a possible path, a life's path, and I accepted it.'

Alex had vision, and the wit, faith and courage to make things happen.
During his time of the Sheiling, there grew up around him a school hall,
four residential houses, a gym hall, more classrooms, a beautiful chapel, a
surgery and a swimming pool, as well as the founding of a Training
School for students aged sixteen to nineteen, a Eurythmy School and Folly
Farm School, now Ringwood Waldorf School.

Christof König remembers what he had heard about the Sheiling whilst
Alex lived there:

*Two founder members of Camphill said of Alex that he was
instrumental to bring about a real and modern Rosicrucian community
in the Sheiling, Ringwood, and I understood that this was unique in
Camphill at the time. Those who lived in the Sheiling at the time Alex
lived there were graced to have been allowed to experience these special
years with him. I understood the remarks about a modern Rosicrucian
Community as meaning that the Spirit has been brought down into the
physical places where people attempt community building. That means,
the ship has dropped its anchor, and comes into the harbour, or the
Spirit has taken in the community, and is not separate from the physical.*

Widening horizon

> *Alex extended his interests to Scandinavia, notably Norway, ... and
> here, his positive qualities in helping and advising young people
> had newer and freer scope to unfold. But also his connection with
> educational and therapeutic circles in Munich developed ... and
> many there availed themselves of his services.*
>
> Anke Weihs

Margit Engel wrote about Alex's relation to Norway:

*From the first day Alex entered Vidaråsen, he tried to listen to our
needs. At that time some of us had a longing to come to a closer
understanding of the Edda. By the time of his next visit Alex had already
done a great amount of work on this subject. He made us speak the
verses in the Old Norse language and he read and interpreted the
images with an ease of recognition, which we were hardly able to follow.*

*It seemed one of the peculiar characteristics of this personality that
his vast insights at times were difficult to get across to those who
listened. His great modesty and sensitivity let him often withdraw what
he could have brought, what he had prepared. Thus, much of his
wonderful power of thinking did not fully reach out to those whom he
met and his sensitive nature suffered over this. But in those moments
when he was at ease and his being could fully merge with those around,
precious things could come about.*[20]

Peter Roth travelled to Norway and Finland with Alex in the autumn of
1975. Alex then travelled on alone to Munich. Later, Peter wrote:

*He was a teacher; first of children, then in the seminar and then a
teacher of teachers, speaking and lecturing in the last years first about
the Edda, then on the* Kalevala. *His last two lectures in Sylvia Koti were
about Lemminkainen, the consciousness-soul-figure from the* Kalevala.

He approached the Edda and the Kalevala *not with philological interest only, but very much with the love, devotion and genius towards creations which contain not just the sorrow of the past but the hope towards the glory of the future, not just the twilight, but the resurrection of the Gods.*[21]

Whilst visiting Munich, on the afternoon of Monday, November 3, 1975, Alex suffered a heart attack and on the following afternoon he died. Alex had planned to conclude his course that Friday, with Shakespeare's *Tempest* and the words: 'Our revels now are ended ... We are such stuff as dreams are made on, and our little life is rounded with a sleep.' *(*IV, i.).

Eva Sachs had come to the Sheiling at the same time as Thesi and Alex. She had worked closely with them for many years and wrote down her experiences around Alex's death:

After his recent visit to Ireland, where he had met many friends from different Camphill places, he travelled to Norway, Sweden and Finland, from where he always used to return inspired with new impulses concerning the future. This time he went to Munich direct from Finland to hold a week's seminar in the Eurythmy School. He had intended to speak about Shakespeare and the consciousness-soul but asked the students during the first morning of the Seminar on Monday, November 3 to be patient until Friday, the last day of the course, by which time they would understand more about the working of the consciousness-soul. On Friday, at noon, the funeral service took place. We had indeed been led through new experiences of the consciousness-soul ...

Swans of great beauty accompanied us on the way to the burial service at the Waldfriedhof. This was a moving picture as Alex had recently given a lecture in the Sheiling about the swan as a messenger between our world and the spirit world. On the table stood a picture of Edvard Munch of a swan, his reflection mirrored in the water and beneath, the head of a youth who had drowned. Now we passed the swans on the way.[22]

Alex's funeral was that Friday. The next day, in a memorial Act of Consecration of Man, the priest, Irene Johanson, gave an address:

Thinking of him, one can think of the parable, that Christ told his disciples and the people: 'The Kingdom of Heaven is like a mustard seed, that a man took and sowed in his field, which is the smallest of all seeds. But when it grows, it is the biggest of all herbs and grows into a tree. And the birds of Heaven come and nest in its branches.'

Looking inwardly at Alex Baum, one can say: He was a man, who took the Kingdom of Heaven like a seed and planted it in the field of his soul. There it grew into a tree which let its roots grow deep into the Spiritual World and whose branches stretched all over Europe, from

Austria in the South to Scandinavia in the North. From Scotland in the
West to Finland in the East. And the birds of heaven, the Spiritual
Beings of innumerable People and their angels could come to him and
find inner strength and peace, orientation and food with him. His name
suited him. Now this tree is felled. But its seeds carried by all the winds
fell into manifold soils, in the souls of children, of parents, of teachers,
of friends. And they will germinate. Now the roots will grow into earthly
destinies and the crown with the branches will reach into the Spiritual
World. We all will be caretakers of this widespread tree-nursery.
Responsible for his seed, Father Baum, who rooted in Heaven and
branched in the earthly realm, will remain connected with those who
root in the earthly realm and strive into the Spiritual with their
branches.[23]

Just as Irene Johanson began to speak about the large tree, birds began
to sing outside, even though it was already November, and they continued
singing whilst she spoke. Then they were silent.

Anke Weihs, concluding her obituary of Alex, wrote:

Like Hans Heinrich Engel and Carl Alexander Meier, Alex, after
many years spent in Britain, went back to the Continent to die; as it
were, back to his language-home, and as I have heard, he must have
had the beauty of a poet in his face as he lay in death in Munich. That
Alex died in Munich has perhaps another kind of significance; for
Munich was the stronghold of that Nazidom by which he was so deeply
hurt in his youth. Perhaps it was one of his acts of goodness and
reconciliation to go there at the end.[24]

Near the end of his life, tapping away with two fingers on his old typewriter, Alex wrote some notes where themes in his life are alluded to; his
first memories, his life with children in need of care, and Christianity:

Where is the sphere where we men are all equal?

The only moment where we all become equal is the moment of death.
I know that it is one of the most impressive things for anybody who has
grown up in Old Austria to witness and to have heard how the burial of
the Hapsburg emperors was. They were the mightiest people of their
time. One of them could say with right: 'In my empire the sun never
sets.' That was Charles V. But when they were dead the procession with
the coffin went through the city of Vienna and when they arrived at the
old monastery of the Capuchins, the gate was locked. The master of
ceremonies knocked three times at the gate. There came from inside the
voice of one of the capuchin monks, asking: 'Who asks to be admitted?'

And then the master of ceremonies quoted the 'long title' of the
emperor: 'Emperor of Austria, King of Hungary, defender of the faith,
King of Jerusalem ...' and so on for pages and pages. And the answer
was: 'I know him not.' And then the master of ceremonies knocked a

second time. And the voice of the old monk came again: 'Who asks to be
admitted?' And then the so-called short title was given that went perhaps
over a quarter of a page. But the old monk answered: 'I know him not.'
And then the master of ceremonies knocked a third time, but this time the
answer was: 'A poor sinner.' And the door was opened. This is the full
statement of equality. And if we insist on equality only we insist that we
all die and not more.

Where are the other spheres? — The sphere of fraternity lies in the
fact that we are all born. And we are all born unequally. Look at our
children! Some are born with brain damage, others are born with other
ailments; everything that the fall of man implies. But it is so; as Christ
went through birth, we should see the brotherliness. Whatever our I.Q.
we sit together, not because we are equal, but because we recognize that
in the other one lives Christ as a brother.

And where is the sphere of freedom? It is the one beyond death. There
we become free, any moment we can unite with the power of
resurrection, because the power of resurrection is the power of freedom.
And there we are not equal either, but at any moment and on any of us
the Holy Spirit may descend and declare our freedom.

Therefore the sphere of brotherliness is: Ex Deo nascimur; the sphere
of equality: In Christo Morimur and the sphere of the Holy Spirit is: Per
Spiritum Sanctum Reviviscimus.

To insist on equality only, means to remain at the cross, remain at
Good Friday and deny the Resurrection.'

Trude Amann

(March 22, 1915 – March 28, 1987)

Peter Howe

'That was the end'

There is an extraordinary passage in Trude's autobiographical sketch of her childhood and youth, written towards the end of her life for the great friend and companion of her later years, Petra Julius:

My good little mother loved me well enough that she never reproached me for leaving Vienna without farewell. Perhaps she had some premonition that this leaving was for good and that we would never see each other again?

Hitler came between — in the next holidays I was not able to return to Austria. Everything that constituted home for me since I was born — everything I owned, books, photographs, school books, everything dispersed forever. My parents had to get out of the apartment and leave the business — my father became ill and died in hospital. Mother landed in Theresienstadt and then in Auschwitz — that was the end — and I went to Scotland and my Camphill destiny began. Later, whenever I read in Rudolf Steiner that each person has a guarding angel who leads and guides him and watches over him, I knew that that was absolutely true.

The inward progression and transformation from 'that was the end' to the confidence and conviction in spiritual guidance and meaning, is the hallmark, not only of this modest and unassuming life, but also of the early Camphill. Hers is a response to the Holocaust which takes one's breath away; the emotional and existential wrestling which must have been needed to bring this about one can only begin to imagine. The social and community struggles that went on in the melting pot of the early Camphill are well documented; the personal grief and struggles to over-come it were never spoken about. From then on, Trude's biography fuses with that of the movement she was instrumental in founding. The details and achievements of her personal life are barely recorded or remembered.

Holiday camp
from c. 1930/31.
Trude (centre),
Lisl (right) who
were helpers.
The girl on the
left is one of the
children.

One could say, perhaps, that like many of the older generation of co-workers, self-effacing and fulfilled in Camphill's chosen tasks, Trude's legacy
is Camphill itself.

The landscape of childhood

Trude Blau was born in spring, the first spring of the First World War, into
the most modest of homes — the family of a struggling locksmith, in the
Jewish district of Vienna. The flat, at Rotensterngasse 22/9, which was no
more than a 'couple of rooms and the kitchen' was home to Trude, her parents and older sister Lizzi, until she left home for Switzerland as a young
woman. There is, though, no hint of deprivation: the loving and able
mother created a warm and ample home even in these strained circumstances. The autobiographical sketch starts with memories of the Sabbath:

On Fridays in the afternoon, however, there was but one main aim:
getting back home from school, quickly bidding adieu to Eva Schreibers
and all the 'very best' friends. Running upstairs and sniffing, yes, it smelt
of freshly baked white bread in the form of a giant plait with tiny black
poppy seeds sprinkled on top, and it smelt of covered apple cake and of
meat! Mutti already had her special dark blue dress on, with some
narrow white lace held by a brooch at her throat. Our flat was a-shine
with 'being tidied' — also my and Lizzi's things were all in their
appointed places once more — nothing lay about unnecessarily. I was

allowed to stand at the window and gaze into the small square of dark blue sky, until I saw 'it,' the first star. Only then Mutti would speak the blessing over the lit candles with a deeply festive mien and hands outspread. The light of the candles shone on her hair. Nearly always she and I were alone in these few moments, a steadfastness of faith flowed to me through her, for always. This blessing of the candles and the bread was the upbeat for the Sabbath. There followed a festive evening meal, a quiet Saturday until once again the first star showed in the darkening sky.

Sunday was quite different ... an early breakfast, the rucksack packed, the apartment locked. We took the tram to the terminus: Grinzing. In hot sun and through the green wood up on to Kahlenberg. Under the dense and high beeches the ground was covered with white and purple violets, delicate pale green sorrel, whose leaves tasted so refreshingly sourish! We were rested and well pleased. Up on the mountain the first weariness began but I didn't really give in to it, there was too much to look forward to in the picnic, well stowed in the rucksack!

From the two windows of the flat the young girl gazes out, from the very first an observer of the world rather than a doer, perceptive of nature and human nature, rejoicing in life.

[She saw] and experienced much; the world expanded and opened out: the small section of sky, blue in spring, many swallows flitting across; the thick carpet of big, soft snowflakes falling unceasingly to earth until roofs and streets and everything were muffled in thick white snow. Then the world became so silent and so clean. And then I knew; now it is November and soon the chocolate figures of St Nicholas and Ruprecht would appear in the lit-up shop-windows. Then in the evening, before we went to bed, we would quickly draw back the curtain in order to see the many clear stars sparkling in the cold winter sky.

But it was unbearably sad when it poured from the grey sky, pouring mercilessly in torrents, when just this Sunday we wanted to go up the Kahlenberg, there to pick primroses, violets and lungwort ...

... Late spring in Vienna! Bright sunshine over the city. Renewed joy of life rises in everybody ... On such spring days I was intoxicated by the very air and left the dark apartment for the road. Alone, or the two of us, the way went over the Swedish Bridge to the inner city — along the Kärntnerstrasse, round the corner, past the Opera House, along the Ring — always the whole way along the Ring! On one or the other corner stood an old woman with posies of early snowdrops and dark, sweet-scented violets. When I had decided on one of the posies and bought it, I lived in the delight of it the following days ... But the sun set early in the afternoon and we quickly picked handfuls of scented, dark violets and wood anemones, whose heads would droop before we got home. But there were so-o-o many on the Prater meadows in spring. And it was on

such an early spring day that I experienced something which never went from my feeling again. In thinking about it, when I try to imagine at what age this experience might have happened, it seems to me that I am not more than three, or at the most four years old.

I feel myself toddling behind my mother along our narrow street. I was holding on to her skirts with one hand. Then suddenly she stopped in front of the tiny greengrocer's on our street and suddenly I look up. Something new comes into my view. On a wooden trestle, facing the road, there are baskets and shallow bowls filled with early vegetables, to tempt customers. Amidst the bright green, there stand stripped branches about which the first early cherries are wound shining brightly, drawing the child's eyes with their magic. Then, suddenly, mother's skirt moves again and my hand does not let go. All at once though, I feel my knees stretch and with a shock when we go further I feel a quite strong, overwhelming feeling of walking, with straight, stretched-through legs! From toddler with flabby knees to a walking child — this was given to me consciously and connected me forever with the strong experience of the gleaming red cherries placed amidst the bright green.

Was that then the earliest experience of my own 'I'?

Again and again, Trude remembers the flowers, the seasons, the festivals, the birthdays — the landscape of childhood, which will be obliterated for her at a stroke, but which she will spend a lifetime re-creating for generations of children.

At school, she meets one teacher who gives her a lesson which will become inscribed in her and lay a foundation for the curative teacher who will encourage and challenge countless pupils and young co-workers in the years to come. For years she receives top marks at school, not by dint of much effort, but because she is liked by her teachers.

And then suddenly a flash of lightning out of the clear sky: with the first report after Professor Noel's entry to our class as French teacher, there was a resplendent 'insufficient' among all the marks. Horrified, I blinked at the mark: 4! It didn't change, there it stood, black on white. The longer I looked, quite uncomprehending the 4 seemed to mock me. When I got home I put the whole report with its envelope into my bottom drawer ... The following day it was back to the Gymnasium, full of a devout hope that it might after all have been a mistake. Perhaps the 4 was really meant for another pupil? Then Prof. Noel called me to the teacher's room in the break and explained (using the polite form 'Sie'): 'I know you don't quite understand and therefore I shall explain it to you. You have worked just as little in my lessons as in all the other subjects, and thought it would continue as in previous years. I, however, know that you could work if you wanted to. This time you have earned the mark 4; if however you wake-up and begin to learn I shall straightway be

Trude with her class in 1931 (she is second from left)

prepared to write a one in your next report. But only if you earn it, not just mechanically because you are Trude Blau. Do you understand?' Oh yes! I had understood with my soul, with my mind, with my will. And I was terribly ashamed, embarrassed and at the same time I was furious!

... I had myself learned far more out of this kind of treatment, learned far more for my whole life than learning French would ever have taught me. At last I had met a teacher who was above all a fine person and to whom I could look up because he had seen through me.

Was it a coincidence that he was called 'Christmas'?

'You must come and help me, I am doing something wonderful'

As the youthful heart awakens, friendships arise, encounters happen, the worlds of music, theatre and dancing open up, love stirs, and the inner voices of a future vocation begin to call.

An early friend was Hans Schauder, who seems to have been instrumental in leading Trude to many of these experiences. Together they attended a rehearsal of Mahler's Eighth Symphony, conducted by Bruno Walter:

Our purses were too lean to buy tickets for the actual performance but our souls were wide open and when the orchestra began to play under Bruno Walter's dancing baton, oh then my heart began to beat ever more loudly; the whole world around my head vanished and the heavens were opened. After the last sounds died it was silent for a long while and in me something new was born: the certainty that life was good and was also beautiful and that I myself would want to live it in that way, so that my

A passport picture

'being-good' would always be helpfully there for other people. An endless strength was in me, awoken and confirmed by this wonderful music.

Another of the group of young friends attending the concert was Willi Amann, himself an enthusiastic musician and violinist, which 'he does much better than speaking.' An innocent young love blossomed between them. Together they queued for concerts, swam in the icy cold Danube, and walked for hours 'in order to bear the feeling of indescribable happiness.' Willi brought her branches of blossoming lilac and long-stemmed roses, which she was happy to accept 'as though life of course owed me that.'

But it was with Hans, who was a few years older, that she went to the Christian Community, to an Act of Consecration of Man in which the priest, Dr Frieling, spoke in his New Year's sermon about 'the three gifts of Man': uprightness, speech and thinking.

As he came to an end everything in me said, 'Yes' — even to Dr Frieling presenting Christ as the helper of Humanity for the attainment of these three attributes.

From this moment on something became ripe and matured in me. The Judaism in me began to become the past and what bore the future had begun. The name 'Christ' suddenly meant something to me — but I also knew that it was the first more profound experience that I would not be able to share with my mother. This knowledge remained painful for many, many years, growing pains that to this very day have not entirely gone.

On leaving school, Trude worked as an apprentice and qualified as a tailor and dressmaker, work which she loathed so much that afterwards she never made another dress in her life.

Then, crucially, Hans insisted that she attend a particular lecture with him: 'just because Hans says "Trude you *must*." That is a magic word.'

The lecturer demonstrated and explained curative exercises carried out at his home for 'children in need of soul-care' in Switzerland. He was Werner Pache from the Sonnenhof.

Like a lightning flash his words went into me. In this moment a fog had been lifted from me. I knew it clearly, distinctly, without any doubt, 'That is where I must go, that is what I want to learn and do in my life.'

Still in the same night I wrote to the Sonnenhof.

After an initial refusal because of her youth, and then her insistence that she must come now, she at last received an acceptance.

Very rarely in my life has such a wave of joy risen in me as in this moment when I held the letter in my hand with its momentous content.

Even before this, at a still tender age, Trude was already a secure and confident presence with children and young people and her contemporaries. Barbara Lipsker describes meeting her for the first time, Barbara then being eighteen:

Hans and Lisl said I must meet a wonderful young girl. And when I did, I can say, she did not look so very different from how she was when she grew older: bright eyes, pink cheeks, short hair, a sturdy body, and with an inner warmth and energy. She said 'You must come and help me, I am doing something wonderful.' So I went with her to the Arbeiter Kinderheim, which was a barracks with lots of children, twelve or

In Arlesheim, February 1949

thirteen years old, some rather rowdy. And Trude stood there in the midst of them like a rock, in absolute command, emanating a natural authority, and an accepted friend to whom they looked up. I was very impressed and though I was older, she seemed to tower in maturity and I wondered, How is this possible? From this experience I could derive help for myself — through her warmth, strength and security.

Although Trude mixed socially with several of Karl König's youth group, and was introduced to anthroposophy by Rudi Lissau, she makes no mention of group meetings. Undoubtedly she was part of the 'first youth group' for it was only later that she met the Roths, Carlo Pietzner and Thomas Weihs. By the time they joined the group, in late 1936, she would already have left for Arlesheim. When exactly she met König remains unclear, but one can imagine his enthusiasm and support for her choice of career.

Arlesheim — Kirkton House — Camphill

So, at the age of twenty-one she made her way to Arlesheim, Switzerland, seeking her future with children in need of special care, and with anthroposophy. She made the decision whilst on holiday in Switzerland with Willi, and informed her parents by letter. She could not know that it would be nine years before she could return to Vienna, and by then everything would be different.

After an arduous journey, the warm and welcoming community at the Sonnenhof greeted her:

My glance was caught by a young girl, who at every step she took there on the lawn, threw up her arms, her legs going in all directions, she squinted violently and tried to speak to me — in English! She was the first child with cerebral palsy I ever saw and came from Birmingham. She was called Elma. At this moment my three year course in the Sonnenhof began, each moment of which I loved. But next to Elma who moved so very strangely, my glance happened to range over the walls of the Sonnenhof, past the vineyards in the distance and was caught by the Birseck [Castle] and the dark woods and green meadows that stood roundabout, shimmering in the midday heat, the Eremitage!
— My destiny with children in need of special care of the soul had begun and my thankfulness has never ceased.

During the three year course in *Heilpädagogik* she would have been instructed by Pache, Bort, Ita Wegman and the other pioneers in the new discipline of curative education, which had been initiated only a dozen years previously by Rudolf Steiner. It set the course for the whole of Trude's working life; she had found her vocation.

In 1938, a few days before her twenty-third birthday and in the second

Kirkton House Group 1939. Standing: Willi Amann, Peter Roth, Anke Roth, Thomas Weihs, Alex Baum, Tilla König. Sitting: Trude Blau, Marie Blitz, Alix Roth

year of the course, the Nazis invaded Austria. Her mother was to die in Auschwitz, her father in hospital, while her sister Lizzi found her way to America and became a doctor.

Trude was invited to join the circle of friends from Vienna who planned to start curative work in Scotland. During a brief holiday with Willi in Paris, there was the occasion where Peter Roth, Thomas Weihs and Trude Blau — red, white and blue — met for the first time. The story became part of the folklore of Camphill: the tricolour, the revolutionary virtues of Freedom, Equality and Brotherhood, which were to underlie Camphill. Equally, the three names are a poignant reminder that the Jewish community in Austria were obliged to adopt the names of colours in place of their true names in order to be allowed some degree of freedom and equality. (In Germany, names of trees were often used; in Spain, flower names.) This would become a characteristic gesture of the Camphill community: to take on the destiny of the outcast, the outsider, and transform it into a healing social force.

The life of the embryonic community in Kirkton House is well documented. Trude's role was a particular one. Anke Weihs later remembered her with:

... a jacket with big orange and brown squares, unforgettable! This jacket had big, deep pockets and all the while we were scrubbing Trude kept her hands in her pockets. And I remember Tilla König hissing like

Outside Camphill House 1942

an angry pussycat, 'Why can't she take her hands out of her pockets?'
But this was not Trude's way. In scrubbing, as in dressmaking, Trude
had no ambitions.
Yet she represented the clear pure waters of anthroposophical
curative education. Not that we had too many subjects to practice it on!
Trude was imperturbable and strong. In her gait she stepped very
manfully on her heels. Her hands had long tapering fingers — not the
hands of a charwoman! — soft and cushioned. But they were not weak
hands, but could hold a child, and in this holding could give a child an
enormous sense of security, holding the child in a very definite way.
Hands that were comforting in appearance. Trude, coming from a very
different Viennese background and having been in the Sonnenhof, was
alien to me, although perhaps we were all alien to each other! Yet Trude
was outspokenly one of the Early Brothers of the Camphill Community.
She was there, playing her part in this building up in the early and
crucial years, especially in Camphill Estate.

Those of us who knew her in later years can recognize in this description that the formidable matriarch, devastatingly successful with the
wildest children, unflinching in her convictions and absolutely secure in
her self-belief, was already fully formed in the young woman. It must
have taken a remarkable sense of purpose and self-possession to oppose
Tilla König's own indomitable will. And it must have been difficult for the
desperately overworked group to understand and accept her 'lack of ambition' for practical work. Her strength lay in her observation rather than in

With a lyre

practical activity, and Anke Weihs also recalled that Trude was the first one of the group whom König asked to become a Service Holder for the lay services which were soon being conducted. She was also, of course, one of the fabled six women who sat around the candle in Kirkton House, debating the decision to move to Camphill House.

Trude had one advantage over the others, in that she was the only one trained in working with children with special needs. As Barbara Lipsker said later, 'Next to her, only Dr König could extend that recognition and inner conviction for the child. What could be difficult in Trude, at times, was out-shone by that which she could give to the children.'

The young group, with its emerging vision of community building in the widest and most profound sense, experienced traditional anthroposophical curative education as a limiting, restricting thing. Yet Trude's considerable achievement was to hold fast to curative education whilst recognizing the greater vision of what would become Camphill. Using the 'scrubbing' as a metaphor for the energetic and youthful will of the early Camphill, Peter Roth said:

Scrubbing was full of prophecy, containing — like an egg — the

With one of the children

*future of Camphill, the impulse and the community. Trude ... would not
scrub, but she experienced that what was in the scrubbing was
worthwhile. She had a great understanding with Dr König in that they
both knew curative education. Trude knew something had to be added
to curative education, therefore she lived with us. Yet in the first years
she asked herself, 'Is it right that I give my experience with
handicapped children to Camphill?'*

Not a renunciation, then, of her gifts and previous training, but a willingness to put them at the service of a greater social whole — Trude's
achievement, which was an extraordinarily difficult balancing act in a
close-knit community, was again a quality which became a hallmark of
the early Camphill.

In 1940 Trude heard for the last time from her mother before she died
in Auschwitz. Near the end of her life, Trude's memories of her mother
resurfaced:

*She was so small, so quiet, so always there — I hardly experienced
her consciously and yet — I was protected, I was loved.*

*And now as I get older, I experience her more strongly with every
passing year.*

*I know that in my innermost being, there where I am strong, it is
because she believed in me so strongly. Ever and again even now I find
my way back to myself because her love carried me, without ever
doubting, throughout my childhood.*

*Thus she was able in March 1940, in the year Hitler's hordes were
poisoning Vienna, to write me a letter so full of love:*

With Anke at the St John's picnic

'*My dear dear Trudl!*

Today before anything else I would wish you as many happy returns as I am altogether able. When you first saw the light of this world 25 years ago, it was just such a sunny morning, so that I asked the midwife whether the sun was shining in your face, and might harm your eyes. Naturally she denied it. It was the beginning of spring! And thus I wish you my dear Truderl that your whole life's course may only be shone upon by the sun. Keep yourself well, fresh and joyful and may you be as happy as I could wish you and as you yourself might wish.

I am so sad that I am not permitted to send anything, as I used to send you, but that is now also not possible. I hope you will be well, really well on this day, your birthday and have an especially lovely day.

Yours, your loving Mutti'

This was my last birthday letter from her, before she died in Auschwitz — thus I wander back into that space in my life which was completely filled with my mother and it gives me strength. I know that also my 'being able to believe,' my 'religion' have only become firm and real because her essence flowed from her into me during my childhood.

For that I am boundlessly grateful!

It was also during these early Camphill years that Trude and Willi were married, but it was sadly short-lived. Willi left Camphill as part of the group with Hans and Lisl Schauder who started the Garvald project near Edinburgh. Trude kept his name.

During these tumultuous years, König wrote for Trude the imagination 'Brother and Sister,' which is an extended contemplation of the painting by Raphael, *Madonna del Belvedere* (or *Madonna in the Meadows*) which hangs in the Kunsthistorisches Museum in Vienna and would have been well known to them. By any standards this poem is an extraordinary work of art, of such profundity and complexity that it defies description. Although it can be read on many levels, knowing that it was written for Trude reveals that it sprang also from König's deep and lively involvement with her destiny. Above all, it is about the ability of the human being, in union with Christ, to transform wretched and bitter experiences of destiny into life-affirming, healing strengths. One can imagine that its wisdom and depth of feeling gave Trude leitmotivs that led her very far in life.

Camphill

After the War, during the rapid expansion of Camphill's activities and the spread of its work, one can imagine Trude coming into her own as one of the first generation of Camphill 'matrons.' With her perceptive eye, her instinctive understanding for the children and young co-workers, and her general unflappability, she could pour her motherly warmth, her interest and her moral authority into the task. Generations of young volunteers attest to the profound influence Trude had on the lives and development of both themselves and their pupils. Gerda Holbek, who herself became an outstanding housemother, said:

What was most outstanding was her love for children, the young children of staff as well as the handicapped children. Equally outstanding was the love the children had for Trude.

She had a special way of teaching, strict and demanding, but with love. She knew the people she worked with; she knew that I had to change and that it would have to be the hard way! When there was a difficult situation I could accept it because I knew she knew me and loved me. In my very first dormitory I had a very charming Down's syndrome girl, but I did not like her. I don't know why, but I didn't. This little girl became ill and I looked after her. We were both standing next to Susan's bed and Trude said, 'You know, when a Down's child is not loved, they can die.' That was all she said. Then I nursed Susan and I learned to like her and I also learned that one can get to love every child and every person if one wants to.

Ebba Booth, now in South Africa, describes the profound influence Trude could exert, not through an overbearing will, but through seeing into a person and understanding their deeper desires. After a year in Trude's house, Ebba was more than ready to return to her native Germany:

Trude called me to her office and asked me what my plans were. She let me do the talking, got up, looked me straight, almost sternly in the eye and with the door already open, asked very slowly and solemnly,

What about the children? The door closed and a few minutes later there wasn't a shadow of a doubt in my mind that I wouldn't be leaving.

From personal experience I recollect Trude's great affinity to the 'difficult' children, who had behavioural problems. You didn't dare to complain about the problems you had with a particular child in your dormitory, as this was almost like affronting her. You could ask her for help and she would quietly take the child, sometimes asking you to come along. It is difficult to put into words the transformation that took place in the child; to witness it was remarkable. Trude radiated such peace, love and compassion that for a moment it almost felt as though she and the child became one entity.

Clearly, life with Trude was not a soft option! Her uncompromising belief in not only the children's potential, but also your potential, came before all, even friendship. But then, this is the very highest form of friendship: friendship as it is described in the New Testament, John 15:12–17, a text that is central to the spirituality of Camphill.

For most of her life Trude was based in Camphill Estate, but in 1952 Camphill was asked to help with the running of a small children's home, Brockham End near Bath, a project which lasted just a few months. From there Trude joined the group who were starting the new Camphill centre at Thornbury House. She helped to build up this community until 1960 when she returned to Camphill Estate where she would spend the rest of her life.

For ten years, Trude became a class teacher in the St John's School in Camphill, where the younger children of co-workers were taught alongside the pupils with special needs. Equally skilled and assured in the classroom as in the home, Trude's creativity and love for music, colour and drama found even fuller expression.

In an article in *The Cresset* Trude wrote:

... the pupil is gradually introduced to the discipline of painting — and I use the word 'discipline' with great emphasis. In our time much stress is laid on the young child's 'freedom' to choose their own materials for their first artistic ventures, out of a bewildering manifoldness. The child's path to 'free expression' is paved forcefully at an early age by modern teaching methods. This is done especially at the time when the school child is trying to find in his teacher one who 'knows'— who knows what is beautiful, what is ugly.[1]

Given this framework of discipline — which is the teacher's inner discipline over herself — pupils flourished. Another article about poems in Class 8 demonstrates this, along with the other side of Trude which was perhaps less obvious to colleagues, but could find full expression with her children — her sense of fun and joy in life:

It was in Class 3 that I first encouraged the children to make up their own little poems. The response was joyous and quite a number of the

*class came forward with four-line rhymes. Five years later we took it up
again. It was the birthday of our Eurythmy teacher and the children
wanted to bake her an apple-cake, her favourite. I suggested they write
a funny poem to present with the cake.*

*The response was immediate and overwhelming. One girl said: 'Oh,
that's easy, I can make dozens of poems and always do so for myself in
the evening before going to sleep, but I forget them again.'*

*I called her to the blackboard and then it was I who gasped. One
poem after another just spilled out and the pace of her writing was far
too slow compared with the wealth of rhymes. Other children followed
and the result was nearly the same. It was as if the lid had been removed
and at long last these fourteen-year-olds could unburden themselves of
all that had been stored in their minds.*[2]

One of the children's poems from that issue of *The Cresset* is repro-
duced here:

The Wind and the Waves
The wind is a thing we can hardly see,
The waves are very strange for me,
But I don't mind so very much about the wind and waves
And such and such —
If you go out on a summer day
You'll hear the wind far, far away.

                                                  Gillian Epstein (aged 14)

It is touching, then, to discover that on hearing of her teacher's death, seventeen years later, Gillian sent another poem:

Dedicated to the memory of Trude Amann
I'll miss your smile
and friendly laugh
I'll miss you a whole lot
And a half,

If it wasn't for you
I wouldn't care
You taught me to love
The people there,

You taught me the difference
Between right and wrong
And I still remember
The German Elephant song,

Trude and
Petra Julius

Sleep well, My Dear Teacher
One day you will see
We'll all be together
The whole class, you and me.

Camphill Estate — Petra — The Special Class

Those of us who met Trude towards the end of her life, recall a somewhat
stately, white-haired figure. Her step, as she crossed the lawns of Camphill
Estate, was a conscious and measured one, with a certain indomitable
quality. Her speaking, too, was considered and economical, wise almost
like an oracle, yet with a kindness and a bubbling laughter not far from the
surface. She was never abstract, always referring to real human experiences, often using a story or an image. She was a private person, whom
few got to know well. To young co-workers, in particular, a somewhat
remote figure, and not a little daunting.

During the last phase of her life, Trude lived in the extremely modest
little building known as 'The Dispensary.' Just along the corridor was the
classroom for a group of children very close to her heart — the 'Special
Class.' This was a group of perhaps two to six children of mixed ages
who were too disruptive or too sensitive to cope in their mainstream
class. They were the children 'whom we love but of whom we despair'

A relaxed moment

par excellence, and it is characteristic of this seemingly demure and straight-laced Viennese lady, that she chose to have this wild bunch, the ultimate outcasts, in the next room!

For much of her life, Trude seems to have been a private and self-sufficient person. Then, in her later years, a friendship blossomed with a vivacious young eurythmist — Petra Julius, (undoubtedly the recipient of the apple cake). Trude described Petra's arrival:

On the last day of the year 1966 she came. Tall, with open curious eyes, inquiring into everything, wanting to join everything and spreading laughter and gayness. Where Petra appeared there was constant movement and high waves of badly pronounced English mixed with very loud German talk poured over children and adults. Soon Camphill raised its head: 'Who is this new co-worker who wants to join absolutely every activity and does not wait for an invitation?'

In one way the attraction of opposites — the staid matriarch and the 'over-the-top' youngster; yet also a meeting of two ardent, youthful hearts.

In time, Petra moved into the Dispensary, Trude called her 'my daughter,' and one rarely mentioned one of them without the other: 'Trude and Petra.' The relationship became that rare thing, a friendship that embraces and enriches the whole community.

Trude with Alix Roth

One can, then, barely imagine the bitter blow of Petra's tragic early death, in a train accident in Germany on August 12, 1984, at the age of forty-three. Even before then, in her memoir, Trude had written, 'an air of loneliness blows on me which I never knew in earlier times.' Now her friend was gone and her own generation, 'the founders,' also began to go in the mid 1980s. The illness with which she struggled for some time worsened and she finally had to lay down her task as a Service Holder. After a last struggle with illness and doubt, there was a final period of acceptance and peace before her death, a few days after her seventy-second birthday. It was spring.

A kingdom of childhood

The characteristics of the youthful Trude — her passion for music and flowers, the love of festivals and birthdays, of walking, swimming, sledging, and joy in companionship — in maturity became inward qualities: interest, humour and a genuine wisdom. Her confidence in life and in the ultimate goodness of destiny, which had been tested and forged through personal disappointments and bitter life experiences, enabled her to perceive the potential and the purpose in difficult human lives. The greater the disability of a child and the more extreme the problems, it seemed the louder the voice of destiny was heard by Trude. The difficult children she loved were living proof of Christ's words, 'Neither hath this man sinned, nor his parents: but that the works of God should be made manifest in him' (John 9:3).

In the ordinary sense, few traces are left of Trude's life, even so soon after her death. She was neither a writer nor a speaker; she was a private person whom few knew intimately; the memories we have of her are of the personal qualities we met in working life. Yet, Trude's qualities, quiet and withheld, not dissipated in gossip or ceaseless activity, became a force which profoundly influenced her community.

Camphill Estate has, to this day, a unique atmosphere. It is above all a place for children — a children's village — where all that belongs to childhood in its original and true sense, can blossom; made possible by the inner discipline of teachers who are observant, interested and conscientious; a place of peacefulness and playfulness, of maternal, nurturing forces and the creative world of the imagination.

Something of the mood of the *Madonna in the Meadows* exists there and, from there, has gone with Camphill throughout the world. The serene Madonna nurtures and guides the two infants — the one who will give Himself for mankind, the other who serves Him — the landscape is light and calm, yet there is also an air of seriousness.

All this belongs to the spiritual foundation of the Camphill community and has been sustained by many people over very many years. I believe it is also Trude's legacy.

Conclusion and Outlook

Friedwart Bock

This book speaks to all generations through the story of each founding member of Camphill. As a group they became an archetype of community builders, who had the will to create a social organism, together with those 'children of Kaspar Hauser,' whose needs they wanted to meet. This aim united them even though they were not, to begin with, 'like-minded.' It took time to submit each individual will to the greater will and to follow a common vision.

The young men and women around Karl König were fired by an impulse to build a community for the future. In 1938 the first steps were taken to find a country where this impulse could be brought to life. As the political situation in Austria worsened, Karl König applied to the governments of Cyprus, Ireland, and even France.

While the threat increased around them they waited, but no positive reply was forthcoming. Cyprus did not respond and Ireland turned them down. France was too close to Nazi Germany. The Annexation of Austria on March 11, 1938 led to the making of quicker decisions than they had imagined. The outer threat accelerated the realization of a plan. They dispersed into different places of temporary safety to await the call to rejoin once a place had been found to start their community.

While Karl König was in Switzerland, he unexpectedly got permission to enter Britain, together with an invitation to go to the north-east of Scotland from the Haughtons, who were friends of Ita Wegman's. Dr Ita Wegman was the leader of the Medical Section at the Goetheanum. Karl König wrote to each member of the Youth Group on December 18, 1938. He had found solace and acceptance of this haven while reading the translator's preface of the Authorised Version of the Bible: 'To go forward with the confidence and resolution of a Man in maintaining the truth of Christ, and propagating it far and near ...'

They all responded, making their way to Scotland. Individually each one brought his, or her own past and destiny. They were filled with a selfless spirit knowing they were preparing the way for future generations. They described themselves as the 'preparers of the preparers' in the spirit of John the Baptist.

Once they had found their way to Scotland the nine young men and women around Dr König had to learn how to tackle practical tasks which they had never before faced in the shelter of their previous homes. They had to learn to serve the needs of the growing community. König had shown them the way of self-development with the help of anthroposophy.

Thomas Weihs, a medical doctor, took on the farming work together with a group of delinquent boys. He learnt the skills of husbandry, and gained an insight into farming, and this in turn inspired others.

Anke Weihs-Nederhoed, a dancer, took on the laundry with great energy and dedication. Peter Roth, a medical student, taught the children; and Alex Baum, a chemistry student, learnt the rudiments of gardening so that the community could live off the produce of the land. Carlo, an artist, acted enthusiastically as cook.

Alix Roth, a trained photographer, took on the study of nursing. Hans Schauder, a medical doctor, gave music lessons and led the choir. Tilla König and Barbara Lipsker were model mothers to their own families and became the home-makers of the community for the children and the co-workers. Trude Amann was the only one who had been trained in curative education. She was fully engaged in work with the children who soon started to arrive. This was to become the main task of the community.

In 1940 Karl König wrote about the truly wise person who knows no specialization and will do any task asked by their community. He or she will endeavour to bring order into life. This can lead to a kind of sacramentalism that enhances the lowliest task into a significant and meaningful contribution.

Karl König himself was willing to work in many areas. As a doctor with vast experience he gave direction and substance to the common study work. The administration of the community's income and expenditure was in his capable hands for many years until he was able to pass this on to Thomas Weihs. König's musical expertise was applied when he played the piano for Irmgard Lazarus' eurythmy lessons with the group. Later, König formed an orchestra which he conducted superbly from the conductor's desk, or from the grand piano. Among Dr König's contributions were also the plays he wrote for the festivals. For the Michaelmas Play (1942) he cast each member of the community in that role which mirrored most appropriately their own being.

May these founder portraits speak to young people and to those who stand in responsible positions. May these portraits bring to life the memory of these individuals who shared such a unique destiny, and who, with Karl König's help, formed a modern community in our time.

Friedwart Bock
Camphill, February 2004.

Brothers of an Earlier Age!
May your work become our Wisdom
We will use the means of the circle's roundness
and the directing power of the straight line
by taking these from your royal art.
May the work you have accomplished
be strength in our soul,
strength for our hands.

Brothers of the Present Time!
In that you are wiser than we are
Let your wisdom light up in our souls
So that your God-inspired thoughts
will become ever more revealed in us.

Brothers of the Future!
In as much as you carry the building's plan in your will
Let your strength flow into our limbs
So that we may embody the great Souls.

Rudolf Steiner (January 3, 1924)

About the Authors

Nick Thomas: Born in 1941 in England, he is by profession an electrical engineer. Nick is General Secretary of the Anthroposophical Society in Great Britain.

John Baum: Born in 1945 in Aberdeen, Scotland. He studied botany and has taught in state schools and a Steiner school in Norway. Later he attended the Priest's Seminary of the Christian Community and was ordained in 1987. John works as a priest in Oslo, Norway. Having grown up in Camphill and later having worked for some years in a Camphill Village in Norway, he has an ongoing connection with Camphill.

Christof-Andreas Lindenberg: Born in 1932 in Berlin, Germany. He studied composition for a time in Munich and joined Camphill (Aberdeen) in 1950. In the 1960s he studied elements of music therapy with Prof. H. Pfrogner in Germany and with Dr H.H. Engel in Camphill. He is a co-founder of the Free Music School (Freie Musik Schule) in Europe (1972) and the founder of the Dorion School of Music Therapy (2001). During his years in Camphill in Scotland, Ireland and U.S.A. he has composed numerous songs as well as music for the lyre. He lives at Camphill Special Schools, Beaver Run, U.S.A.

Margarethe von Freeden: Born in 1928 near Rostock, Germany, Margarethe trained for two years in agriculture and joined Camphill (Aberdeen) in 1951 where she obtained the Camphill Certificate in Curative Education. Margarethe lived and worked in Camphill Villages in Scotland and England and now resides at Camphill Houses in Stourbridge.

Cherry How: Born in 1948 in Auckland, New Zealand. She gained her MA in English and French at Auckland University. After travelling for a year she arrived in Northern Ireland in 1972. She worked for many years in Glencraig, Mourne Grange and Ballytobin. Since 1990 she has been in Clanabogan.

Marianne Sander: Born in 1930 in Breslau, Germany, she grew up in Holland, where she studied at the School for Arts and Crafts and obtained its certificate. She joined Camphill (Aberdeen) in 1952, where she attended the Seminar in Curative Education. Some years later she took a years intensive course in speech and drama at the Marie Steiner School in Germany. She has lived and worked in various Camphill Communities in Britain and abroad and is now resident at Ochil Tower School in Scotland.

Christine Polyblank (née Weihs): Born in 1943 near Aberdeen, Scotland. She trained to become a teacher, and taught for some years in Botton School,

Yorkshire. Then, responding to a call from Alex Baum at the Sheiling Community in Ringwood, England, she became the founder teacher of Ringwood Waldorf School, with which she is still involved today. Having grown up in Camphill as Thomas Weihs's daughter, she has a long-standing and lasting connection with Camphill.

Deborah Ravetz: Born in 1957 in Zambia. She took a degree in Literature and Philosophy at York University. Deborah lived and worked in Camphill for 13 years most of which was spent in Botton Village, Yorkshire. Later she studied painting and printmaking in Edinburgh and Aberdeen and now lives and works as a painter and a teacher of history of art in Stourbridge, England.

Claudia Pietzner: Born in 1957 in Vienna, Austria. After joining Camphill in Aigues Vértes, Switzerland in 1977, she obtained the Camphill Social Therapy Certificate and later, after moving to Camphill in the U.S.A. she studied massage. Claudia works professionally as a massage therapist and lives at Camphill Soltane, U.S.A.

Hartmut von Jeetze: Born in 1928 in Pilgramsheim near Breslau, Germany. He studied agriculture in Germany and then joined Camphill (Aberdeen) in 1950 where he took the training in curative education. Hartmut emigrated to the U.S.A. in 1961 to help pioneer the work of Camphill in Copake N.Y. for a number of years, and then in Minnesota. From 1990 he taught in Camphill Village Kimberton Hills in Pennsylvania. He now lives in Camphill Triform, Hudson N.Y.

Nick Blitz: Born in 1943 near Aberdeen, Scotland, he grew up in Camphill (Aberdeen) and later studied at Aberdeen University and at McGill University, Canada. Initially he worked as a research scientist in Canada and then London. In 1980 Nick qualified in medicine and became medical officer for the Camphill Schools, Aberdeen. At present he is the medical adviser to the Camphill Communities in Ireland and he lives at Carrick-on-Suir Camphill Community, Co. Tipperary.

Peter Howe: Born in 1951 in London, England. Peter lived and worked in Camphill (Aberdeen) from 1971 until 1995. He obtained the Camphill Certificate for Curative Education and later took the Hauschka Training for Artistic Therapy and then practised as a therapist. At present Peter is studying for a degree in fine art in Newcastle-upon-Tyne. As the editor of *Camphill Correspondence* he is in regular contact with Camphill.

Friedwart Bock: Born in 1928 in Stuttgart, Germany. He studied biology and geology at the universities of Tübingen and Stuttgart. Friedwart joined Camphill in 1949, where he obtained the Camphill Certificate in Curative Education and has since worked as a house parent and teacher and in various other capacities in the Camphill Schools, Aberdeen.

Endnotes

For full details of publications see the Bibliography (p. 312)

1 The Youth Group in Vienna
Several visits to Vienna, conversation and correspondence with Hans Schauder in the last three years of his life, conversation with Rudi Lissau and his wife Hedda in 2001, as well as information Rudi contributed whilst reading the manuscript in 2003, forms the background for this chapter. Correspondence with Barbara Lipsker, Stella-Maria Hellström, Agathe Dawson (née Schauder) and Marjatta van Boeschoten (née Lissau) has also been helpful. If no reference is given to a quotation it comes from these sources, with my grateful thanks. Also my hearty thanks to Friedwart Bock, Christine Polyblank (née Weihs) and Sally St Clair for many a good suggestion and to my wife, Gerd Eva Thoresen, for invaluable help on visits to Vienna and to Hans Schauder in Edinburgh.

1 König, Karl, 'Rudolf Steiner's Childhood and Youth' Lecture in Vienna, October 18, 1964. Translated by Friedwart Bock.
2 Schauder, *Vienna.*
3 Lefébure & Schauder, *Conversations on Counselling.*
4 Schauder, *Vienna.*
5 Schauder, *Vienna.*
6 König, 'The Candle on the Hill.'
7 Hoy, Andrew, 'Kimberton Hills Diary,' 1988.
8 Steiner, *The Course of my Life.*
9 Lipsker, *Personal Memories.*
10 König, 'The Candle on the Hill.'
11 Schauder, *Vienna.*
12 Zuckmayer, *Als wär's ein Stück von mir* (translated by Friedwart Bock).
13 Schuschnigg, *The Brutal Takeover.*
14 Schauder, *Vienna.*
15 König, 'The Candle on the Hill.'
16 Schauder, *Vienna.*
17 Zuckmayer, *Als wär's ein Stück von mir* (translated by Friedwart Bock).
18 König, Karl, letter to his young friends (translated by Friedwart Bock).
19 König, 'The Candle on the Hill.'
20 Weihs, *Fragments.*
21 *Camphill Correspondence,* March/April 2003.
22 Translated by Friedwart Bock.

2 Karl König
1 König, 'Candle on The Hill.'

3 Tilla König
A full account of Tilla König's life has been prepared by Nina Rowley.
1 Weihs, *Fragments.*

4 Barbara Lipsker
Unattributed quotations are from Barbara Lipsker's 'Red Copy Book' and 'Personal Memories.'
1 Veronika van Duin, *Camphill Correspondence,* Sep/Oct 2002.
2 Veronika van Duin, *Camphill Correspondence,* Sep/Oct 2002.
3 Müller-Wiedemann, *Karl König.*

5 Anke Weihs
1 Weihs, *Whither,* pp. 14f.
2 Weihs, *Whither,* p. 6.
3 Weihs, *Whither,* pp. 16f.
4 Weihs, *Whither,* p. 18.
5 Weihs, *Whither,* pp. 37f, 43.
6 Weihs, *Whither,* p. 75.
7 Weihs, *Whither,* p. 80.
8 Weihs, *Whither,* pp. 110f.
9 Weihs, *Whither,* p. 148.
10 Weihs, *Whither,* p. 87.
11 Weihs, *Whither,* pp. 203–5.
12 Weihs, *Whither,* p. 256

13 Weihs, *Whither,* pp. 261f.
14 Weihs, *Whither,* p. 264.
15 Weihs, *Whither,* p. 269.
16 Weihs, *Whither,* p. 269.
17 Weihs, *Whither,* p. 271.
18 *The Cresset,* Michaelmas 1966.
19 In Weihs, *Whither,* p. 7.
20 Müller-Wiedemann, Hans, *Karl König,* 1992. Part 2, Kirkton House chapter.
21 Letter with memories of Anke.
22 Sleigh, *Camphill Correspondence,* July/August 1988.
23 Bock, *Camphill Correspondence,* July/August 1988.
24 From a letter.
25 Bould, *Camphill Correspondence,* July/August 1988.
26 Kate Roth, *Camphill Correspondence,* July/August 1988.
27 Gisela Schlegel, *Camphill Correspondence,* July/August 1988.

6 Thomas Weihs
1 Opening and closing words spoken by Thomas as part of the Camphill Rudolf Steiner Schools'Annual Report 1975–76.
2 Weihs, Thomas, 'Healing & Teaching,' Lecture 4 at Sylvia Koti, May 1, 1981.
3 Weihs, Anke, 'Thomas Weihs,' a talk in Vidaråsen, October 19, 1986
4 Weihs, 'Healing & Teaching,' (Note 2)
5 Müller-Wiedemann, *Karl König.*
6 Schauder, *Vienna.*
7 Rudolf Steiner, lectures of November 21 & 23, 1911, Berlin
8 Weihs, Thomas, 'Three Lectures on the Inner Path,' Camphill Hall, April 23–26, 1969
9 Schauder, *Vienna.*
10 *Camphill Correspondence,* November/December 1987
11 Müller-Wiedemann, *Karl König.*
12 Weihs, Anke, 'Thomas Weihs,' (Note 3)
13 Tapp, Michael, 'Thomas Weihs,' *Threshing Floor,* July 1983.
14 Weihs, Anke, 'Thomas Weihs,' (Note 3)

15 Weihs, Thomas, '*Ex Deo Nascimur,*' address at Camphill Hall, November 30, 1979
    Other sources for the material used in this chapter include Weihs *Fragments,* various Annual Reports and letters of Karl König, Thomas & Anke Weihs, Anke's Diaries 1983–87 and Henny's papers.
    Special thanks to Friedwart Bock and John Baum for the immense amount of help and encouragement they gave. Also to Graham Calderwood, Karin Gretton, Rudi Lissau, Jonathan Stedall, Valerie Daniels, Nick Blitz and Sally St Clair.
16 Weihs, Anke, 'Thomas Weihs,' (Note 3)

7 Peter Roth
1 Editorial, *The Cresset,* Vol. 3, No. 1, Michaelmas 1956
2 Monteux, Angelika, 'The Search for the True Self,' a lecture.
3 Steiner, Rudolf, *Royal Art in a New Form.*

8 Alix Roth
1 Weihs, A. *Camphill Correspondence,* March/April 1988.
2 Roth, P. *Camphill Correspondence,* March/April 1988.
3 Weihs, A. *Camphill Correspondence,* March/April 1988.
4 König, Karl. Poem dated 1959.
5 Weihs, A. *Camphill Correspondence,* March/April 1988.
6 Byrde, John, *Camphill Correspondence,* March/April 1988.
7 Engel, Margit, *Camphill Correspondence,* March/April 1988.
8 Roth, P. *Camphill Correspondence,* March/April, 1988.
9 König, Karl, letter of June 20, 1948.
10 Roth, Alix, letter of April 12, 1950.
11 König, Karl, letter of December 25, 1952.
12 Lipsker, Barbara, *Camphill Correspondence,* March/April 1988
13 Schlegel, Gisela, *Camphill Correspondence,* March/April 1988.
14 Roth, Peter, letter of June 19, 1945.

9 Carlo Pietzner

1 Steiner, *Inner Aspects of the Social Question,* lecture 5 (June 12, 1919).

11 Alex Baum

Where no reference is specifically given, contents and quotations come from conversations or correspondence with the following, who are heartily thanked: Thomas Baum, Friedwart Bock, Reg Bould, Morwenna Bucknall, Hanne Drexel, Heinz Frankfurt, Henning von Gierke, Marianne Gorge, Stella-Maria Hellström, Peter Howe, Christof König, Barbara Lipsker, Edith Polke (née Rubik), Christine Polyblank (née Weihs), Angela Rawcliffe (née Baum), Eva Sachs, Lotte Sahlmann, Hans Schauder, Dorette Schwabe, Sally St. Clair, Sandra Stoddard and Gerd Eva Thoresen.

1 Karl König, 'Autobiographical Fragments.'

2 *News Sheet for Members of the Anthroposophical Society in Great Britain* (Jan–Feb 1976).

3 *Camphill Correspondence,* December 1975.

4 Transactions of the Faraday Society 34, 797–99, July 1938.

5 *Camphill Correspondence,* December 1975.

6 *Camphill Correspondence,* December 1975.

7 Steiner *The Mission of Christian Rosenkreutz,* from the lecture of January 29, 1912.

8 Allen, *A Christian Rosenkreutz Anthology.*

9 There were 45 large transports from Vienna during the war, and a number of smaller ones. By the end of 1942, only about 8000 of the 200,000 people considered Jews by the Nuremberg racial laws remained in Austria. Most of them had intermarried or were exempted from deportations for having one 'Aryan' parent. A large majority of the Austrian Jews lived in Vienna. Some 135,000 fled the country, *ca.* 65,000 were deported and almost all of them were killed.

(Information from: Florian Freund and Hans Safrian, *Expulsion and Extermination. The fate of the Austrian Jews 1938–1945.* Issued by Austrian Resistance Archive, Vienna 1997.)

10 Translated by Friedwart Bock.

11 Irmgard Lazarus, in a conversation with Chris Baum, in 1988.

12 Steiner, *Overcoming nervousness,* from a lecture of January 11, 1912.

13 *Camphill Correspondence,* July/August 1988.

14 Alex Baum, 'Nation and Race,' a lecture at Antioch College, Ohio, August 1965.

15 Alex Baum, New Years address, December 31, 1964, in the Sheiling, Ringwood.

16 Allen, *Living Buildings.*

17 Letter of January 28, 1966.

18 *Camphill Correspondence,* January 1976.

19 Polyblank, Christine, 'Beginnings,' *Ringwood Waldorf School Magazine* 1999.

20 *Camphill Correspondence,* December 1975.

21 *Camphill Correspondence,* December 1975.

22 *Camphill Correspondence,* December 1975.

23 Translated by Thesi Baum.

24 *Camphill Correspondence,* December 1975.

12 Trude Amann

1 'Colour in Childhood,' *The Cresset,* Christmas 1969.

2 *The Cresset,* St. John's 1970

Bibliography

Allen, Joan deRis, *Living Buildings. An Expression of Fifty Years of Camphill.* Camphill Architects, Aberdeen 1990.

Allen, Paul M. *A Christian Rosenkreutz Anthology,* Rudolf Steiner Publications, New York 1981.

Bradley, J. *One More Turn.* Self-published 1992.

Gerstler, Sali, 'Personal Memories of the Years 1928–39 of Vienna,' *Camphill Correspondence,* July/August 1998.

Hansmann, Henning. *Education for Special Needs.* Floris Books, Edinburgh. 1992.

König, Bertha. *Meine Kindheits- und Lebenserinnerungen.* Private publication. 1966.

König, Karl, 'Autobiographical Fragments,' 1960.

—, *Being Human.* Camphill Press, Botton and Anthroposophical Press, New York. 1989.

—, *Brothers and Sisters.* St George Books, New York 1963 (reprinted Floris Books, Edinburgh 2004).

—, *First Three Years of the Child.* Floris Books, Edinburgh. 1984.

—, *In Need of Special Understanding.* Camphill Press, Botton Village. 1986.

—, 'The Candle on the Hill,' *The Cresset,* Vol. VII, Summer 1961.

—, *The Human Soul.* Anthroposophic Press, New York. 1973 (reprinted Floris Books, Edinburgh 2004.)

Lefébure, Marcus, and Schauder, Hans, *Conversations on Counselling between a Doctor and a Priest,* T & T Clark, Edinburgh 1990.

Lipsker, Barbara, (Sali Gerstler), 'Personal Memories of the Years 1928–39,' manuscript, Karl König Library, Camphill.

—, 'The Red Copy Book,' unpublished autobiographical memories.

Luxford, Michael. *Children with Special Needs.* Floris Books, Edinburgh 1994.

Müller-Wiedemann, Hans, *Karl König, A Central-European Biography of the Twentieth Century,* Camphill Press, Botton 1996.

Pietzner, Carlo. (Ed.) *Aspects of Curative Education.* Aberdeen University Press. 1966.

Pietzner, Cornelius (Ed.) *A Candle on the Hill. Images of Camphill Life.* Floris Books, Edinburgh 1990.

Rowley, Nina, *Tilla König's Life and Work,* unpublished account at Camphill Village, Dassenberg, South Africa.

Schauder, Hans, *Vienna — my Home* (edited by H.W. Franke, translated by Christian von Arnim) private publication, Edinburgh 2002.

Schuschnigg, Kurt von, *The brutal Takeover. The Austrian ex-Chancellor's account of the Anschluss of Austria by Hitler,* (translated by Richard Barry) Atheneum, New York 1971.

Stedall, Jonathan. *In Defence of the Stork*. BBC films. 1971.

—, *Candle on the Hill,* BBC films, 1990.

Steiner, Rudolf, *The Course of my Life: an Autobiography* (translated by Olin D. Wannamaker) Anthroposophic Press, New York 1951.

—, *The Inner Aspects of the Social Question,* Rudolf Steiner Press, London 1974. Translated by Charles Davy.

—, *The Mission of Christian Rosenkreutz,* (translated by Dorothy Osmond) Rudolf Steiner Publishing Co., London 1950.

—, *Overcoming nervousness,* (translated by R.M. Querido and Gilbert Church) Anthroposophic Press, New York 1969.

—, *The Royal Art in a New Form,* Lecture, Berlin, January 2, 1906.

Weihs, Anke, *Fragments from the Story of Camphill,* Elidyr Press, Llangadog, Dyfed *(c.* 1975).

—, *Whither from Aulis,* Floris Books, Edinburgh 1989.

Weihs, Thomas. *Children in Need of Special Care*. Souvenir Press.

—, *Embryogenesis in Myth and Science*. Floris Books, Edinburgh 1986.

Whitmont, Edward, *Return of the Goddess*, Crossroad, New York 1982.

—, *The Symbolic Quest: Basic Concepts of Analytical Psychology*, Princeton University Press, New Jersey 1978.

Zuckmayer, Carl, *Als wär's ein Stück von mir,* Fischer, Frankfurt 1969.

Index

Italic page numbers refer to photographs

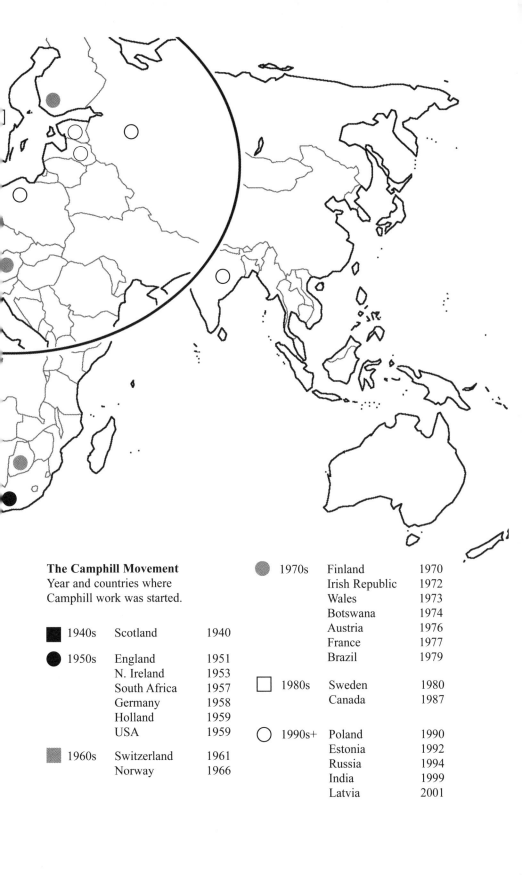

The Camphill Movement
Year and countries where
Camphill work was started.

⬛ 1940s	Scotland	1940
⬤ 1950s	England	1951
	N. Ireland	1953
	South Africa	1957
	Germany	1958
	Holland	1959
	USA	1959
🔲 1960s	Switzerland	1961
	Norway	1966

🔴 1970s	Finland	1970
	Irish Republic	1972
	Wales	1973
	Botswana	1974
	Austria	1976
	France	1977
	Brazil	1979
▢ 1980s	Sweden	1980
	Canada	1987
◯ 1990s+	Poland	1990
	Estonia	1992
	Russia	1994
	India	1999
	Latvia	2001